Discourses, Dialogue and Diversity in Biographical Research

Research on the Education and Learning of Adults

Series Editors

(On behalf of the European Society for Research on the Education of Adults)
Emilio Lucio-Villegas *(University of Seville, Spain)*
Barbara Merrill *(University of Warwick, United Kingdom)*
Henning Salling Olesen *(Roskilde University, Denmark)*
Cristina C. Vieira *(University of Coimbra, Portugal)*

Editorial Advisory Board

VOLUME 10

The titles published in this series are listed at *brill.com/esre*

Discourses, Dialogue and Diversity in Biographical Research

An Ecology of Life and Learning

Edited by

Alan Bainbridge, Laura Formenti and Linden West

BRILL

SENSE

LEIDEN | BOSTON

Cover illustration: *Blue Corner*, artwork by Jon L Bird

All chapters in this book have undergone peer review.

The Library of Congress Cataloging-in-Publication Data is available online at http://catalog.loc.gov

Typeface for the Latin, Greek, and Cyrillic scripts: "Brill". See and download: brill.com/brill-typeface.

ISSN 2542-9345
ISBN 978-90-04-46589-3 (paperback)
ISBN 978-90-04-46590-9 (hardback)
ISBN 978-90-04-46591-6 (e-book)

This book is printed on acid-free paper and produced in a sustainable manner.

Printed by Printforce, United Kingdom

Contents

The European Society for Research on the Education of Adults
    (ESREA)   VII
Acknowledgements   IX
Notes on Contributors   X

Introduction: Towards an Ecological Perspective on Learning and the
Stories People Tell   1
    Alan Bainbridge, Laura Formenti and Linden West

PART 1
Discourses of Ecology and Learning

1   When Lake Erie Is Polluted, We Are Too   23
    Laura Formenti and Linden West

2   Biographical Interviews and the Micro Context of Biographicity: Closely
    Listening for Meaning, Learning, and Voice   39
    Rob Evans

3   Narrative Regimes: An Alliance between Descriptive Phenomenology
    and Biography   53
    Hervé Breton

4   Biographical Research at the Boundary: A Careful Listening for the
    Micro, Meso, and Macro in End-of-Life Care   65
    Kjetil Moen

5   Trying to Capture the Value of the 'Live' Conference Using an Ecological
    Approach   77
    Hazel R. Wright and Marianne Høyen

PART 2
Dialogue on Learning Together, and Its Distress

6   Dynamic Ecologies of Person and Place: Dialogic Ethnographies as
    Public Engagement   95
    Richard D. Sawyer

7   Beyond Truth: A Pragmatist Approach to Narrative Pedagogy in
       Professional Learning for Healthcare Practitioners   107
           Laura Mazzoli Smith

8   A Key? Conflict, and the Struggle for an Ecology of Dialogue, Learning
       and Peace among Israeli Jewish and Palestinian Educators   121
           Alan Bainbridge and Linden West

       PART 3
       Diversity as a Content and as a Feature of Biographic Enquiry

9   Understanding Women's Lives through Critical Feminist Perspectives:
       Working-Class Women Students in Higher Education   143
           Barbara Merrill

10   Some Reflections on the Meaning, Limits and Challenges of Critical
       Biographical Research   157
           Fergal Finnegan

11   Storytelling, Culture, and Indigenous Methodology   170
           Adrienne S. Chan

12   Profession Reimagined: Tackling Adult Educators' Alienation through
       Multimodal Ways of Knowing   186
           Gaia Del Negro

13   The PhD and Me: A Liminal Space   203
           Paula Stone

       Conclusion: An Evolution of Ideas: The Transformative Ecological
       Imagination in Adult Learning, Education, and Research   217
           Alan Bainbridge, Laura Formenti and Linden West

       Index   227

The European Society for Research on the Education of Adults (ESREA)

ESREA is a European scientific society. It was established in 1991 to provide a European-wide forum for all researchers engaged in research on adult education and learning and to promote and disseminate theoretical and empirical research in the field. Since 1991 the landscape of adult education and learning has changed to include more diverse learning contexts at formal and informal levels. At the same time there has been a policy push by the European Union, OECD, UNESCO and national governments to promote a policy of lifelong learning. ESREA provides an important space for these changes and (re)definition of adult education and learning in relation to research, theory, policy and practice to be reflected upon and discussed. This takes place at the triennial conference, network conferences and through the publication of books and a journal.

ESREA Research Networks

The major priority of ESREA is the encouragement of co-operation between active researchers in the form of thematic research networks which encourage inter- disciplinary research drawing on a broad range of the social sciences. These research networks hold annual/biennial seminars and conferences for the exchange of research results and to encourage publications.

The current active ESREA networks are:
- Access, Learning Careers and Identities
- Active Democratic Citizenship and Adult Learning
- Adult Educators, Trainers and their Professional Development
- Between Global and Local: Adult Learning and Development
- Education and Learning of Older Adults
- Gender and Adult Learning
- History of Adult Education and Training in Europe
- Interrogating Transformative Processes in Learning: An International Exchange
- Life-history and Biographical Research
- Migration, Ethnicity, Racism and Xenophobia
- Policy Studies in Adult Education
- Working Life and Learning

ESREA Triennial European Research Conference

In order to encourage the widest possible forum for the exchange of ongoing research activities ESREA holds a triennial European Research Conference. The conferences have been held in Strobl (1995), Bruxelles (1998), Lisbon (2001), Wroclaw (2004), Seville (2007), Linköping (2010), Berlin (2013) and Maynooth (2016).

ESREA Journal

ESREA publishes a scientific open access journal entitled *The European Journal for Research on the Education and Learning of Adults* (RELA). All issues of the journal can be read at www.rela.ep.liu.se. You can also find more information about call for papers and submission procedures on this website.

ESREA Books

ESREA's research networks and conferences have led to the publication of over forty books. A full list, giving details of the various publishers, and the books' availability, is on the ESREA website. ESREA's current book series is published in co-operation with Brill.

Further information on ESREA is available at www.esrea.org

Emilio Lucio-Villegas
Barbara Merrill
Henning Salling Olesen
Cristina C. Vieira

Acknowledgements

We would like to acknowledge the work of all our colleagues in ESREA, and especially those belonging to the Life History and Biography Network, in the genus of this book. It is the outcome of a collective quest since 1993 for deeper illumination and understanding of adult learning and educational processes, in diverse contexts. We wish to acknowledge the spirit of collaboration too, across national and language communities, which include the whole of Europe and a wider world. We celebrate the continuing influence of founding fathers and mothers who helped build such a vibrant, sustaining ecology of research, life, and learning; especially Peter Alheit, Agnieszka Bron, Pierre Dominicé, Marianne Horsdal, Barbara Merrill, and Henning Salling Olesen.

Notes on Contributors

Alan Bainbridge
began working in Higher Education in 2001, having previously taught in secondary schools for 18 years. He is interested in the contested space between psychoanalytic thought and practices and education in its widest sense. He has written on how life history influences the development of educational professional practice and is currently using ideas linked to the Marxian and Freudian fetish to explore education processes. He is also interested in the interconnection between human learning and the "natural world". He is a co-coordinator of the European Society for Research on the Education of Adults (ESREA) Life History and Biography Network.

Hervé Breton
is Associate Professor in Education Sciences at the University of Tours. He is a member of the research team Education Ethics Health (EA7505) and President of the International Association of Life Stories in Adult Education (ASIHVIF). His research work questions and examines the effects of descriptive and narrative practices on the processes of self-formation and the formalization of experiential knowledge.

Adrienne S. Chan
is a Professor in the School of Social Work and Human Services, at the University of the Fraser Valley, Canada. Her research focuses on working with Indigenous peoples, racialized groups, and feminist and narrative storytelling processes. She is particularly interested in anti-racism, diversity, social justice, institutional change, and addressing normalized discourses within higher education.

Rob Evans
was born in London and studied Russian and History at Leeds and Tübingen. After working in adult, further and higher education as a freelancer he taught Academic Writing in English at the University of Magdeburg, Germany until 2019. His main research interests include biography research methods, the language of narrative, memory, conversation analysis and discourses of learning. Publications include books, chapters, journal articles, and edited books and journal special issues, most recently *Before, beside and after the Biographical Narrative* (Nisaba Verlag, 2016) and a chapter in *Discourses We Live By* (edited by Hazel R. Wright and Marianne Høyen, Open Book Publishers, 2020).

Fergal Finnegan

works at the Department of Adult and Community Education, Maynooth, National University of Ireland where he co-directs the Doctorate in Higher and Adult Education and the PhD in Adult and Community Education programmes. Before becoming an academic Fergal was a community adult educator and literacy worker for a decade and these experiences have strongly shaped him My research interests include biographical methods, social class, access and equality in higher education, popular education and social movements as well as critical realism and Pierre Bourdieu. He is active member of the European Society Research on Education of Adults (ESREA) for a decade and is a co-convenor of the network on *Active Democratic Citizenship and Adult Learning*. He has a longstanding interest in critical pedagogy and transformative education and an editor of the *Journal of Transformative Education* and of *RELA*.

Laura Formenti

is Professor of General and Social Pedagogy at the University of Milano Bicocca, Italy; President of the Italian Universities' Network for Lifelong Learning, Joint Convenor of ESREA's Life History and Biography Network with Linden West and Alan Bainbridge; Chair of ESREA from 2014 to 2019. She developed a compositional and cooperative approach to adult education, aimed at social justice and mixing participatory and arts-based methods with biographical writing, embodied experience, critical reflection, and Socratic dialogue. She co-edited books on *Stories That Make a Difference* (2016), *Embodied Narratives* (2014) and wrote with Linden West (2018) *Transforming Perspectives in Lifelong Learning and Adult Education: A Dialogue* (2019 AAACE Cyril O. Houle Award). She is working internationally on various projects on sensobiographic methods, feminist methodologies in museums, migrants' trajectories of inclusion, and empowering professionals in Residential Child Care through competence-based training.

Marianne Høyen

is Associate Professor at Aarhus University, Denmark, and has significant experience teaching adults, frequently those who work in educational settings. She is a Bourdieu specialist interested in the sociology of the professions and, particularly, the differing views on nature that professionals hold. An interdisciplinary academic (her PhD was situated within the philosophy of science and addressed professionals' self-understanding), Marianne's chapter "Teaching about nature across generations" (in Formenti & West, *Stories That Make a Difference,* Pensa Multimedia, 2016) combined both these interests. With Hazel Wright, she co-edited *Discourses We Live By: Narratives of Educational and Social Endeavour* (Open Book Publishers, Cambridge, 2020).

Barbara Merrill

is an Emeritus Academic in the Centre for Lifelong Learning at the University of Warwick, UK. Her research interests include issues of class and gender in relation to the learning experiences and the learner identity of adult students, particularly in higher education, European comparative research as well as bi-ographical narrative approaches to research. Barbara is a member of the Steer-ing Committee for ESREA (European Society for Research on the Education of Adults) and co-ordinates the ESREA Access, Learning Careers and Identities Network.

Kjetil Moen

is a Lecturer and Researcher at the Faculty of Health Sciences, the University of Stavanger, Norway, where he teaches ethics and care to current and future health-care professionals. Moen is also working as a chaplain in mental health-care at the University Hospital in the same city. His main research interests focus on relation-intensive work, in particular how working in boundary situa-tions triggers existential and moral philosophical concerns among profession-als. Moen is the author of *Death at Work: Existential and Psychosocial Perspec-tives on End-of-life Care* (Palgrave Macmillan, 2018).

Gaia Del Negro

has a PhD in Education at Canterbury Christ Church University (UK) and col-laborates with Milano-Bicocca University (Italy). Her research interests lie in the relationship to knowing and culture in professional lives. She is passionate about auto/biographical and transformative research methodologies. She also works as teacher of Italian as a foreign language and independent social re-searcher in Milan. She is about to complete her training in integrated somatic practices in nature.

Richard D. Sawyer

focuses on reflexive and transformative curriculum within transnational con-texts, especially those related to education, identity, and neo-liberalism. He recently developed a critical self-study methodology, called duoethnography. In 2015 he received the outstanding book award for this qualitative methodol-ogy from Division D of the American Educational Research Association. In addition, he studies how educators begin to change their thinking and their teaching in relation to diversity. More recently, he is editing a special issue of the *Northwest Journal of Teacher Education*, around the theme of "A Critical

Reimagination of Teacher Education for Sustainable Social Justice in a Time of Crisis."

Laura Mazzoli Smith

is Assistant Professor in the School of Education at Durham University, UK. Her research interests are in adult education and professional learning, out-of-school learning, issues of social inclusion and equity, and education as holistically conceived. Methodologically her research uses interpretive and participatory methods including auto/biographical research, narrative inquiry and digital storytelling. She has published widely in the field of education and is currently engaged in an inter-disciplinary European project to develop a narrative-based training platform for healthcare practitioners.

Paula Stone

is a Senior Lecturer in Education at Canterbury Christ Church University. Paula teaches on postgraduate programmes for pre-service and in-service teachers. Paula's research interests, based on her biography, lie in narrative research and social inequality in education. Paula completed her auto/biographical PhD in 2018. The thesis was an exploration of the inter-relationship between class transition and education in a bid to understand the impact of both in the formation of the self and identity. Paula argues that auto/biography provides a legitimate means of illuminating the minutia of self/other encounters to challenge the discourses about the 'other'.

Linden West

is Professor of Education at Canterbury Christ Church University in the United Kingdom and has worked in many universities. He was Visiting Professor at the University of Milano-Bicocca, the Université de Paris Nanterre, and Michigan State. He served as a member of the ESREA Steering Committee and has jointly coordinated the ESREA Life History and Biography and Transformative Processes in Learning and Education Networks. His main contemporary interest is in applying auto/biographical and narrative enquiry, and interdisciplinary psychosocial perspectives, to notions of learning, change, and transformative processes. In 2016 he won an award for his outstanding contribution to the theory and practice of transformative learning. He has authored diverse books and articles, including *Distress in the City, Racism, Fundamentalism and a Democratic Education; Beyond Fragments, Adults, Motivation and Higher Education, a Biographical Analysis*; and, most recently, *Transforming Perspectives in Lifelong Learning and Adult Education: A Dialogue*, written with Laura Formenti. The book won the 2019 Cyril O. Houle prize for outstanding literature in adult and continuing education. In 2020 Linden was inducted into the International

Adult and Continuing Education Hall of Fame. He is also a registered psycho-analytic psychotherapist.

Hazel R. Wright
is a Visiting Fellow at Anglia Ruskin University in Cambridge, UK where she was a Senior Lecturer in Education following an earlier publishing career. She pursues three key research areas: adult (particularly women's) education; childhood which she accesses through contemporary children and memory work with adults; nature, space and sustainability from a human perspective. Author of many articles and chapters, she has written two monographs: *Women Studying Childcare* (Trentham Books, 2011) and *The Child in Society* (Sage, 2015). With Marianne Høyen, she co-edited *Discourses We Live By: Narratives of Educational and Social Endeavour* (Open Book Publishers, Cambridge, 2020).

Towards an Ecological Perspective on Learning and the Stories People Tell

Alan Bainbridge, Laura Formenti and Linden West

1 ESREA's Life History and Biography Network

ESREA's Life History and Biography Network has a long, compelling story to tell. Telling that story in the light of our chosen book title, is important for engaging with the various chapters. Our Network's conferences began in 1993, bringing together a diverse group of scholars from all over Europe who were using biographical methods, albeit in varied ways, often with different assumptions about the nature and purpose of research. The idea was to share their research experiences on wide-ranging topics relating to adult education and learning in the broadest sense, informal, non-formal and formal.

The Network has been meeting for more than 25 years, with annual conferences, centred on the role of biographical narratives, auto/biography, storytelling, subjectivity and intersubjectivity, as well as memory, in researching lives and experiences of learning. Thematic, methodological and disciplinary interests alongside dissatisfaction with many traditional research methods and epistemologies – have drawn this community of researchers together, from different contexts, language communities and with varying preoccupations. The book is a testimony to the depth and variety of contributions that participants bring to discussions. Over the last few years, we have moved to considering biographical struggles to define and live sustainable lives, located within families, communities, cultures, politics and our relationships to the natural world. Our book is an attempt to illuminate what amounts to an ecology of life and human flourishing, no less, in a world that can be tortured, fractious, fragmented, fragile and yet still provide rich resources of hope.

Doing biographical research is no isolated, individual, solipsistic endeavor but is shaped by larger ecological interactions – in families, schools, universities, communities, societies and networks – that sustain or destroy hope. Sustainability is often to do with creating sufficient hope in individuals and communities by building meaningful dialogue and creating good enough experiences of togetherness, across difference. We have become more aware, in our research meetings, that telling life stories or listening to them celebrates the complexity, messiness, ecological challenge but also rich potential of learning lives. But we have grown more concerned about the rapid disruption of sustainable ecologies, not only 'natural', physical, and biological, but also psychological, economic, relational, political, educational, cultural, and ethical. We live in a precarious, frightening, liquid Covid world and believe that our kind of research can both chronicle this while also illuminating how resources of hope are created in deeper, aesthetically satisfying ways. Biographical research offers insights, and even signposts, to understand and transcend the often ignored or defended darker side of the human condition, alongside its inspirations.

We note how the Life History and Biography Network is set within a changing conceptual field of adult/lifelong education and learning. Our work is framed (and constrained) by local, national, European and global influences. Particularly, the changing nature of network membership and preoccupations, in the face of neo-liberalism, including in universities and education; and of declining trust in politics, institutions, experts and the future in Europe and beyond. Rightist populism and fascism are on the march once again. So, our reflections on the evolution of our community, and our dilemmas as researchers and adult learners, in present times, point to a considered and determinedly positive interplay with these wider forces. This is part of the book's rationale: to generate insight into people's fears and anxieties but also their capacity to keep on keeping on and to challenge forces that would diminish our humanity. We, as researchers, teachers and citizens, are embedded in a liquid, runaway, fractious, anxiety ridden world but have responsibilities to struggle towards something better, grounded in social justice.

Nicoll and Biesta's (2014) '(His)story of ESREA' report highlighted the difficult relationship between research, policy, and practice within many ESREA networks. There has been much questioning, and different positions articulated, in relation to how research should be defined and orientated, and the role of academic research in relation to policy and practice. There is no one agreed answer to the question of how – and if – academic activities such as conferences and publications (should) contribute to the 'field' of policy and practice. Such relationships and debates are part of what we refer to as researching and illuminating 'the ecology of living and learning'. This is different from the early years of the Network when the main concern was to establish and validate life history and biographical methods, either to illuminate the dialectic of subjectivity and social structures, or their role in the training of educators. While important questions remain, for instance about doing biographical narrative interviews, the bigger issue is how these methods can offer meaningful feedback on different adult education practice and theorising, encompassing the political, economic, intersubjective as well as ideological worlds in which learning lives are located. Maybe, as a result, helping transform practice and theory in the struggle for better, more sustainable learning and living ecologies.

In different ways, many members of the Life History and Biography Network already strive to "make a difference" (Formenti & West, 2016) in their varying contexts, via evolving practices of narrative and auto/biographical research. New methodological and epistemological debates have emerged around arts-based, performative, as well as interpretative inquiry. This includes the researcher's experience as a site for research, in struggles to create resources of hope (autoethnography, auto/biography, duoethnography, etc.). Narrative methods have proved themselves to be highly appropriate and richly genera-tive in illuminating the complexity of life, and its enhancement, in inclusive ways. This has been done by providing "stories" (often beyond words, or the "classical" interview) with rich contextualized interpretation, illuminating not only how adults learn to live within their personal, cultural and professional worlds, in subjective and private ways, but how they can create new social and political knowledge to build more inclusive communities. How people can be empowered to find voice, to talk back to power, and create new resources of hope in struggles for sustainable lifeworlds is a, if not the central preoccupa-tion across the chapters.

Our worlds are complex. Stories can sustain our understanding of the indi-vidual (micro) level, and of relationships in families, workplaces, communities, organizations (the meso level); and of the big processes of change in history, in the larger society, and even the whole planet (macro level). We include the virtual world. So, 'living' may be understood within complex interactions with others, and otherness, and with diverse processes, systems and encounters with the physical as well as virtual world. This is the complexity of life and living that the Life History and Biography Network seeks to investigate, which raises a question in turn about the ecological vitality of the network itself. How much, in other words, does the Network enliven and enrich the educational, social, political and ecological imaginations of those who participate?

2   Early Preoccupations

There was a need, at first, in the Network, to establish or reinvigorate research on adult education because it remained a marginalized field in the academy. If biographical methods were beginning to gain more attention across the social sciences, and within adult education and in studies of professional lives, including teachers, then its standing was never strong (Merrill & West, 2009). There was also the desire, among this 'family' of researchers, post the fall of the Berlin Wall, to contribute to building a better, more inclusive Europe, by bringing scholars and research students together, from East and West, North and South, as a contribution to the bigger project.

Beside such shared zeal, there was always and inevitably tension. The question of what was an acceptable definition, or even a scientific standard, for "biographical" or "life history" methodologies was frequently raised. Some researchers were focused on illuminating and developing educational practice and valued the relationship between research and intervention, interviewer and interviewee, while others positioned themselves as "pure researchers" seeking to gain greater recognition and credibility within academic disciplines and institutions. A number of researchers came from the colder lands of Northern Europe, bringing, maybe, more of an objectivist imperative, alongside standardized empirical practice, and strong interpretative procedures. Others, from the sunnier shores of the Mediterranean, had different backgrounds and a penchant for an applied philosophy; for less standardization and for a relational creativity (and sometimes messiness) in doing research. In the Western archipelago of Europe, researchers were attracted by the apparent rigor of German biographical approaches in sociology, but there were others who preferred the more relational emphasis of feminist methodologies. There was a kind of tension between methodological and epistemological coherence and celebrations of diversity. Any attempt to determine a common methodology or disciplinary framing, in some perspectives, risked being anti-experimental and even anti-ecological. It was best to celebrate various research forms and practices if they could bring new life, insight, epistemological sophistication as well as aesthetic satisfaction. Like the American pragmatists, what mattered was the search for the good and beautiful, and what enhanced life and learning.

The 2018 LHBN conference theme 'togetherness and its discontents' provided a space to explore such tensions, with its echoes of Freud's (1930) *Civilisation and its Discontents*. Freud emphasized a living contradiction between what we might call personal instinctual desires, and a sort of social necessity, in which individuals needed to adjust to social realities, and often repress various desires – sexual or aggressive – in the interests of social harmony and their own well-being. We wonder if there is a parallel in the urge for greater consistency in research design, compared to the more eclectic, experimental, and idiosyncratic in research. Where id is, ego shall be; maybe. Whatever the reason, the Network has struggled with but also benefited from various discontents and vigorous debate: over purpose (a more practical or academic orientation), objectivity and subjectivity, (minimizing or enhancing the researcher's presence, for instance), and or attaining rigorous respectability in the academy, as against enabling a thousand flowers to bloom.

There were Network conferences where dissent was particularly marked. At a Triennial Conference of all ESREA Networks, there was fracture in the leadership of the Network. There were issues, as suggested, to do with the intellectual and methodological inclusivity of our work, with especial reference to Southern European traditions. At one Conference there was a major debate about the scientific quality of our conferences. Each conference in fact raised crucial issues about the Network's identity, its inclusivity, and the intellectual influences at work in engaging with the stories people tell. These issues remain alive today, in the Network and of course beyond.

The original leaders of the Network – Pierre Dominicé and Peter Alheit – were progressive and collaborative in their work. They used a metaphor of 'patchworking' (West et al., 2007), and applied this to the work of 'educational biography' and the struggle for agency across lives. In Pierre's perspective, it represented a deep search for self and a quest for cultural identity and professional competence. The point was to conceive our biographies as the potential locus for meaning and authenticity, and a resource for the broader education of self as well as the capacity to work humanely with others.

Pierre Dominicé (2000) developed educational biography workshops at Geneva, in which a range of people, actual and would-be professionals, came together. They told stories in small groups, and worked over time, iteratively, to create written biographies, drawing on their own lives but also the educational resources of the group. They were offered theoretical resources like Paul Ricoeur and hermeneutics. Ricoeur wrote of writing as an act of testimony about one's own life and identity. Educational biography was not primarily a tool for better knowledge of adult development or adult psychology and did not belong either to the domain of psychology or sociology. Instead it offered insight into what it means for an adult to become more of a subject in his or her life. Doing biographies can be a process of subjectification, as against socialization, where the latter has to do with fitting people into to the established order, maybe by learning to be a good employee, or citizen. Subjectification is about learning from here and now experience, surrounding our capacity for agency, for being a person and citizen in our own right, if never in conditions of our choosing.

Peter Alheit is a sociologist, who looked back to the Chicago School and American pragmatism. He engaged with the ideas of Ulrich Beck, Pierre Bourdieu and Fritz Schütze (Alheit & Dausien, 2007). Peter wrote of the feeling we have of being the organizers of our life course. We are planners, whether for the dream job, a political career, homebuilding or finding a good match. We even plan to lose 10 pounds in weight or give up smoking... creating the impression that we hold our own lives in our hands, that we are the authors of our own biography. But this is partly illusion. Fate can deal us a blow at any time, like illness, the loss of a loved one or a valued job. And our supposed autonomy of action and planning is subordinated to 'processual structures' in our biographies. We influence these only to marginal extents, as in schooling, vocational training, work, or in trajectories of unemployment, a drug career, let alone when facing unconscious desire like coming out gay, late in life.

Structure and subjectivity in interaction, and we are not as free, it was suggested, as we may sometimes imagine. But for Peter Alheit, even within such constraints, we have more opportunities than we will ever put into practice (Alheit & Dausien, 2007). There are unlived lives within our biographies and we can become aware of the structures, or unquestioned certainties, or discourses, functioning in and constraining our lives. The habitus can be reflexively understood and our unlived lives have the potential to become socially explosive forces for change as well as of profound personal significance. This is a political as well as personal ambition of Alheit's framing of biographicity.

There were discontents in the Network, as noted. The educational emphasis clashed with the more scientific search for patterns or regularities across large samples. Or with what biographies teach us of the workings of the social order (Alheit, 1995). Especially in a world of enticement and promise, as well as illusions around the self-authorship of a life. Peter Alheit was pre-occupied with the status of biographical research in the discipline of sociology. If there was a turn, a looking back to the Chicago School and forward to the potential for biographicity, there remained many in the academy who questioned the value of personal testimony or biographical work. We need to remember German history: it is always possible to demonstrate the illusions that surround and infuse the stories people, we, tell. Hannah Arendt (1958) wrote of what happens in totalitarian societies, like the DDR, when a neighbor goes missing: no one wants to know, memory can be obliterated and highly selective stories are told.

There was rarely a tension between senior and junior researchers, or older members and newcomers, however. The narrative of the Network has always stressed inclusivity, which is not always the case with research groupings. Laura was shocked in her first meeting in 1993, as she has mentioned on many occasions: coming, as she did, from an Italian and very patriarchal academy, where a beginner PhD student was asked simply to listen and learn; here she was welcomed even though her ideas were still very sketchy and her research was still-to-be-completed on using biographical methods to sustain adult learning.

There were other tensions, reflecting no doubt different language communities, academic cultures, paradigms, and occasionally conflict and struggles for power. We struggled to attract more colleagues from the Francophone world, although many efforts were made (González-Monteagudo, 2008). A small number of colleagues left the Network over the question of scientific standards and the kind of conferences we held. Too much art, collage, music and movement were not to everyone's taste. Even so the Network survived and thrived, for almost three decades now. Many of us use the word "home", or "family" to express what this community means to us (Formenti & West, 2018). How did this happen? We can say, if with varying degrees of emphasis, that our objects of study and our research methods – narrative, biographical, auto/biographical – are strongly relational, touching depth in human experience; while doing research can be transformative for both researchers and the subjects of enquiry alike. So, we learned – as coordinators – to manage the struggles, conflicts and self/other relationship demands. But this is not the whole explanation. Educators are not simply "good people". Researchers are not either. Togetherness is always a challenge. Creating and maintaining a community, as a learning space for adults, requires perpetual effort of taking care of complexity in a collaborative, responsible and developmental way. The complexity of the process must and has been acknowledged: of different needs, of the play of emotions and different expectations, and recognition of external pressures on the group. Discontents and centrifugal forces are always and inevitably there, alongside the urge for community, dialogue, respect for difference and the desire to learn from each other.

The pioneers of adult education knew some of the above rather well: the workers tutorial class movement in the UK, the adult education circles in Italy, the feminist groups working towards self-consciousness, community adult educators all over the world, know this too but also how difficult, tricky, messy, and fragile human togetherness is. When Linden became the Convenor of the Network, followed by Laura and more recently Alan, he brought an awareness that the quality of the space – physical, symbolic, and relational – of conferences mattered greatly. We know many conferences where people participate for the sake of their presentations alone. They do not particularly listen to each other, let alone learn from the experience of the conference itself. There are clear hierarchies in the structuring of sessions. This is deeply unsatisfactory, especially for people who work in education. It represents a kind of dismissal of the very nature of learning and research. Research is in fact a form of learning, in its own right, while creating a community involves maximizing the potentiality of learning from experience, from otherness, as well as self. What do we learn from our participation in the academic system? What kind of people are we and do we become? Which values should we celebrate and why, are constant questions in the Network's life.

So, we have tried to enable the LHBN Network to become a vibrant community, critically engaged in a reflexively collective as well as individual process.

A community serving as a good enough ecology of learning and life, to help researchers develop their ideas and identities. There can be, from time to time, a strong feeling of connectivity, of good practice and conceptual sophistication to inspire and make a difference to research in the troubled world "out there". The evidence is to be found in the following, diverse chapters.

Empowering researchers is a prime task for this community: the goal is to encourage the development of meaning-full research in the struggle for a better society, as in ESREA's overall rationale. It is not simply achieving excellent results in research (as our institutions constantly insist, we must, but occasionally in ways that are destructive to lives, well-being and the quality of research itself). Remembering, too, that the Network was forged out of a desire to contribute to building a better Europe, and to heal the centuries old wounds between the Francophone and German speaking world as well as to transcend the demons of destruction haunting the European imagination. Pierre Dominicé, from Romandie, represented the French speaking world, and Peter Alheit, the German. We are living in times where Europe is once again fragile and fractured and the old demons of nationalism, racism and xenophobia rear their heads.

Struggling for social justice has been another goal for the Network. We are a microcosm of the whole and try to create good enough learning, dialogical and just spaces across our differences. Understanding intimate relational processes has also been a preoccupation. Alan and Linden are psychoanalytic psychotherapists while Laura trained in the Milano School of systemic therapy. What happens intersubjectively between people, and in their inner worlds, and how this can be theorized has mattered, alongside, or maybe as part of the struggle for social justice and a fairer share of the planet's resources. Some people emphasize the socio-cultural, others the intersubjective and psychic, but these differing dimensions all matter, in learning from each other. Too often the sociological is separated from the psychological, and academic disciplines act like warring tribes. We can often only seek reinforcement of our existing perspectives, to the neglect of others. Maybe because our Network's focus is on people, in context, and the difficulties, even mystery of not understanding why they may act as they do, we understand that collaboration is essential. But such qualities have not always been evident, and it has been a struggle to practice what we preach. We have engaged with complex political and personal questions about research and adult education in struggles for a better world. We have explored how narratives are deeply embodied (not simply formed in the mind); and how people and their stories are embedded in cultures and ecologies of precarious life (the topic of a conference in Odense, 2013; see Formenti, West, & Horsdal, 2014). We moved explicitly to questions of the politics of biographical narrative research, in Magdeburg, 2014, in a divided, increasingly unequal and troubled continent (Evans, 2016). And we considered the transforming potential of stories in Milano, 2015 (Formenti & West, 2016); and in Canterbury, in 2016, where resources of hope might lie in research and contemporary adult education. In 2017, in Copenhagen, we critically engaged with the theme of the discourses we live by, including the ecological, and asked whether our lives enhance or help destroy, and if our meso worlds are really open to diversity (Wright & Høyen, 2020). Across all this work, arts-based methods have been more confidently woven into the repertoire. We continue to search for the 'good' and beautiful in adult education, in our research and wider lives and action, recognizing, always, that what we do is a perpetual experiment in creating more satisfying social forms.

We are aware of the relative absence of colleagues from particular countries in this collection, and that our evolution does not appeal to everyone. The German speaking world and Eastern Europe are under-represented. It is worth recalling that the Network's first book, published in 1995, in Vienna, by Verband Weiner Volksbildung, had various German speaking contributors, but a number of these researchers were never involved again. What to do about under-representation from certain countries is a constant question, as are concerns about the Network's life future. Adult or popular collective education, of a questioning and critical kind – a tradition from which many of us come and to which our biographical work often relates – has been perpetually marginalized, over decades: at the same time as forces in Europe that have little or nothing to do with civility, democracy or conviviality have strengthened. 'There are populist currents with dangerously fascistic tendencies', wrote Peter Alheit, Pierre Dominicé, Agnieszka Bron and Elisabeth Brugger in their introduction to the 1995 book. The political turn in some of our recent conferences suggests disturbing trends have worsened, and the need for subtler understanding of why, and how they can be resisted, has strengthened.

We should mention, again, that any turn to biographical and narrative research can count for little among policy makers in some parts of the world; or it continues to be treated sceptically by many academic colleagues. Strange, really, given its power to illuminate how people's hearts and minds are often colonized by demeaning discourses of racism, gender or fundamentalism, but that the means can be found for resistance, sometimes in surprising places like a sewing class, or women's health group (West, 2016). Our work chronicles and illuminates the dystopic, destructive as well as generous, inclusive, learning possibilities in lives, across Europe and beyond.

The idea of this book was born in 2018. We were meeting in Turin, during a snowstorm in the city. There were old and new people sharing their research, thoughts and experiences on togetherness, connectivity, belonging, cooperation, conflict, and separation. The Network felt "like home" again. We used our intelligence as researchers, educators, and humans, to consider the joys of togetherness, but in no simplistic Pollyanerish way. This book brings to life what was then done, and embodies the writing of diverse colleagues, in their struggles for togetherness as researchers, in classes, and diverse groups; to create, in other words, vibrant ecologies of life and learning. There was in fact a powerful and poignant reminder of darkness in the Research Foundation in Turin where we working at this time. It was the location for a violent attack by the Red Brigades, which had emerged in Italy in the 1970s, in the name of liberation and hatred of bourgeois democracy. People were murdered in this place. We were reminded of what can happen when dialogue breaks down and hate captures hearts and minds. Some take it upon themselves to lead the people, cavorting with a Kalashnikov or grenade. Our work and Network are grounded in a vastly different ideals: of practicing and illuminating adult education for social justice and peace, and as the means to learn our way to more sustainable, inclusive futures.

And so, these stories of a network's struggles and successes have been brought together, to think about ecologies of learning, research and conviviality. The book is divided into three overlapping parts, on Discourse, Dialogue and Difference: these three broad themes have emerged from our recent conferences. They provide a context for all the chapters, offering a contribution to evolving theoretical assumptions, methodological nuance as well as fulfilling the Network's aspirations. The part on *Discourse* represents the philosophical, theoretical and thematic perspectives that inform our work on stories, and a whole panoply of methodological stances.

3   Discourse

In Chapter 1 Laura Formenti and Linden West consider the link between ecological and psychological crises. They reflect on a dominant epistemology, which has narrowed to very linear, narcissistic and reductive assumptions about the good. Unbridled consumerism has increased individualism, exploitation of the poor, and the narrowing of education to economic instrumentalism. It serves the needs of capitalism, rather than encouraging citizens to learn, recognize and cope with actual and impending ecological, democratic and cultural catastrophe.

Neo-liberalism, it is argued, fuels an 'ecology of bad ideas', and our world, as researchers, is not exempt from this. Critically challenging ideas are marginalized by functionalism and marketization. Objectification and obsessive quantification make it impossible to recognize the wholeness of phenomena, or of experience. Drawing on a dialogue around the ideas of

Gregory Bateson and psychoanalysis, they illuminate how psychological problems are often interlinked with wider ecological ones: when Lake Erie is polluted, so too are our psyches. And we may not want to know about the damage we do.

In Chapter 3, Evans combines the work of Alheit, Löw and Schiffrin to investigate how past experiences are used to provide meaning in the present and even to consider future actions. Evans' research focuses on the close analysis of the micro context of an interview interaction, from which the meso and macro of experience emerge. Drawing on Alheit's theory of biographicity, here is a biographical self that can only, to a limited extent, consciously shape decision-making. Guided by Löw's (2001) notion of synthesis and Schiffrin's (1996) focus on verbalization, voices from the near and far are embedded in biographical (self) knowledge that although not necessarily known to the narrator, can be identified. Such work shows how lives shaped by macro forces can be found in the minutia of micro contexts. Evans uses the narrative of a Polish teacher to indicate how the complexity of time, space and culture dovetail, to make more sense of a situated learning ecology.

The reporting of experience changes over time and what was once immediate sensory awareness becomes distant memory, but this can be brought back to life through narration. Hervé Breton's chapter explores a paradox between immediacy and memory by examining two "narrative regimes": the first uses words as a descriptive phenomenology of lived experience. The second focuses on hermeneutical attempts to understand the wider ecological, social and historical dimensions of lives. Within the context and comparison of micro-phenomenology and biographical narrative – focused on the same event in a coffee shop in New York – Breton highlights the oscillation between phenomenological description and biographical narrative elaboration. This is then used to illuminate the construction and understanding of lifelong learning processes. A distinction is made between embodied experience, lived before it is thought about and described; and subsequent recall where such moments are re-cast within complex social and cultural worlds. The micro-phenomenological is shown to expose the 'strata' of singular experience as embedded in ecological and socio-historical worlds.

Any study of the ecology of life should include the consideration of end of life moments. How death and dying are approached and what can be learnt from them. Death has moved from being an everyday aspect of lived lives to being separate and managed within large institutional structures. Moen's chapter focuses on professionals who care for those at the end of their lives, paying attention to how past personal experiences influence professional judgments. It is noted how heavily defended individuals – patients and professionals – can be when faced with the inevitability of death. The troubling subject of death is dealt with by either avoidance or fantasy. Moen uses the Biographical Narrative Interpretive Methodology to provide participants with opportunities to reconnect aspects of their own stories, about life and death, that due to defensiveness, may have been lost. The role of the end-of-life-professional is presented as inhabiting the meso level, having the potential to humanize and reconnect individual (micro) experience of dying and death, to the demands of organizations (neso/macro).

Wright and Høyen engage in an ambitious project to explore the ecological dynamics of a specific LHBN conference. By drawing on experience over many years, initially as novice delegates, through to conference organizers and book editors, they consider the external and internal motivators and inhibitors of the life of a conference. Beginning with Bronfenbrenner's four-level model, representing everything from the micro to the macro, Wright and Høyen seek to describe the lived-experience of delegates at a particular Life History and Biography conference. They ultimately struggled with the Bronfenbrenner model. While finding it theoretically interesting it failed, in the context of neoliberal policy, to represent the fluid interconnectivity between delegates' professional and personal lives alongside the demands of their institutions. Their thinking is transformed by a realization that the conference reflects a coming together of disparate elements, including the interrelation of people, places, papers, plenaries and social events. Of note is the under-representation of mid-career academics and the problem of how to involve and engage more such people in the activities of the network.

4   Dialogue

The next three chapters are concerned with dialogue's possibilities and preconditions in struggles to create good ecologies of life, learning and democratic social forms. In Chapter 8, Richard Sawyer argues, in the face of ecological disaster, that research claiming to be neutral and value free no longer suffices. He dialogues with researchers who interrogate different spaces within a College of Education, part of a bigger university. Richard raises questions about life histories and their intertwined relationship to diverse ecological contexts in the university. He and colleagues seek to elaborate what a more inclusive ecology of person and place might look like by walking the campus. The College can be a place of exclusion, which can also be subverted. We can shape our own spaces via forms of symbolic welcoming, in which, among other things, black and indigenous lives are made to matter. What is invisible becomes visible while inclusive symbolism is made concrete, aesthetically, via a picture, poem, artefact or poster etc. The chapter draws energy from several academic fields, including environmental and place-based education, curriculum theory, popular culture and life history research. The challenging dialogue engenders a transformative pedagogy of hope and resistance.

In Chapter 9, Laura Mazzoli Smith takes us into the possibility of dialogue between different epistemologies, often considered incompatible in the world of health care. Between the medical model and narrative understandings, for instance. She suggests that to know what patients endure, in illness, requires doctors to enter the imaginative worlds of patients and to see and interpret these worlds from the patients' point of view, rather than regarding them as an irritant or step towards real knowledge. Narrative knowledge offers a rich, resonant grasp of another's situation and frames of meaning, as these unfold in time. But scientific knowledge of a narrow kind can hold sway. Unlike scientific or epidemiological knowledge, which seeks to discover things about the natural world that are universally true, or appear true, narrative knowledge enables one individual to understand particular events, not as an instance of something universally true but as meaningful in its own right. However, negotiating different regimes of truth in health care is difficult because realist medical knowledge often devalues narrative ways of knowing, dismissing it as anecdote. So how to use narratives in manageable, applicable and developmental ways in health care, so as to create more substantial and eclectic ecologies of care and learning is the prime task.

Laura Mazzoli Smith turns to pragmatic philosopher Richard Rorty for a possible solution. For the pragmatist, questions of truth, or the innate essence of things, is supplanted by the question of which vocabularies and cultures can produce new and better ways of thinking and acting. In this sense, pragmatism is anti-essentialist and opposed to the idea that there is an intrinsic nature to things. Rorty maintains that we can engage with different ways of knowing without thereby losing our grip on effective standards of inquiry, or useful norms of behavior and so on. Ontological and epistemological traditions are just that – traditions. Pragmatism views science as one genre of literature, albeit a powerful one – or, put another way, literature and the arts are forms of inquiry in their own right, on the same footing as, and complementary to the scientific. Some inquiries generate propositions, some narrative insight, others evoke painting, literature and the poetic. Dialogue becomes more possible, in pragmatic perspectives, in that no one truth is absolute. Professional learners unfamiliar with narrative pedagogy, even when working with narratives, seem to find confidence in pragmatist eclecticism, if this is presented as a kind of anti-foundationalism in truth claims. It offers reassurance against stark dualism, and hence epistemic (and perhaps even ontological) threat. Dialogue between scientific knowledge and narrative ways of knowing, creates a better, more beautiful ecology of learning and health care.

In Chapter 10, Alan Bainbridge and Linden West focus on experiments in auto/biographical, narrative teaching and research in the context of a project called CURE, set, in part, against the backcloth of wider conflict between Israelis and Palestinians. Here dialogue most often breaks down or seems impossible. CURE was a European Union financed project to create spaces for civic education, democratic values and dialogue within teacher education in Israel. The project involves, inter alia, groups of Israeli and Palestinian educators living in Israel. But it is set against the dark historical backcloth of what remain living traumas: the Holocaust and Al Nakba (or the Catastrophe, the forced evacuation and death of many Palestinians in the 1948 War and since). Israeli Jews can continue to be haunted by the memory of the 'final solution', in the middle of the last century, as well as centuries of oppression. There can be deep and continued anxiety over security, playing out in the present. Anxiety and fear drive nationalism and colonialist oppression, religious fundamentalism, intolerance, and violence against Palestinians. Palestinians in turn can feel there is no alternative to violence, as the world turns its back on their oppression.

Trauma is thus visited onto present and future generations. It may be the failure of Israeli Jews to process deep traumatic memories that drives what is oppressively done in their name today. How much adult education, even of an intensive, in-depth therapeutic kind, might address these issues is a basic question in the chapter. Alan and Linden play with the metaphor of a key – from an old Sufi proverb about our need to search for solutions in the darkness of human experience. They have created a potential key: a playful, experimental adult education space for generating stories and a culture of listening to self, and the other. The work was palpably meaningful to many involved, but Alan and Linden struggled to transcend silence and silencing among particular Jews and Palestinians. Keys were found for some therapeutic, educational, relational, narrative, playful, even poetic dialogue: where disturbance could be managed, and people felt seen. But if the proverbial light from a candle flickered more brightly, for a moment, the darkness surrounding the conflict and in particular lives never truly receded.

5   Diversity

Part 3 is on diversity as a constant feature of biographic enquiry. Understanding lives and learning through biographic lenses, in fact, means celebrating diversity in human experience, and across a variety of contexts and life worlds. It is about avoiding easy generalization and the blurring of difference that often comes with mainstream research and in its essence informed by ecological assumptions. It also means that biographical and narrative methods and perspectives are plural by definition, and able to initiate and sustain processes of nuanced diversification. So, the authors we meet in this part of the book are diverse and especially attentive to diversity in the stories they tell.

Chapter 9 is by Barbara Merrill, a pillar of our community and a critical feminist researcher, who has engaged in a lifetime's task of promoting deeper, humanistic, and subjective understanding of women's lives using biographical methods. She illuminates the interplay of class, gender, ethnic backgrounds, and structural dimensions in shaping subjective experience. But also coping strategies in Higher Education. Using feminist lenses, Barbara brings a specific contribution to the diversity of biographical methods by giving voice and richness to women's experience at university. It reveals the collective beyond the subjective, and the role of agency and structure in everyday lives, at the intersection of micro, meso and macro worlds. In fact, for more than twenty years, Barbara has chronicled experiences of working class women from different ethnic backgrounds, and their struggles and contradictions in attending courses in elite middle-class universities. But this is alongside the capacity to cope with challenging diversity in their living contexts: of family, work, university, community, and the larger society. In this chapter, she summarizes the distinctiveness of feminist theories and methodologies, and provides exemplary stories. She argues that higher education (especially in the social sciences) is a powerful experience for women. Many of the women she met, indeed, enjoyed their academic experience and became more aware of the dialectics of agency and structure, and power dynamics, shaping them and what they do. Hence, the academy can offer a transitional space enabling them to reflect upon past, present and possible futures, embracing, not rejecting their working-class identity, if in more critical ways.

In Chapter 12, we meet Fergal Finnegan and his personal commitment to criticality and critical research, as a specific approach in biographical inquiry. Fergal explores various meanings and traditions of critical research, from the Frankfurt School to Freire's pedagogy of the oppressed. In his discussion of the diversity of critical paradigms, he places some distance between what he considers the most abstract and academic exercises, and his embrace of Bhaskar's notion of "critical realism". Complexity and emergence characterize the approach: in fact, he suggests that a plurality of agents, things, events, and powers always combine in unpredictable ways. What critical biographic research can do is to grasp the ongoing interaction of structures and subjectivities within stories of self-understanding and self-monitoring. Emancipatory social science looks for explanatory depth as well as for the aims and practices of good education: human flourishing, care, solidarity, emancipation, voice, and resistance to dominant logics. In this framework, critical biographical research is always concerned for the larger social context and frames the biographical interview as an intersubjective encounter, where the researcher brings his/her own values, desires, position, within an institutional space. Then, the process of analysis becomes a key phase in the research process, entailing a recursive iterative movement in which the researcher brings his/her methodological, ethical and theoretical positioning. The process is far from being neutral or objective.

Biographic critical research is powerful: Fergal witnesses how it has altered his identity as a researcher and multiplied internal voices; besides, it had an impact in the field, illuminating topics of adult learning (such as the experience of non-traditional students in Higher Education), alongside better understanding of the stratifications of agency and structure. While its impact on society or the academic institution is still debatable, it seems to fuel activism as a "natural fallout".

Another crucial topic for diversity is doing biographical research with a variety of communities, whose cultural backgrounds defy the taken for granted. This is a challenge for biographical researchers, as well as an opportunity to learn and to revise our epistemological assumptions, maybe in more comprehensive and ecological directions. We should interrogate the often implicit colonialism of academic literature on "stories"; the idea of biography is itself strongly rooted in the history of Europe, in Western philosophy, epistemology, and literature. It tends to disconnect self and other, human and non-human, culture and nature. Adrienne Chan illustrates, in Chapter 11, how a researcher who has been shaped by the Anglophone academy, and worked for many years using an auto/biographic framework, is suddenly challenged and brought to reflect and to re-think her own relationship with stories. This is thanks to a 'land based' program of intervention within a community of First Nation People. Reading her chapter, we better appreciate the deep relationship of culture with "homeland", not as a mere background for human action, or even worse a resource to be exploited: but as a source of culture and life itself. And yet, due to the trauma of colonization and the violent separation of Indigenous people from their land, culture, language, and values, the work of healing is now necessary, and the programme invites younger generations to have renewed relationship with the land and the elderly. Storytelling seems a very reasonable way to overcome feelings of dispossession and hopelessness for many young people. So, in the programme, ancient practices of storytelling are re-actualized, allowing participants to take care of themselves in relationship with others, the elderly, the ancestors, and the environment. Indigenous epistemology praises storytelling: but the relationship with a story is different, less individualistic, connecting to traditional themes and rituals. However, an immense effort of understanding was needed, in a long (and still ongoing) process of what we can call co-learning, with humility, curiosity, and respect on the researcher's side. The researcher's journey within this territory and community of Stó:lō became a personal, collective, and political endeavor.

Another way to celebrate diversity, with a methodological focus, is proposed by Gaia Del Negro. She presents her PhD study of professional epistemologies of knowing and becoming, and the role of emotions, relationships, and imagination in this. She uses cooperative inquiry with two groups of adult educators in Italy (Milano Bicocca University) and the UK (Canterbury Christ Church University). She describes a participatory process of narrative aesthetic research, aimed at co-building knowledge on the research topic. This is an exploration evoking similar experiences, as in Dominicé's work in Geneva. But she does this with a stronger aesthetic and feminist thread. Once again, the researcher is actively and deeply involved in the process: her own quest for meaning and the desire for a new positioning in how we best know and are open to experience and the ecological, is shared with the participants. All of them face the potential beauty and deep challenges of their profession, and its 'irreducible uncertainty'. She invites them to explore, individually and collectively, professional experience, and the emotions it entails. She encourages stories through a panoply of approaches – narrative, metaphorical, embodied, aesthetical, and reflexive. As feminist scholars and humanistic psychotherapists have maintained, dominant Western epistemologies can alienate, as we become disconnected from who we are, as well as the other and her context. Education, here, is instead a relational process, entailing encounters with otherness, inside and outside ourselves, cultivating authenticity in how we respond. But educators 'in the patriarchal West' often learn from an overly intellectual curriculum where emotions, intuition, and creativity are marginal. There can be distance towards the other (and self). Gaia suggests 'practicing multiplicity' instead: by engaging with a variety of cultural objects, by encountering the other (the group setting is a must, in this way of working), and through 'transcoding', i.e. using different languages to tell the same story. In the process of facilitation, Gaia reflects, it became possible for her to learn how to engage with her own ambivalence, alienation, and fears.

The last chapter is about another piece of PhD research, and connects with the first in this part (Barbara Merrill's). In fact, Paula Stone could have been one of Barbara's participants: she uses auto-diegetic narrative to chronicle her own transformative experience – intellectual and cognitive, but also spiritual and emotional – as a student and academic in Higher Education, and then a PhD researcher. Playing the researcher and the researched, Paula analyses her path as a woman of working-class origins who learnt little by little how to recognize the structures of inequality acting upon her life, and her desire for recognition that was, finally, the leitmotif which allowed her to thrive in academe.

Bearing a social stigma as an 'illegitimate' daughter of an extremely poor single mother and having to carve out her own place in society, meant that nothing in her life was taken for granted. She explores the conditions that made it possible for her to find her own way and claim her space and voice in the academy. Self-narrative creates a 'third space', a 'site of exploration and struggle' where meaning can be rearticulated and self can be re-interpreted within 'broader ecological interactions, including my past, my family, and my work'. Connectedness matters, both in shaping one's life, and in reshaping it.

Yet, she writes, this is not simply one individual story; it is also collective, and any academic woman coming from a working-class background might find very similar dynamics in their own lives. In fact, Paula's story can be taken as a kind of universal narrative of inequalities, transition, and negotiation: these are common elements in the contemporary world. Where class transition, migration, life crises, environmental disasters struggle to be heard. The core issue in transition is diversity: in entering a new world, new experience, we face other frameworks of meaning, and we lack the rules of the game. Feeling like a fish out of water is a widespread human experience, in the contemporary world, far beyond class and gender. Paula suggests ways to tackle such feelings: besides telling our stories, by embracing illuminative concepts and ideas from writers who become theoretical friends, as with Axel Honneth and his concept of recognition. Love matters in dialogue and good enough relationships with supervisors. As does reciprocity in recognition, and the feeling of emotion and conflict being legitimate, alongside a capacity to imagine future possibilities.

Paula provides an appropriate end to our introduction by acknowledging our Network, as a community where she experienced 'concern, mutual respect and solidarity', allowing her to overcome the frightening feelings of vulnerability that surfaced in her first conference presentation. Intersubjectivity, rights, and solidarity are ingredients of good adult education which allow, in the longer run, for people like her to claim space, notwithstanding the careless, dismissive culture of the neo-liberal world and, at times, within it, the university.

References

Alheit, P. (1995). *Taking the knocks, youth unemployment and biography – a qualitative analysis.* Cassell.

Alheit, P., Bron, A., Brugger, E., & Dominicé, P. (Eds.). (1995). *The biographical approach in European adult education.* Verband Wiener Volksbildung.

Alheit, P., & Dausien, B. (2007). Lifelong learning and biography: A competitive dynamic between the macro- and micro-level of education. In L. West, P. Alheit, B. Merrill, & A. Siig Andersen (Eds.), *Using biographical and life history methods in the study of adult and lifelong learning* (pp. 57–70). Peter Lang.

Arendt, H. (1958). *The human condition.* University Press.

Dominicé, P. (2000). *Learning from our lives; Using educational biographies with adults.* Jossey-Bass.

Evans, R. (Ed.). (2016). *Before, beside and after (beyond) the biographical narrative.* Nisaba Verlag.

Freud, S. (2002). *Civilisation and its discontents.* Penguin.

Formenti, L., & West, L. (Eds.). (2016). *Stories that make a difference. Exploring the collective, social and political potential of narratives in adult education research.* Pensa Multimedia.

Formenti, L., & West, L. (2018). *Transforming perspectives in lifelong learning and adult education: A dialogue.* Palgrave Macmillan.

Formenti, L., West, L., & Horsdal, M. (Eds.). (2014). *Embodied narratives: Connecting stories, bodies, cultures ad ecologies.* University Press of Southern Denmark.

González-Monteagudo, J. (Ed.). (2008). Approches non-francophones des histoires de vie en Europe. *Pratiques de formation/Analyses, 55.*

Löw, M. (2001). *Raumsoziologie.* Suhrkamp Verlag.

Merrill, B., & West, L. (2009). *Using biographical methods in social research.* Sage.

Nicoll, K., & Biesta, G. (2014). *(His)story of the European Society of Research on the Education of Adults (ESREA): A narrative history of intellectual evolution and transformation in the field of adult education in Europe.* Research report. Retrieved May 10, 2018, from https://www.esrea.org/wp-content/uploads/2016/11/ESREA_HISTORY_REPORT_SUBMITTED.pdf

Schiffrin, D. (1996). Narrative as self-portrait: Sociolinguistic constructions of identity. *Language in Society, 25*(2), 167–203.

West, L. (2016). *Racism, fundamentalism and a democratic education.* Trentham/UCL Books.

West, L., Alheit, P., Merrill, B., & Siig Andersen, A. (Eds.). (2007). *Using biographical and life history methods in the study of adult and lifelong learning.* Peter Lang.

Wright, H. R., & Høyen, M. (2020). *Discourses we live by: Narratives of educational and social endeavour.* Open Book Publishers. https://www.openbookpublishers.com/product/1110

PART 1

Discourses of Ecology and Learning

∵

CHAPTER 1

When Lake Erie Is Polluted, We Are Too

Laura Formenti and Linden West

Abstract

We live in times of profound crises: ecological, political, material, educational, spiritual and epistemological. A virus stalks the earth, and we are struggling as to how best to respond and understand. We are suffering from an epistemological malady of narrow, solipsistic thinking, under mantras like 'evidence-based practice'. We separate ourselves off, as humans, from nature, from each other and even from ways of knowing. We find difficulty in creating deeper, psychic, intersubjective, social, ecological and spiritual sensibilities towards ourselves and our behaviors as well as myriad relationships. What is Lake Erie to us, what are we to Lake Erie? This chapter is about the power and ubiquity of turning away, of denial and the death wish, alongside the potential power of stories, and dialogue, to create interconnectedness and awareness of what we are called to do, and learn, in such times.

Keywords

systemic theory – psychoanalysis – macro, meso and micro worlds – resistance to knowing – stories

1   Introduction

There is an ecology of bad ideas, just as there is an ecology of weeds, and it is characteristic of the system that the basic error propagates itself. It branches out like a rooted parasite through the tissues of life, and everything gets into a rather peculiar mess. When you narrow down your epistemology and act on the premise "what interests me is me, or my organisation, or my species", you chop off consideration of other loops of the loop structure. You decide that you want to get rid of the by-products of human life and that Lake Erie will be a good place to put them. You forget that the eco-mental system called Lake Erie is a part of your wider eco-mental system – and that if Lake Erie is driven insane, its insanity

is incorporated in the larger system of your thought and experience.
(Bateson, 1972, p. 484)

We live in difficult times, when the coronavirus stalks our lives, and we feel
vulnerable and deeply dependent on each other. We are finalizing this chapter
still in lockdown, painfully aware that the world can go on without us. So, we
are even more persuaded now, that a healthy life is not simply about solipsistic
human beings but has to do with the air we breathe, the soil we use and the
water and food that sustains us. There is a need for the human species to de-
centre and take responsibility for the health of a whole ecosystem called Planet
Earth, threatened by deforestation, global warming and melting ice caps. The
ecological crisis – and now this tiny virus – seems to invite us to reflexively
learn our way to a holistic sensibility and a whole set of new relationships with
diverse others, with the natural world, and with our own possible complicity
in the present ecological insanity. It might include questioning economic and
behavioral assumptions about capitalism's illusions of infinite growth, collid-
ing with a groaning, fragile, depleted creation.

In this chapter, we reflect on the dominant epistemology, which has narrowed to very linear, overly narcissistic and reductive assumptions, even worse
than in Gregory Bateson's time. Unbridled consumerism has increased individualism, exploitation of the poor, and the narrowing of education to economic
instrumentalism. It serves the needs of capitalism, rather than encouraging
citizens to learn, recognize and cope with the impending ecological, democratic, and cultural crisis. Neo-liberalism fuels an 'ecology of bad ideas', and
our world, as researchers, is not exempt from this. In fact, research, education,
and learning, as values per se, are dismissed or marginalized by functionalism
and marketization. Academics are called to demonstrate that they, we, have
an 'impact', quantitively, no matter if much of what is meaningful in our job
is lost. Objectification and obsessive quantification make it impossible to recognize the wholeness of a phenomenon, or our experience. Even the worlds
of music, poetry and art seem to have lost their educating power and healing
potential, for many, in a rapacious, frequently insane world.

This crazy context, shaped by linear presuppositions, produces pathologies
and shortcomings, particularly in and through education. Evidence Based Education is the dominant paradigm of sense making in many countries; it too
easily becomes an undisputed discourse nurturing acritical and falsely neutral
positions regarding 'evidence'. It disempowers theory and subjective experience, our whole selves, in fact, separating theory from practice and subjectivity
from objectivity. This insanity is especially damaging for adult education and
learning. Adults are constantly building theories by telling stories about their

experience, and so do we. In this historical moment, more so than ever, we feel the need to develop a satisfying theory/narrative of who we are, as individuals, researchers, and as members of the human species; and about the ground on which we stand, the quality of the air and ideas we breathe, and how much we nurture those around and beyond us, as academics and a research community.

Stories are ways to reconnect. Nowadays, dis-connection is evident in the construction of material and symbolic walls between groups, keeping the other, the migrant or people of a different colour, as well as difficult thoughts and feelings, at bay. The separation of 'us' and 'them', based on religion, ethnicity, ideology, paradigms, or whatever, builds closed communities creating a limited understanding of the human condition and its manifestations. The need to define one's own 'field' or territory nurtures defensive strategies vis-à-vis the stranger, who becomes like an intruding body (West, 2016). Even coronavirus is in a certain sense our creation, thriving destructively because of negligence in how we prepare our food, how we might slaughter other species, and how we might fly, hubristically, from one place to another, without fear of the consequences. The wildlife market of Wuhan sold snakes, bats, beavers, badgers, cats, foxes, lizards and scorpions in an unregulated trade that played to people's naïve belief in their health benefits, without regard to microbiological evidence (Yu, 2020).

As we said, stories have the power to reconnect. But denial and repression of troubling thoughts can be strong: we often refuse to face the consequences of what we do. Our stories are not neutral. They reveal hidden presuppositions. And, to repeat, when we fail to recognize Lake Erie's groaning, or Polar Icecaps melting, or the extinction of species, we deny our own biology, experience, our potential to learn and ethical responsibilities to self, others and a whole world (Formenti & West, 2018).

The power of disconnection is central to psychosocial, including psychoanalytic thinking, as it is to systemic thought. We learn to tell disconnected stories and we come to deny our capacity to know, at a social, political, cultural, ecological and personal level, maybe because of fear and anxiety that understanding is too difficult or attempts to learn frighten and expose us to ridicule. We fear rejection in our closed communities. It may be easier to indulge the desire for instant gratification, and immediate answers; while experience might feel too difficult to process – especially if we are isolated. So, we may be frightened of the truth of our actions, because, child-like, we do not want to be disturbed or face the consequences of what we do. Knowing, in such terms, is a difficult business and we easily escape into a kind of Oceanic bliss of ignorance and or forms of religion or ways of seeing that offer superficial comfort but do not challenge us in any depth.

In this chapter, we reflect on this context, and argue for a situated ecology that encourages openness of thought and feeling, through storytelling, and a concern for diversity and dialogue. At the heart of good education, we claim, is a freedom to tell our stories, and to think about them collectively, in the company of others. Stories have the power to reconnect, to offer a thick and meaning-full representation of reality, bringing together the micro, i.e. the local and subjective, with the meso level of interacting systems, such as families and other institutions, including schools and universities; and the macro, i.e. history, the socio-cultural and ideological contexts and meta narratives shaping what we say and do. A narrative power enabling us to weave wider, reflexive understanding of self and culture, an ecological sensibility too, maybe even wisdom (Fraser, 2018; Tisdell & Swartz, 2011). Or not, as the case might be, in capitalism's worship of greed and Mammon (McCarraher, 2019).

Stories convey implicit values and perspectives, our epistemology, our ways of thinking and acting; they are shaped by ongoing interactions with the environment at large, natural and social. Shaped, to greater or lesser extents, by what McCarraher (2019) calls the seductions, illusions, and even enchantments of Mammon: capitalism as the all-pervasive religion of modernity. By listening to our stories, and interrogating them, we can re-create a good epistemology, celebrating complexity, circularity, and participation in a cycle of life rather than avaricious consumption. Stories are an antidote to dis-connection, to linearity, and to the closure of heart and mind.

2   Wrestling with Dis-Connection

> We face a world which is threatened not only with disorganization of many kinds, but also with the destruction of its environment, and we, today, are still unable to think clearly about the relations between an organism and its environment. What sort of a thing is this, which we call 'organism plus environment'? (Bateson, 1972, pp. 448–449)

Half a century after this was written, the human species is witnessing pandemics, ecological catastrophe, war, terrorism, mass migration, increasing inequality and poverty, desperation, and political ugliness, worldwide. Our insane epistemology – what Freud and Klein labelled, if in slightly different ways, the death instinct, Thanatos above Eros (Bainbridge & West, 2012) – has created the conditions for the extinction of human life, polluting the spaces where we live, our relationships and minds. Ideas are very concrete, they produce effects, out there and inside us. This is what education should take as a primary concern. What is the human condition? What enables us to flourish? What inhibits human flourishing? How did we arrive at a point of such desperation? What can we do about it? And what has it all to do with adult learning?

The dominant Western metaphor of control and conscious purpose is born out of being in thrall, addicted, stuck, while also imagining that we can be omnipotent. Surrendering might be required to regain mental health and groundedness: as in the 12 steps of Alcoholics Anonymous (Bateson, 1972), admitting vulnerability, and accepting a greater power, to enable us to manage our addictions. Philosophical and spiritual leaders as well as depth psychologists have often articulated the importance of a language of meaning, of real belonging, of hope amidst the fears, limits, conceits and defeats of life. Acknowledging our vulnerability, and yet finding power, recognition, glimpses of larger truths and ethical responsibility, could constitute moments of existential, embodied as well as relational transformation, even of transcendence. But these are hard won, individually and collectively, over a life.

Both Freudian psychology and Bateson's epistemology expand our notion of "mind", the former inwards, the latter outwards. "And both of these changes reduce the scope of the conscious self. A certain humility becomes appropriate, tempered by the dignity or joy of being part of something much bigger" (Bateson, 1972, p. 461). We need to re-think then, the individual mind, as "immanent but not only in the body. It is immanent in pathways and messages outside of the body; and there is a larger Mind of which the individual mind is only a subsystem. This larger Mind [...] is immanent in the total interconnected social system and planetary ecology" (p. 461).

How does a lake 'think'? How do 'I' or 'we' think? Every system – a human being, a forest, a society – has its epistemology. Bateson tried to challenge his interlocutors by interrogating theirs. In this, he was an educator. His method was abductive, based on stories and metaphors, since 'thinking in terms of stories' (Bateson, 1979, p. 14) is what we do when we try to (re)connect to the world around us. A satisfactory theory of adult education and lifelong learning must re-compose meaningful pictures of the whole, celebrating connections, fostering creative, generative compositions of stories, of ideas in relation to them, and levels of understanding transcending micro, meso and macro demarcations. Interdependence, not separation, is the key feature of living. The 'unit of learning' is a whole formed by organism-plus-environment (Bateson, 1972); hence any individual change depends on other changes in the larger system. And vice-versa.

As researchers and adult educators, we have had a long-term and passionate engagement with narrative and auto/biographical methods. We practice auto/biographical research in different ways, since we are different: a man and a woman, from different roots, learning paths as well as cultures. Our prime task is chronicling and theorizing struggles to learn, in professional, higher, and adult education and community contexts (Formenti & West, 2018). We have recently explored concepts like lifelong and transformative learning, over a three-year journey – a kind of pilgrimage – to consider what these terms might mean. Transformation is an overused word and is easily commodified. In our writing, we asked if transformation is a kind of consumerist illusion, a marketing trope. Are we really transformed or more likely seduced by a new car, a mobile phone, a new outfit, or partner, or even a degree? Transformation might, on the other hand, be a lifelong, lifewide quest for meaning, truth, agency, and authentic selfhood. It might have to do with taking responsibility and accepting our obligations, in Simone Weil's (1952) terms, long before our rights.

But are we able to transcend who we are? To leave behind the child, or the particular man or woman we have been? Are we able to let go of obsession, addiction, narrow epistemology, cultural presuppositions, and to question inherited values and why we act as we do? Or, for that matter, to engage with unconscious fears, anxieties and delusions? There could be a strong case for pessimism, here, alongside an optimism of the will, in our struggles to know; maybe life and learning are a mix of both. Knowledge is a difficult business, never complete. It may partly have to do with acknowledging our limitations and the defensive postures of hubris, omniscience and omnipotence. Negative capability, in the poet Keat's phrase, learning to live in doubt and uncertainty, might be crucial to transformative experience, as strange as this might sound (Formenti & West, 2018).

We rely on dialogue to celebrate our diversity, and compose a richer, more embodied and relational understanding of the stories we tell (Formenti, West, & Horsdal, 2014), not least to make a difference in the world where we live (Formenti & West, 2016); maybe to heal our hubris, narrowness and disconnection. Our epistemologies are different, rooted in systemic theory (Laura) and psychoanalysis (Linden): but difference can be a trigger for reciprocal learning. All the great adult educators (Paulo Freire in South America; Raymond Williams and R. H. Tawney in the UK; Danilo Dolci and Aldo Capitini in Italy) and myriad feminists (Barbara Merrill, Luisa Muraro, Adriana Cavaro and Edmee Ollagnier) – insist on a dialogic pedagogy, rooted in lived experience and – here lies a difficult word – love for the other. They understood that adults learn with each other, by sharing stories about their experience, hence multiplying their possible meanings, and challenging and teaching each other in the process. When we search for a higher order learning, a perspective transformation, or psychological integration, we need another's point of view to be able to question and change our own. But the relationship must be one of mutual respect, of acceptance, equality, of listening. Which is problematic, not granted once and for all. For Paulo Freire and Tawney, drawing respectively on liberation theology and Anglicanism, there is a potential divinity in the other, however obscure and disguised (Leopando, 2017; West, 2017). Education, in Martin Buber's (1922/1937) terms, is a perpetual search for I/Thou relationship at all levels, with others and in the symbolic world.

We have questions, however, about this. We work with stories, and cultivating an ecological epistemology is far from a given in narrative, life history or auto/biographical enquiry: stories are easily de-contextualized, objectified, simplified, even narrowed down to counting how many metaphors are used; or stories are reified, used as if they were 'true'. So, we decided to juxtapose, here, our narratives and perspectives to show how they shape our theory and practice of education and research. More specifically for this book, we use a rich narrative ground to interrogate our choice of life history and auto/biography and its power in considering the construction and re-construction of meaning, identity, knowledge, values and even selves.

3   Laura and Questions of Ecological Loss

The ecological narrative, today, is of loss. Many people are feeling the effects of the ecological crises, alongside Covid-19, which has brought death to many families in places like Lombardy where I, Laura, live. I remember doing biographic work, almost twenty years ago, in an Alpine village. I met a group of 10–12 elders once a month for two years, telling and writing stories to create a local archive of memories. Those old men and women were deposits of traditional practices and ideas, of a form of wisdom indeed. They mourned their lost childhood, the appearance of the land, of the woods, when the paths uphill to the mountain were clear, and daily care for water and animals a necessity. They were even nostalgic for the cold winters during the Second World War. They kept saying this or that had disappeared. They were fully aware that those changes were irreversible. In some cases, there was self-blame and shame. They were witnessing the invalidation of a long-standing, inherited transgenerational knowledge, and they felt they had not been good enough in passing it on to new generations, with a coherent sense of culture. It hurt.

The loss of a space where we can flourish brings *solastalgia* (Galway et al., 2019), like being homesick while still in the self-same place. For me, it goes back to my father, the youngest child of a miller. At six, he was given a sheep to care for. And years later, when he had already enthusiastically embraced modernity, he still loved the woods, animals, and they loved him. I can recognize, now, that he suffered solastalgia: he kept telling stories of what was before. Is this a deep family reason for my addiction to stories? Was telling stories, then, a form of healing and is it the same now?

Our personal experiences of the environment are shaped by biographical, relational, cultural, economic and social factors. There is often no space to talk about our feelings. We can even lack the words to give them voice. How can we name ecological losses, particularly when they are so ambiguous – since civilization undoubtedly brings advantages? This question becomes more urgent with climate change and species extinction. What might be the role of education, of learning, as a resource of hope? Some of us are changing our habits, caring for garbage and energy, bringing more attention to the life of plants and animals, listening to our bodies. But what of our psyche? And soul? How is our mental health and well-being influenced by such changes and the narratives, practices and assumptions that surround them?

A new branch of psychology studies the impact of climate change on mental health (Clayton et al., 2017), signalling an increase of depression, suicidal ideas, post-traumatic stress, as well as feelings of anger, hopelessness, distress, and despair. The Alpine area where I worked has the highest rates of suicide in Italy. Cunsolo and Ellis (2018) coined the term 'ecological grief' to address feelings related to experienced or anticipated loss in the ecosystem, especially when meaningful landscapes are submitted to irreversible change. They undertook research with Inuit people in Arctic Canada and farmers in Australia, in locations where climate and environmental changes are dramatic: they found commonalities despite the differences as people struggle to cope with ecological loss and the prospect of an uncertain future. They grieved in fact for lost landscapes, ecosystems, species, or places that carry personal or collective meaning. If you are living off agriculture, or hunting, as many peoples in the world do, you may be worried for your future. But there is more: living in contact with the land is part of life, within as well as without. For Indigenous peoples, the land is foundational to their way of life and values, hence for mental health and cultural belonging, as Chan shows in her chapter in the present book. Climate change – and before it, industrialization and the exploitation of finite resources – can make activities like hunting, fishing, or cultivating impossible. The impact is more than economic: it is cultural, and there is anger, sadness, frustration, and hopelessness when life is disrupted. It is unbearable to see something you love – your farm, your favourite place, your world, maybe a link with ancestors – blown away.

But what happens when one is already disconnected? People like me, who go to the mountains for a holiday, who maybe have a pet, but never learnt the bond of dependence with 'Mother Nature'. Can I go on thinking that I do not depend on the land for my living? Many people experience 'the land' as exotic, an 'other' place, to which they do not belong. If we have no relationship, or a very mediated one, can there be 'grief'?

I have been doing research with Silvia Luraschi using *sensobiographic* methods (Murray & Järviluoma, 2019; Formenti & Luraschi, 2020), walking together with participants, using senses, and evoking biographical memories about the place. This way of doing research nurtures my sensitivity to the land, to the changes occurred in the area where I live. The stories reveal how people are structurally coupled with their physical environment. We ask them to choose 'a place of the heart', and the relationship between inside and outside is immediately evident. No matter if you do not have an ecological education, or you were not born there, you still feel the wounds. Knowing, being sensitive, means mourning: is this why so many people prefer not to know and keep anaesthetizing themselves? Is it possible that we underestimated the psychological effects of distancing ourselves from nature? We need more research to understand our relationship to the landscape, to the more-than-human environment, and what we learn by and through our relationship to it.

We are connected to our environment, no matter how conscious we are, and when this bond is threatened, we react in different ways, to be understood at a micro, meso and macro level. These feelings are healthy: not 'symptoms' of insanity, but the sign of a connection. The real insanity, as Bateson said, is disconnection. A collective experience of 'ecological grief' could bring a strengthened sense of commitment to the places, ecosystems, and living beings that inspire, nurture, and sustain us. I believe that the global pandemic will exacerbate this need.

3.1 *Linden, My Space*

I, Linden, am a psychoanalytic psychotherapist, a researcher and adult educator. Freud, the father of psychoanalysis, believed in the principles of the Enlightenment, of the importance of reason's triumph over illusion but was aware that empiricism often lacked a language to explain mental phenomenon. Science he observed had little or nothing to say about sexuality, for instance, towards which not one ray of a hypothesis had penetrated this dark hinterland (Symington, 1992). Freud heroically wrote about this taboo subject, shocking the bourgeois world of his time (Kahr, 2020). Yet Freud was something of a romantic and returned, despite himself, to classical and other literary myths, to explain clinical phenomenon, famously the Narcissistic and Oedipus complexes.

How we are caught in our own idealized image, locked into empty worship of self, closed to life, love, others and experience. Freud thought the infatuation in one's own person, including one's genitals, could helpfully draw on the

Greek myth of the beautiful youth dying of self-infatuation, and in the process, killing love, represented by Echo. The narcissist loves what s/he is, and was, and would like to be (Gay, 1988). Or, in the case of the Oedipus complex, we get trapped in the triangle of traditional parental relationships: captured and enraptured by the mother, for instance, against the father whom we might learn to hate. What Freud had in mind, (his ideas developed over time), was ubiquitous evidence of sibling rivalry, rivalry between mothers and daughters, fathers and sons, and even death wishes against other members of the family. This was the stuff of myth and literary tragedy. Such dynamics find expression in the rivalrous academy, and in education, in our ambivalence towards teachers, knowledge and our rivalries with other students. Transformation, from a psychoanalytic view, has to do with engaging with the unconscious, with what is difficult to see and acknowledge – like our sexuality or competitiveness – and to release some of the energy consumed by repression. It is a choice for life over death, Eros over Thanatos, learning over denial.

One trouble with psychoanalysis has been a tendency to stick too rigidly to the micro, and maybe meso level, although Freud wrote about culture too (Freud, 1919/2009). The micro-level is insufficient, if important, when thinking about sustainability in our lives and our relationships to others and a fragile earth. The other dimensions, one way or another, get in the way of seeing things afresh and more openly: whether familial, socio-cultural, economic, political, psychological, spiritual or ecological. There is no clear boundary between external and internal worlds, the social and psychological, the human and non-human. I use a psychosocial/cultural as well as historical frame in the search to understand others, and myself. I am increasingly aware of how modernity's religion is called capitalism, with its passion for unregulated growth, which evokes destruction, despoliation and profound feelings of anger and loss.

What lies 'out there' – the 'context' – shapes the internal world as well as vice versa. All that we know is a product of our perception, which is mediated by the body, by cultural presuppositions, by previous learning. I am a product of a profound disassociation with the natural world called industrialization. As I write these words, I feel torn by complex, confused auto/biographical feelings: partly of anxiety about Coronavirus, but also of loss alongside memories of the ugliness of the industrial revolution, with its many benefits, too in reducing domestic drudgery, as Raymond Williams (1989), the adult educator and cultural historian, forcefully reminds us. I grew up in a city landscape disfigured and polluted by unregulated mining, pottery manufacture and iron and steel production. I was surrounded by slag heaps, as well as new housing estates that embodied, after the Second World War, a spirit of a New Jerusalem. A world of trade unions, cooperatives, workers education, municipal confidence, and socialist politics, much of which has dissipated. It was a world of a reactive commitment to nature, too: of ramblers' associations, cycling in the country-side, and a love of gardening and ecological beauty, in the presence of ugliness. Not on everyone's part, for sure, but many. Now, biographically, I see a different kind of ugliness and neglect in this post-industrial city, called Stoke-on-Trent, in the English Midlands, like many other similar places, wounded by over-rapid deindustrialization, neo-liberal austerity, poverty, individualism and the decline of the welfare state. Basically, by lack of care.

It was a world where adult education was once strong, created by commit-ted men and women who dreamt of a better world and strived for a meaningful well-lived life. Their stories have been of forms of education, different to now, where groups of learners constituted microcosms of a better social order, even of the Kingdom, where beauty or truth could be experienced, however fleet-ing and contentious. Where organized religion still held some sway and the churches, especially the non-conformist, provided hope and spirit in the diffi-cult business of adult education (Goldman, 2013; Rose, 2010; West, 2016, 2017). Questions were asked such as, how can we create a better socially just world? What does history have to teach us? Does life have meaning? Why is there suf-fering and death? How can we pursue happiness? What is the 'good enough' life? Why do events so often feel beyond our control? And what of hate as well as love in our relationships? And what of taking better care of the land, the soil, the water where we live? Questions like these still matter.

Psychoanalytically, I am well aware of the difficult business profounder forms of learning can be. Knowledge is often resisted as well as embraced. Trou-bling thoughts are often repressed, alongside the feelings that prompt them, but anxiety is ever present, even if anaesthetized by alcohol or other drugs. If in Freud's fin-de-siècle Vienna, anxiety surrounded sexuality, and dangerous desire in a rigid bourgeois world, in our world, it might have to do with narcis-sism, fuelled by capitalism's seductive enchantments, false gods, and antipathy to thought. There can be antipathy to thought even in educational contexts, where the cash nexus shapes interactions with students, who, as customers, demand an easily digested product. Zygmunt Bauman (Formenti & West, 2018) has written of the seductions of junk food, of cheap, easy to digest educational sound bites, of a conspiracy against troubling thoughts. Keep it simple, get the grades, sell the institution. Creation groans.

The neglect of the spiritual dimensions of human experience also matters. Secularism, at least of an overly rational kind, may be insufficient when inter-rogating profounder forms of learning. It is interesting that Paulo Freire – so central to radical struggles to learn, in many parts of the world – is often secu-larized and stripped of his fundamental grounding in liberation theology. Irwin

Leopando (2017) writes of how Freire had a deep sensibility towards the divine in everyone. His convictions were rooted in faith, not least in a God coming down to earth in solidarity with the poor. This God died the most brutal of deaths, on a cross but transcended this, mythopoetically, in ways signifying life, strength, and solidarity in the face of hubris and brutal, raw power. Suffering as strength, learning as transcendence: here lie ways to revitalize and sustain education practice. R.H. Tawney, the British adult educator, saw glimpses of the divine in the other too, while Raymond Williams, the humanistic Marxist, was spiritual in his attachment to dialogue and I/Thou dynamics in good adult education practice. Tawney and Williams may in fact have had more in common as educators than what divided them ideologically (West, 2017). What may be happening in our time is a kind of re-sacralization of our relationships with one other, and with the ecologies of which we are a part. Extinction rebellion and other forms of activism are forging a new language of I/Thou-ness, to encompass the other and otherness, diverse species, forests, mountains, oceans, lakes, and the air we breathe. The health of Lake Erie matters in these terms to our own well-being, to our *live*lihoods as well as to the fish and diverse species that rely on clean water in a profoundly interconnected eco-system.

4   Weaving Our Ideas Together

An image of a golden thread helps both of us to weave together fragments of knowledge about ourselves, unconscious life, and the other, of what s/he represents, as well as to appreciate the wisdom of nature. This resonates with Bateson's idea of the sacred as a celebration of wholeness (Bateson & Bateson, 1987). Something not excluding science, mathematics, technology, or conscious purpose, or for that matter reason, but woven together with aesthetics and ethics, unconscious, narrative, mythopoetic and spiritual imaginations. An epistemology of the sacred reasserts certain values and insights lost in the Enlightenment's embrace of positivism and narrow empiricism: if there lies an element of the sacred in all human beings, maybe other species, perhaps in the natural world too, in the sense of an astonishing, connected but vulnerable whole, then this is worthy of recognition and respect. It becomes easier to compose universal ethics emphasizing responsibility and obligation, a sense of shared sacredness, and the unacceptability of oppression, objectification, commodification and environmental abuse.

We have tried to celebrate the possibility of many truths, including subjective truth, so often silenced in evidence-based mantras. Rituals, metaphors, and poetry are relevant here: they can heal the splits of inner and outer, objective and subjective truth, by conveying experience that includes elements of mystery, that cannot easily be communicated in words. Presentational knowledge (Heron, 1996) can liberate our complex, lifelong struggle to understand, including ourselves. What does it mean when Lake Erie is poisoned our psyches are poisoned too? What is happening when a pandemic threatens us all? What does it mean for a species to be annihilated or a rain forest desecrated? There is a sense of tragedy on an epic scale here. But we can recover feelings of awe, mystery, epistemological desire, and transcendence by taking time to notice, to see eternity in the palm of a hand, in Blake's evocative phrase. And through participation in enactments, rituals and ceremonies of resistance and healing, including in adult education. These are not optional extras, but fundamental necessities in the struggle to protect a whole fragile ecology and ourselves. We need myths to teach humility, and our place in the sacredness of a fragile earth, replete with goodness but also danger. Myth and ritual can inspire us to action, to keep us keeping on when everything seems hopeless, and others are contemptuous of what we do.

5   An Enhanced Form of Selfhood

We also need to recognize the limits of individual minds. Deeper collaborative learning is necessary, including re-evaluating the relationships among us, and with the more-than-human world. And in facing our shadows, and capacity for evil, the death wish, and destruction. In our relationships, in our work, we often witness violence and destructiveness, even in university committees redolent with petty spite and competitiveness. It has to be faced and challenged, not avoided. Openness and reflexivity, and encounters with darkness are important disorientating dilemmas (Mezirow, 1991). Sometimes learning of a higher order, as Bateson noted, is like a 'conversion', which Buddhism terms an 'awakening', Jung, 'individuation', and other psychoanalysts, 'integration'. Encounters with the suffering of a lake, the Amazon ablaze, or Covid-19's power – are painful but essential to profounder forms of learning. We mean by this to seek qualities of learning that embrace both life and death, the damage we do alongside the possibilities of reparation. It is an intellectual, imaginative, reflexive, emotional, practical, material, relational and spiritual transformation of perspectives. It is a kind of soul work.

Here lies a task for adult education: the nurturing of qualities like curiosity, emotional openness, critical and self-reflexivity, responsiveness, respect, the capacity for listening and cooperation. Such qualities need good enough, shared spaces to grow. They depend on experiencing (in childhood and adulthood) the good enough love of the (m)other, the attentiveness of a teacher/

educator, the presence of a loving, caring but also curious and courageous group of fellow pilgrims on a quest for enlightenment. To retain hope in such a task, we need faith to imagine that reparation and healing are possible, however difficult our fragile lives and ecologies can seem. An agentic, questioning, challenging, authentic and empathic selfhood, formed in the company of others, can be reborn in adult education, a women's group, a sensobiographic walk, in community action, in psychoanalysis or in respectful research.

6   Conclusion?

Our dialogue has brought us to a complex, changing and fragile landscape. Our different perspectives have been helpful in composing deeper understanding of adult learning, education and the ecology of life, and death. Our quest is limited by who we are, the experiences we have had, the languages we speak, and the hidden perspectives we enact. But we are determined to learn our way to a better place, with the help of our ESREA Network, via our writing and encounters with the darkness as well as sweetness and light of being human.

Transformation might lie in questioning our relationships and the stories we have inherited from our families, groups, and wider cultures, as well as in our growing relationship to diverse eco-systems and a whole planet. Maybe it is too late, and pollution and destructiveness, as well as thoughtless globalization and worship of capitalism, have gone too far. Maybe it is wiser to be a pessimist in such times. We disagree with this, at least in part. As researchers, adult educators and human beings, as mothers, fathers, grandparents, sons and daughters, we recognize a responsibility to struggle and to seek a re-connection of what is pathologically separated: selves, souls and ecologies; minds, hearts and bodies; the social, cultural and the psychological; the conscious and unconscious, human life and the 'natural' world. The auto/biographical narrative research we do offers glimpses into the complex stories of learners, including our own, and heroic struggles to face the damage done, and to consider how this might be repaired, individually and collectively. The ESREA Life History and Biography Network itself represents a whole and vital ecology of learning and life, to inspire us on our way.

References

Bainbridge, A., & West, L. (2012). *Psychoanalysis and education. Minding a gap.* Karnac.
Bateson, G. (1972). *Steps to an ecology of mind.* Ballantine Books.

Bateson, G. (1979). *Mind and nature. A necessary unity.* Bantam Books.

Bateson, G., & Bateson, M. C. (1987). *Angels fear. Towards an epistemology of the sacred.* Macmillan.

Buber, M. (1937). *I and thou.* T. & T. Clark. (Original work published 1922)

Clayton, S., Manning, C. M., Krygsman, K., & Speiser, M. (2017). *Mental health and our changing climate: Impacts, implications, and guidance.* https://www.apa.org/news/press/releases/2017/03/mental-health-climate.pdf

Cunsolo, A., & Ellis, N. R. (2018). Ecological grief as a mental health response to climate change-related loss. *Nature Climate Change, 8,* 275–281.

Ellis, N., & Cunsolo, A. (2018). *Hope and mourning in the Anthropocene. Understanding ecological grief.* http://theconversation.com/hope-and-mourning-in-the-anthropocene-understanding-ecological-grief-88630

Formenti, L. (2018). Complexity, adult biographies and co-operative transformation. In M. Milana, S. Webb, J. Holford, R. Waller, & P. Jarvis (Eds.), *The Palgrave international handbook on adult and lifelong education and learning* (pp. 191–209). Palgrave Macmillan.

Formenti, L. (2019). Perspectives on context: Metaphors, epistemologies, and theoretical definitions. In B. Merrill, A. Nizinska, A. Galimberti, J. Eneau, E. Sanojca, & S. Bezzari (Eds.), *Exploring learning contexts: Implications for access, learning careers and identities* (pp. 45–58). Université Rennes 2.

Formenti, L., & Luraschi, S. (2020). Migration, culture contact and the complexity of coexistence: Asystemic imagination. *European Journal for Research on the Education and Learning of Adults, 11*(3), 349–365.

Formenti, L., & West, L. (Eds.). (2016). *Stories that make a difference. Exploring the collective, social, and political potential of narratives in adult education research.* Pensa Multimedia.

Formenti, L., & West, L. (2018). *Transforming perspectives in lifelong learning and adult education. A dialogue.* Palgrave Macmillan.

Formenti, L., West, L., & Horsdal, M. (Eds.). (2014). *Embodied narratives. Connecting stories, bodies, cultures and ecologies.* University of Southern Denmark.

Fraser, W. (2018). *Seeking wisdom in adult teaching and learning: An autoethnographic inquiry.* Palgrave Macmillan.

Freud, S. (2009). *Totem and taboo.* Camino Classics. (Original work published 1919)

Gay, P. (1988). *Freud, a life for our time.* Dent and Sons.

Galway, L. P., Beery, T., Jones-Casey, K., & Tasala, K. (2019). Mapping the solastalgia literature: A scoping review study. *International Journal of Environmental Research and Public Health, 16*(15), 2662. https://doi.org/10.3390/ijerph16152662

Goldman, L. (2013). *The life of R. H. Tawney. Socialism and history.* Bloomsbury Academic.

Head, L. (2015). The Anthropoceneans. *Geographical Research, 53*(3), 313–320. https://doi.org/10.1111/1745-5871.12124

Heron, J. (1996). *Co-operative inquiry. Research into the human condition.* Sage.

Kahr, B. (2020, June 19). How Freud would have handled the Coronavirus. *The Freud Museum.* https://www.freud.org.uk/event/how-freud-would-have-handled-the-coronavirus-lessons-from-a-beacon-of-survival/

Leopando, I. (2017). *A pedagogy of faith, the theological vision of Paulo Freire.* Bloomsbury.

McCarraher, E. (2019). *The enchantments of Mammon: How capitalism became the religion of modernity.* Harvard University Press.

Mezirow, J. (1991). *Transformative dimensions of adult learning.* Wiley & Sons.

Murray, L., & Järviluoma, H. (2019). Walking as transgenerational methodology. *Qualitative Research, 20*(2), 229–238. https://doi.org/10.1177/1468794119830533

Rose, J. (2010). *The intellectual life of the British working classes.* Yale University Press.

Steffen, W., Crutzen, P. J., & McNeill, J. R. (2007). The Anthropocene: Are humans now overwhelming the great forces of nature? *Sciences Module, 36*(8), 614–621.

Symington, N. (1992). *The analytic experience. Lectures from the Tavistock.* Free Association Books.

Tisdell, E., & Swartz, A. (Eds.). (2011). *Adult education and the pursuit of wisdom.* Jossey-Bass.

Weil, S. (1952). *The need for roots. Prelude towards a declaration of duties towards mankind.* Routledge.

West, L. (2016). *Distress in the city. Racism, fundamentalism and a democratic education.* Trentham Books, UCL Institute of Education Press.

West, L. (2017). Resisting the enormous condescension of posterity: Richard Henry Tawney, Raymond Williams and the long struggle for a democratic education. *International Journal of Lifelong Education, 36*(1–2), 129–144.

Williams, R. (1989). *Resources of hope: Culture, democracy, socialism.* Verso.

Yu, V. (2020, April 16). What is a wet market? *The Guardian.* Retrieved March 17, 2021, from https://www.theguardian.com/global-development/2020/apr/16/what-is-a-wet-market-coronavirus

Biographical Interviews and the Micro Context of Biographicity: Closely Listening for Meaning, Learning, and Voice

Rob Evans

Abstract

The chapter examines the capacity of the biographical/life history interview for understanding closely heard talk in interaction. The chapter seeks to question how the emergence and sharing of biographical discourse in interview talk may be identified and described; what evidence is found in interview talk of biographical self or 'biographicity', a concept derived from Peter Alheit (2006, 2018); what is the relation between language and voice in a biographical narrative, with particular reference to the notions of 'synthesis' (Löw, 2001) and 'verbalisation' (Schiffrin, 1996). To do this, the author presents experiences related and shared in the micro context of interview interaction and for this purpose, a section of a biographical narrative of a Polish teacher is introduced and discussed. The private history of the teacher Daria is understood as biographised talk, which is structured both temporally and sequentially. Through the changing interaction between Daria and the researcher and through the wider out-of-frame interaction of both with their respective social worlds, it can be seen that strong elements of interdiscursivity and insight into wider ecologies of learning and living enrich the work of meaning-making that learning biographies represent.

Key words

biographical interview – biographicity – synthesis – verbalisation – ecologies of learning

1 Introduction

This chapter will seek to examine and assess the fitness of the biographical/life history interview for understanding closely heard talk in interaction. Questions that this chapter will seek to answer are: (a) how the emergence

© ROB EVANS, 2021 | DOI: 10.1163/9789004465916_003

and sharing of biographical discourse in interview talk may be identified and described; (b) what evidence of biographical self or 'biographicity' (Alheit, 2006, 2018) is encountered in the interview interaction; what is the relation between language and voice in a biographical narrative; how do we encounter and recognise biographical learning? A consideration of the temporality, contextuality and reflexivity (Alheit, 2018) of biographical processes will help to comprehend how meaning, learning and voice can emerge from the accumulated layers of experience that represent a stock of resources of experience. These can potentially be 'used' to create a kind of intuitive sense of an own biography, that is self-referential and yet remains 'porous', transforming and being transformed in ongoing interactions.

The emphasis in the following pages will be on the experiences related and shared in the micro context of the interview interaction and for this purpose, a section of a biographical narrative of a Polish teacher will be introduced and discussed. The private history of the teacher Daria (connected with that of the researcher Rozalia Ligus who originally conducted the interview) is listened to and understood as biographised talk, which is structured both temporally and sequentially. Through the changing interaction between Daria and Rozalia and through the wider out-of-frame interaction of both with their respective social worlds, strong elements of interdiscursivity enrich the work of meaning-making that these learning biographies represent.

Context, therefore, is centrally important here. Adopting Norman Fairclough's "three different 'levels' of social organization" (Fairclough, 1989, p. 25) for the production of social discourse, we can see the level of the interview itself to be an acutely interactive context which encompasses the physical setting and the joint accomplishment of understanding in interactive talk. At a further remove, the interview is embedded in wider interactive contexts, including the institutional character of the research interview and its organisation, the workplace, family and generation, region and community. Finally, there is the broader context of social discourses, the social, national or supra-national context in which the participants and the institutions involved live out their roles and positions.

Their encounter in the interview entails very concretely a revisiting in biographical narrative of former communist Poland (1945–89) and its ideological values and language uses told, however, in the personal and professional vernaculars of post-communist Polish society. Thus, the micro interactions of the interview are heard within the meso and macro contexts of complex institutional and social relations, and through the lens of political and personal transformations.

2 The Biographical Interview and Interview Interaction

Qualitative research addresses the most vital areas of individual and group experience of social reality by observing, questioning and recording the testimony of the actors themselves in sites of social interaction chosen for the collection of data. The relationship between social actors involved in processes of change and learning and the researcher is part of any such learning process which is studied through various types of interview. The nature of the interaction and relationship that arises in qualitative interviews has been the object of much research writing through the successive methodological turns of the last few decades. Of particular importance was the move from the more 'realist' kind of ethnographic interviewing originating in the Chicago school to a critically reflexive methodology strongly influenced by feminist discourse (for an early discussion of this transition see, for example, Denzin, 1989). Another important strand of research is represented still at present by the originally German-Austrian sociological 'narrative interview' founded in the phenomenological tradition of Husserl and the 'Lebenswelt' ('life world') (Husserl, 1986), and developed notably by Fritz Schütze in a number of dense methodological articles (e.g. Schütze, 1976, 1981) and since deployed by generations of social scientists and educational researchers (Fiedler & Krüger, 2016, pp. 7–9). This branch of biography research is traditionally concerned to leave respondent data 'uncontaminated' by researcher influence. It can with some justification be criticised for reliance, too, on a relatively narrow and outdated theory of speech practice (e.g. Schütze, 1976, pp. 224–230; Kallmeyer & Schütze, 2016, pp. 173–175) and an inadequate theoretical accommodation of the rich pluri-vocality of interview interaction. While Schütze himself could show a committed openness for the "presentational capacity of autobiographical extempore narration" and its singular modes of expression (Schütze, 2016, p. 112), more frequently the "formal-structural textual features" (2016, p. 112) of narrative come to the fore in this field of research and the researcher's voice is dominant.

The exact nature of the researcher/respondent relationship can vary, of course, though most frequently today it is characterised by the shared nature of meaning-making in (mostly dialogic) interaction, by a participatory, empathetic style of communication, and by a self/reflexive approach to the encounter as a whole and its many-faceted 'results'. Examples of such relationships, whether, by way of example, involving single mothers' narratives in West's or working-class women learners in Merrill's work show how the interview can serve as a catalyst for biographical narratives of change (Merrill & West, 2009, pp. 133–141). The ESREA Life History and Biography Research Network has contributed in the last two decades to an opening of interpretive and analytical methods to encompass more areas of empathetic, creative, psychosocial or therapeutic dialogue in interaction, transcending the single interview form, even if the interview, understood as co-creation of meaning in talk, for the author, remains the cardinal tool for approaching the life stories of others.

As a research methodology, the understanding of discursive-biographical interviewing as a branch of qualitative research assumes, then, that the biographical research interview is interactive, co-constructed, flooded with inter-discursivity, and that it constructs and constitutes local action and meaning-making in the rich ecologies of learning and living.

3   Biography and Context: The Ecologies of a Told Life

The layers of experience of accumulated and consciously accessed biographical resources can be looked upon as a new form of knowledge. This biographical knowledge, emerging out of the precarious balance-act between the life-being-lived and unlived or potentially-liveable life, is nourished by the stock of experience that is not unconditionally accessible, but which nevertheless represents more alternatives for filling out the social field we live out our lives in than we can realistically grasp or take control of. Alheit refers to this as the 'over-spill' of *potential* lives we accumulate that feeds our knowledge of ourselves, our life-stories and their meaning in relation to others (Alheit, 2006, p. 5).

3.1   *The Relational Nature of Biographical Knowledge*
Central to this understanding of biographical knowledge construction is the *relational* nature of biographical narratives and biographical 'work'. Learning and knowledge acquisition, predicated as they are on biographical experience, are embedded in social learning environments or 'Lernumwelten' (Ecarius, 1997). The contexts of learning identity formation are analogously understood here as interconnected 'ecologies of knowledge" (Anspach, 1987, cited in Miller, 1997, p. 167) in which situation-specific interactional meanings are organised. According to this view of things, subjects make use of the resources of different, socially organised settings to which they belong (or to which they are positioned as belonging, for example) in order to discursively constitute and reconstitute themselves and the institutional settings in which they interact (Miller, 1997, pp. 167–169).

To understand such ecologies of knowledge and learning, we must think of the spaces in which talk is unfolded. When telling their lives, people use language to recreate lived spaces in their talk. Martina Löw calls this 'synthesis': speakers establish the spaces in their stories as existing in tension or opposition to their own present-time location as they perceive or claim that to be

(Löw, 2001, p. 214). Such an action of synthesis, which connects, includes or excludes people and things through the acts of understanding, memory and imagination, constitutes and 'fixes' the spaces inhabited by, and accessible to, the subject and others.

Biographies, their narrative forms, and their subjects are conspicuously constructed in relation to 'others' (Mason, 2004). Memory, too, as Halbwachs has argued (Halbwachs, 1997, pp. 65–66) arises in the relationship to others, in the physical and emotional company of collective experience. Ricoeur underlines this centrality of shared experience and shared memory of body and place, of ecologies of knowledge and experience. Memories of places lived in or visited "interlace in one and the same moment an intimate memory and a memory shared among those close to one ...". Our relationship to this intersection of the bodily and the spatial opened up to us in recollection and narrative remains an "arduous" effort of memory work, so to speak, and of perception of the roads followed and obstacles surmounted (Ricoeur, 2000, p. 184, author's translation).

Experience mediated by memory is voiced and constructed in narratives held together by language which draws, in Habermas' words, on 'grammars' of telling (Habermas, 1981, p. 207). These 'grammars' can be thought of as shared language-worlds for telling life-stories and co–constructing biographical knowledge. Shared understanding of narrative practice (how to begin, how to finish, how to express judgement, emotion, reluctance, and so on) is used to build the theories and standpoints that emerge in narratives as pieces of such ongoing effective biographic knowledge (for the discourse components of narrative see Ochs & Capps, 2001, pp. 18–20). Embodied experiential memory, seen like this, is the basis of the life (lived, unlived, to be lived, re-called) told in the interview.

3.2   *Interaction, the Construction of the Social and the Self*
Interactions of all kinds, then, family or work situations, social relations, social or cultural practice(s) must all be seen as sites in which 'doing biography' is practiced, that is, working on the construction of, and deployment and use of, biographical resources. The discourse practices involved in the biographical co-work 'done' in the biographical research interview context reach out across times of the life and connect with the materiality of social life, but their production – in the interview – is local. Therefore, the detail at the micro level serves to document openly how this meaning-making takes place, how this is affected by group belonging, ethnic or cultural discourses, gender, age, political events, global environmental issues, and so on.

The language in which pieces of our life-stories and events which we have experienced directly (or vicariously through the narratives of others) are welded together is 'multivocal' (Schiffrin, 2006, p. 204) and multi-layered. Alheit and Dausien compare the spatial complexity of narratable biographical

resources with a "landscape made up of different strata and regions of different levels of nearness and distance" (Alheit & Dausien, 2002, p. 578, author's
translation). The temporal organisation of discourse, too, involves multiple
time-planes, and non-linear trajectories through lives.

4   Biographicity: Time, Context, Reflexivity

Life stories, Alheit argues, are essentially occupied with the necessity to syn-
chronise two disparate levels of experienced time: firstly, the dimension of
events and experiences which usually have a routine, daily, everyday frame, and
secondly, those which operate on the life-time scale/horizon, which "links long
past events with past experiences, past with present experience and ultimately
present with conceivable future events" (Alheit, 1983, p. 189, author's translation; on frames see Tannen, 1993). To re-work the reserve of experiences with
the newly experienced and bring about new associations between the new and
the already-lived means that the narrator draws on their collected and layered
biographical resources. These resources we can think of as the individual sum
or distillation of many different learning processes. They are the result of the
individual meaning given to experience which produces subjective forms of
knowledge. This knowledge in its turn is the basis of new cultural and social
structures of experience. This social practice of accessing (and constructing)
life-wide biographical resources – 'biographicity' in Alheit's words – enables
and shapes temporal and continually emerging and changing context-bound
reflexivity in order to meet the everyday requirements of an individually
steered life-course. As Alheit points out: "This biographical structure virtually
constitutes the individuality of the self. It can be understood to be a temporally
layered, individual configuration consisting of social experiences – including,
of course, embodied and emotional sentiments" (Alheit, 2018, p. 14).

Accumulated experience cannot simply be understood, however, as an
absolute sum, a mere wholesale collection of impressions, memories, emotions
that can be accessed freely, limitlessly, effortlessly. The laying-down of experience
itself structures ulterior learning processes and narrows or widens the room
for learning. This narrowing and enabling that is a hallmark of 'biographicity'
is interesting, Alheit suggests, because it can only be accessed, used or steered
consciously by the individual to a limited extent. It remains only partially
accessible to Others (e.g. in pedagogical input) and can 'surprise' the 'owner' by
the life-openings it makes possible or, too, those it closes off (Alheit, 2018, p. 15).

Biographical narratives, then, are to a large extent reliant both on the many
details of the everyday and the ambiguous and re-used words shared in interaction with others. As each narrator of a life history dialogues with others

whose voices speak from the near and distant contexts in which the narrated life is embedded, biographical (self-) knowledge is more grasped at through intuition and feeling, more guessed at in language, than 'known' in certainty. Memory and recollection, recall – reaching 'back' to reclaim what has happened in our past – remains always the "enigma of the presence of what is absent" (Ricoeur, 2000, p. 9, author's translation). Recall and memory are incomplete and unreliable, yet, as Ricoeur reminds us, "Put brutally, we have nothing other than memory to show that something took place, happened ..." (2000, p. 26, author's translation). Notwithstanding, recollection of biographical experience through the inclusion of the absent past in the narrated present does provide, Schiffrin writes, "gradual understanding of 'what happened' and leads to reconstruction of the meanings of past experiences" (Schiffrin, 2006, p. 205).

5 Daria's Story

Taking up Schiffrin's remarks and Alheit's notion of the workings of biographicity in life-wide biographical resources, I shall turn now to examine short extracts from one of a number of interviews with Polish teachers carried out by Rozalia Ligus in Polish Pomerania between 2002 and 2004 (Ligus, 2009; for the transcript see pp. 267–277). I provide an impressionistic English translation of the Polish, but analysis of the language refers at all times to the Polish original. The discussion here of the extracts is based on Ligus' transcription. As far as possible, faithfulness to the original language of the interaction and therefore to the intercultural pragmatics of the reception process and the explication of the results of data analysis should be attended to in research of this kind (Pavlenko, 2007, p. 172). Transcription is, of course, as Elinor Ochs pointed out many years ago, theory put into practice (Ochs, 1979, p. 44) and specific transcription methods reflect specific research aims and affect research outcomes. The shape of speech, with all its slurring, accelerations, repetitions, self-repairs, pauses, changes in volume – in short the prosodic-affective features of natural talk (see for example Tannen, 2007, pp. 22, 32) are largely absent in the extracts used here. The language used in the extracts, too, quite apart from any regional or dialectal features, remains a foreign language the author has understanding of without spoken linguistic fluency and as such there are certainly whole dimensions of meaning in the talk that are inadequately understood. It is therefore imperative, when examining the talk of others, to be aware always of these and other constraints on understanding. This is a further reason for serious caution and restraint when offering explanations and interpretations of what is said in the interview.

5.1   *Daria: First Story and Second Story*

Daria, in this part of her story about her decision to become a teacher, is describing an experience which significantly transformed her biography. Daria's account is divided into a 'first story' (for a lengthier discussion of this part of Daria's biography see Evans, 2013, pp. 238–240) and a 'second story'. Daria signals at the outset that this is the beginning/*początek* of a series of experiences. Such signals are an important signpost for a coming structuring of events and are important for the contextualisation of the interaction and enhance the sequential coherence of the flow of narrative. Harvey Sacks draws our attention to the 'work' that such prefacing does in preparing the co-speaker for the outcome which has yet to be unrolled. First stories implicate the telling of 'second stories' (Sacks, 1992, pp. 19–21). The 'outcome' here – Daria's identity as a mature teacher – will be justified in her account by the beginnings. This strong "general teleological focus" is found in all autobiographical narratives, Schiffrin remarks (2006, p. 205), by virtue of which former events in lives assume a greater directedness than they may have had when they first occurred; the story is told/re-told with the "final point" in view which provides the narrative its sense of direction (Ricoeur, 1983, pp. 130–131).

She became a teacher in communist Poland in 1979. By deciding at the age of eight, as she recounts it, to be a teacher, she was looking beyond her regional and family background in which there was no previous history of any higher school education. Her narrative, therefore, must justify the choices she made, must explain her ambition, and has to take account, too, of her path from her family origins and rural social class to her adult self and her current professional identity (for a detailed discussion of Daria see Ligus, 2009, pp. 151–156; see also Ligus & Evans, 2016).

5.2   *Shared Discourse and Ecologies of Knowledge*

Before Daria comes to her 'second story' which will propose a meaningful explanation and justification for her decision to become a teacher, she proposes an equally interesting rationalisation for the 'strangeness' of her career choice. In fact, she chooses the explanation perhaps most expected by both participants – the narrator and the interviewer, Rozalia Ligus. As an example of the notion of 'tellability' (Ochs & Capps, 2001, pp. 33–36), Daria makes explicit reference to social-political frames of reference which she knows will be familiar to Ligus. In doing this, Daria establishes complicity, based on comparable experience, but also based on the assumption (at the start of the 2000s in Poland) that Ligus will understand fully what she says: literally, that her family was working class/country folk and that becoming a teacher represented a significant social 'leap' upwards. The researcher will equally understand the layers of irony and humour (and resentment) that linger on in such terminology in post-communist Poland. They will, it can be assumed, understand tacitly a whole range of arguments about the social 'suitability' or 'political maturity' of the rural population, and will share experience and knowledge of the role and distribution of individual social and political capital in Poland in the 1970s and 80s and how these changed after the fall of communism (Popow, 2015, pp. 26–33). Deeper still, we can assume possible shared knowledge of the post-war history of the region in which Daria's life-history and career was played out (Ligus, 2009, pp. 21–57). Ligus puts it thus: "My choice was made because I presumed it would be easier for me to follow her story, even if I started my career 500 kilometers away from her place of work. That was the reason behind the choice of Daria" (Ligus and Evans, 2016, p. 690).

Daria's narrative leads us very skilfully to an intimate explanation of her early career choice. Daria leads into her 'second story' with a cautious-suggestive *może/perhaps* and proceeds to lay down a description of a significant figure in her life.

Extract 1   Daria's 'second story'

Może w sąsiednim bloku, raczej pode mną, mieszkała taka pani, która już była kształcona właśnie przed wojną.	Perhaps because there was this lady who lived in the neighbouring block quite near me who was educated you know before the war	*Localisation*: w sąsiednim bloku, raczej pode mną *Hedging*. Może *Adverbs of time/evaluation*: już była kształcona, właśnie przed wojną.
Ona była nauczycielką muzyki. Już wtenczas, w tym okresie, była tak, koło emerytury, ale już miała za sobą ten okres ... Mogła odjeść [*na emeryturę*] w każdej chwili.	She was a music teacher at that time in that period it was like that with pensioners but she was already beyond that she could go into retirement at any moment	*Categories of place, profession*: nauczycielką muzyki *Difference*: Mogła odjeść w każdej chwili
		Affective
I ona właśnie była dla mnie takim może (.4.) wzorem – ja wiem?	And she was really for me a possible sort of (4) model – I think	*Hedging:* właśnie, takim może (.4.) wzorem *Negative epistemic position:* ja wiem?

This description begins in a straightforward way: we are introduced to a 'lady' who lived in a neighbouring block of flats. The important content of this introductory description is communicated by a delayed unfolding of the information: for the lady in the neighbourhood was educated *before the war*. The demonstrative adjective used – *taka pani/this woman* emphasises that something is yet to come. She was 'already' – or rather *had been educated/had got her education*, to render the idea in a simple grammatical sense – educated. The simplicity of these words belies – almost – the evaluative force contained in them. The tell-tale modal particles of time and manner (*już already/właśnie just*), however, underline the import of what Daria is beginning to say. Against the background of her own family upbringing, which in her own words (as indicated above) possessed no tradition, no experience of higher education, this lady from the neighbourhood represented an entirely different world of culture, education, and social behaviour. In some European countries, I would argue, the epithet 'pre-war' might be construed as backward-looking, old-fashioned, conservative, or 'pre-democratic' and so on. Raymond Williams, for example, characterises the vote of the British working-class in the UK General Election of 1951, "still in conditions of post-war austerity" as a vote to "reject the conditions of *pre-war society*" (Williams, 1965, p. 356, my italics). This is not necessarily the case in Poland.[1] These words were used by Daria to conjure up a commonly shared and idealised alternative to the degradation of the present. 'Before the war' was an intact world of values, of beauty, of refinement, of culture. 'Old Poland'. All now gone. And doubtless understood by Rozalia Ligus.

Daria evidently does not understand it negatively. Quite the contrary, for – though hedged and ostensibly questioned (*właśnie just/takim może sort of like/ ja wiem? I think*) – this educated lady (*taka pani, … kształcona*) is proposed as her (possible) model who in some way influenced Daria's decision to become a teacher.

6   'Synthesis' and 'Verbalisation': Explanation through Language of Place or Objects or Period

In this next small stretch of talk Daria unfolds an atmospheric narrative that complements the social and emotional reasons she has already proposed for her decision. In her interaction with Rozalia Ligus she is doing significant 'work' of 'synthesis' (Löw, 2001) to construct a coherent story and reach a level of shared understanding. The turn to suggestive detail of place, of time and of person are convincing examples, too, of what Schiffrin calls 'verbalisation'. This is, she says, "the way we symbolize, transform, and displace a stretch of experience from our past … into linguistically represented episodes, events, processes, and states". Bringing cultural knowledge and past experience to bear, verbalisation "provides a resource for the display of self and identity" (Schiffrin, 1996, p. 168). Daria presents the music teacher as cultured and educated, and she puts the person into a highly telling relationship with the cultured space she occupies or is encountered in: *Wykształconą osobą, kulturalną, właśnie z tym swoim domem/An educated person, cultured, and that flat she lived in!* Actual contact with the person and the space is described as rare. The impression left on her is all the stronger, and this is recreated by the almost dream-like inventory of the unusual, thrillingly out-of-the-ordinary objects encountered, no doubt with fascination, the few times Daria was able to see them. The language is strongly evaluative. It works by employing the cumulative effects of listing, of repetition, and the details are allowed to occupy the foreground as Daria recounts her experience as an observer, allowing the interviewer (and us) to see the scene she evokes through her (inquisitive or dazzled) eyes.

Extract 2   Daria's 'second story' continued

Wykształconą osobą, kulturalną, właśnie z tym swoim domem. Ja rzadko bywałam w tym mieszkaniu, ale to było właśnie takie i takie różne stare, stylowe meble, fortepian, były skrzypce, i takie różne	An educated person, cultured, and that flat she lived in! I wasn't often in that apartment but there were really these these different old things stylish furniture a piano old violin and various things like that	*Categories of person, space and objects:* Personal traits: Wykształconą, kulturalną Spaces of difference: z tym swoim domem, Ja rzadko bywałam w tym mieszkaniu A diverse world: takie różne stare, stylowe meble, fortepian, były skrzypce

---

7   To Conclude

Our worlds are complex, we agree. By carrying out micro-analysis of language in interview talk, it becomes possible to hear and see some of that complexity: how biographical discourse emerges and is shared and understood. Attention to evidence of biographical self or 'biographicity' (Alheit, 2018) as it is co-constructed in the interview interaction requires that we recognise the tension of different life-time planes within the narrative; that we are aware of the dovetailing of contexts and spaces that clothe and house the protagonists with the props of power, culture, position; that we can listen for biographical learning taking place in the tension between co-constructed language and an own voice.

The close examination of a biographical narrative such as that produced by Daria and the researcher Rozalia Ligus demonstrates, I argue, how the self-reflexive language of biography is capable of creating in the moment of telling multiple ecologies of learning and living that enrich the understanding, in an immediate sense, of those involved, but which has the potential to reach and influence much broader ecological interactions – in family and work, in education, communities, and at the level of societies – creating hope, defeating exclusion.

When Daria employs carefully-constructed language, with all its incomparable textures and nuances, to recreate lived spaces in her talk, she performs a 'synthesis' (Löw, 2001, p. 214), putting people and things, in the told life into relationships, deploying efforts of understanding, memory and imagination, and, we may hope, providing in this way some view onto different worlds in which learning lives are located. And, quite possibly, her process of building 'biographicity' can be a valuable aid, too, to the researchers who worked with her and with each other on her narrative, and to their ecologies of practice and theory, their colleagues and networks, in the struggle for better, more sustainable ecologies of learning and living.

Note

1   Indeed, a discussion of this transcript with a young Polish sociologist encountered by chance on a Polish train in 2010 brought our very different understandings of the words 'pre-war' very rapidly to the brink of a heated discussion, happily averted in time to alight from the train together with a rapidly enhanced sense of the range of viewpoints possible and necessary in 21st-century Europe (see Ligus & Evans, 2016, pp. 697–698).

References

Alheit, P. (1983). *Alltagsleben. Zur Bedeutung eines gesellschaftlichen "Restphänomens"*. Campus Verlag.

Alheit, P. (2006). *'Biografizität' als Schlüsselkompetenz in der Moderne*. Paper presented at the Universität Flensburg Conference: "Das Leben gestalten. Biografisch lernen – biografisch lehren". http://www.abl-uni-goettingen.de/aktuell/ Alheit_Biographizitaet_Schluessel_Flensburg-2006.pdf

Alheit, P. (2018). The concept of 'Biographicity' as background concept of lifelong learning. *Dyskursy mlodych andragogow, 19*(9), 9–22. https://doi.org/10.34768/dma.vi19.41

Alheit, P., & Dausien, B. (2002). Bildungsprozesse über die Lebensspanne und lebenslanges Lernen. In R. Tippelt (Ed.), *Handbuch Bildungsforschung* (pp. 565–585). Leske + Budrich.

Denzin, N. K. (1989). *Interpretive biography*. Sage.

Ecarius, J. (1997). Lebenslanges Lernen und Disparitäten in sozialen Räumen. In J. Ecarius & M. Löw (Eds.), *Raumbildung Bildungsräume: Über die Verräumlichung sozialer Prozesse* (pp. 33–62). Leske + Budrich.

Evans, R. (2013). Biography research, the qualitative interview and language 'data': analysing dialogic interaction. In A. Szerłąg (Ed.), *Wiełokulturowósc – międzykulturowósc w edukacji akademickiej: Ku nowej jakosci kształcenia* (pp. 231–245). Oficyna Wydawnicza ATUT.

Fairclough, N. (1989). *Language and power*. Longman.

Fiedler, W., & Krüger, H.-H. (Eds.). (2016). *Fritz Schütze. Sozialwissenschaftliche Prozessanalyse: Grundlagen der qualitativen Sozialforschung*. Verlag Barbara Budrich.

Habermas, J. (1981). *Theorie des kommunikativen Handelns. Zweiter Band. Zur Kritik der funktionalistischen Vernunft*. Suhrkamp Verlag.

Halbwachs, M. (1997). *La mémoire collective*. Albin Michel.

Husserl, E. (1986). *Phänomenologie der Lebenswelt*. Reclam.

Kallmeyer, W., & Schütze, F. (2016). Konversationsanalyse. In W. Fiedler & H.-H. Krüger (Eds.), *Fritz Schütze. Sozialwissenschaftliche Prozessanalyse: Grundlagen der qualitativen Sozialforschung* (pp. 151–180). Verlag Barbara Budrich.

Ligus, R. (2009). *Biograficzna tożsamośc nauczycieli: Historie z pogranicza*. Wydawnictwo Naukowe Dolnosląskiej Szkoly Wyzszej.

Ligus, R., & Evans, R. (2016). Daria. A polish teacher and two researchers' stories. In R. Evans (Ed.), *Before, beside and after (beyond) the biographical narrative* (pp. 698–713). nisaba verlag.

Löw, M. (2001). *Raumsoziologie*. Suhrkamp Verlag.

Mason, J. (2004). Personal narratives, relational selves: Residential histories in the living and telling. *The Sociological Review, 52*(2), 162–179.

Merrill, B., & West, L. (2009). *Using biographical methods in social research*. Sage.

Miller, G. (1997). Toward ethnographies of institutional discourse: Proposals and suggestions. In G. Miller & R. Dingwall (Eds.), *Context and method in qualitative research* (pp. 155–171). Sage.

Ochs, E. (1979). Transcription as theory. In E. Ochs & B. B. Schieffelin (Eds.), *Developmental pragmatics* (pp. 43–72). Academic Press.

Ochs, E., & Capps, L. (2001). *Living narrative. Creating lives in everyday storytelling*. Harvard University Press.

Pavlenko, A. (2007). Autobiographic narratives as data in applied linguistics. *Applied Linguistics, 28*(2), 163–188.

Popow, M. (2015). *Kategoria narodu w dyskursie edukatsyjnym: Analiza procesów konstruowania tożsamości w podręcznikach szkolnych*. Wydawnictwo Naukowe.

Ricœur, P. (1983). *Temps et récit: L'intrigue et le récit historique*. Éditions du Seuil.

Ricœur, P. (2000). *La mémoire, l'histoire, l'oubli*. Éditions du Seuil.

Sacks, H. (1992). *Lectures in conversation* (Vol. II). Blackwell.

Schiffrin, D. (1996). Narrative as self-portrait: Sociolinguistic constructions of identity. *Language in Society, 25*, 167–203.

Schiffrin, D. (2006). *In other words. Variation in reference and narrative*. Cambridge University Press.

Schütze, F. (1976). Zur Hervorlockung und Analyse von Erzählungen thematisch relevanter Geschichten im Rahmen soziologischer Feldforschung. In Arbeitsgruppe Bielefelder Soziologen (Ed.), *Kommunikative Sozialforschung* (pp. 159–261). Wilhelm Fink Verlag.

Schütze, F. (1981). Prozeßstrukturen des Lebenslaufs. In J. Matthes, A. Pfeifenberger, & M. Stosberg (Eds.), *Biographie in handlungswissenschaftlicher Perspektive: Kolloquium am Sozialwissenschaftlichen Forschungszentrum der Universität Erlangen-Nürnberg* (pp. 67–157). Verlag der Nürnberger Forschungsvereinigung e.V.

Schütze, F. (2016). Biography analysis on the empirical base of autobiographical narratives: How to analyse autobiographical narrative interviews. In W. Fiedler & H.-H. Krüger (Eds.), *Fritz Schütze: Sozialwissenschaftliche Prozessanalyse: Grundlagen der qualitativen Sozialforschung* (pp. 75–115). Verlag Barbara Budrich.

Tannen, D. (Ed.). (1993). *Framing in discourse*. Oxford University Press.

Tannen, D. (2007). *Talking voices. Repetition, dialogue, and imagery in conversational discourse*. Cambridge University Press.

Williams, R. (1965). *The long revolution*. Penguin Books.

CHAPTER 3

Narrative Regimes: An Alliance between Descriptive Phenomenology and Biography

Hervé Breton

Abstract

The wholeness of a narrative can be thought of from different parameters. One of them use to be underestimated or absent in biographical narratives: it is the ecological sphere from which the narrator experiences the "physical world". Integrating the dimensions of the sensitive life into the practices of self-telling requires a combination of different narrative regimes. The processes of this form of inquiry are the subject of the study proposed in this chapter.

Keywords

biography – ecoformation – narrative regime – microphenomenology

1   Introduction

Narrative inquiry can be, and is more often, understood as an investigation referring to an epistemology of singularity. By paying attention to life history and to the lived experience of human people, in fact, narratives contribute to understanding, from the subject's point of view, the process of self-development and the constitution of experiential knowledge. However, as Pineau (1983/2012) suggested, it is possible to consider each story's singularity and subjectivity as containing/contained by the collective and social as well as biological life: this ecology is central to Pineau's proposal, his tripolar theory being inspired by Rousseau's three masters and Bachelard's work on imagination and matter. This led Pineau to coordinate four collective books devoted to human formation in contact with the four elements: earth, water, air and fire. Part of his work on "ecoformation" is marked by the concept of formative transaction, which implies an awareness of the relationship maintained with the environment, this relationship being taken in a dialectic between the habit of exploitative relationships and those relating to the awareness of an ecosystemic and reflexive world.

In this chapter, I will address the ecologic dimensions of human lives and learning that can be grasped by comparing and combining different narrative regimes, namely in analysing my own experience and epistemology about narratives, time, and the constitution of a researcher's identity and thought. I will propose a dialogue between different frames, that together may enrich our view of narratives and biographies. I will refer mainly to the French speaking world and the long-standing tradition of *histoires de vie*, that is a way to frame life histories in adult education and learning by developing settings for self-narration. This brings French – and maybe Southern Europe's – biographical researchers nearer to the field of intervention, if compared with other traditions of inquiry in Northern Europe. In this approach there is no rigid separation between research and education, and no claim for the researcher's distance or objectivity, but a desire to celebrate complexity and relationality in human lives and learning. The learner is a researcher of his/her own life, indeed (and viceversa, a researcher is a learner).

In the French speaking tradition of histoires de vie, the biographical account is largely used to design life history group sessions, where narratives allow to grasp the social, cultural and historical determinants of individual lives and learning. This narrative approach seems to leave aside aspects that are nevertheless fundamental for experience, in particular the sphere of bodily experience,[1] which makes it possible to apprehend the world through perception, in direct contact with matter, impressions and "atmospheres". Understanding embodied experience through words and language may be difficult, and this is a challenge for the biographical researcher. The ecological reciprocity – both physical and phenomenological – between human life and the physical environment (animate and inanimate) falls within the sphere of the sensitive. To be grasped, and recovered from oblivion, it requires a thorough description of the perceptions, impressions and inferences produced in the subject by the lived situation. Descriptive phenomenology (or microphenomenology when this description aims to name sensorial experience) is a way to translate the processes of affordance and enaction into language.

Indeed, whether it is from the concept of enaction founded by Varela (2017), which postulates a co-emergence of the world in relation to the dynamics of perception of the subject, or from the concept of affordance (Gibson, 1979), which deals with the potentialities perceived in the environment by the individual (human or animal) to orient his actions, it is possible to find what Chalmers (1995) has called "the hard problem of experience": what is given to living in the environment is perceived in the mode of the obviousness, while the processes of donation, which is a matter of the sensible and the incorporated (Merleau-Ponty, 1969), remain unnoticed.

Based on these considerations, I propose to examine the complementarity – and maybe the generative dialogue – of these two "narrative regimes" – the description of lived experience and the narration of life history – and their specific contribution to the understanding of the ecological, social and historical dimensions of human lives. The first encourages the use of words to describe embodied experience (Merleau-Ponty, 1976) and brings to words the primary roots of existence, i.e., the sphere of sensitive life, based on perceptions and sensations emerging from body-matter interactions. The second form of narrative, derived from hermeneutics and biography (Ricoeur, 1986; Pineau & Legrand, 2019), promotes meaning by weaving the historical conditions, social interactions, and experiential learning process.

2 The Narrative Regimes: Phenomenological Description and Biographical Narration

Each experience told within the life story can be grasped as a temporal unit, a more or less extensive fragment of the person's story. The temporal dimension is a crucial one in human experience, correlated to the narrative process and necessary for the investigation of the different aspects of daily experience. In his book on the constitutive relationship of time and narration, Ricœur (1986) considers the reciprocity between different forms of temporalisation of experience and the relative narrative processes. The theory developed by Ricoeur is the following: the narration of the lived experience presupposes establishing the temporal structure of the experience on the basis of a principle: that of succession. It is this principle of succession that orders the facts experienced in time and prefigures the causality connections whose function is to associate the facts among themselves in order to ground the story and configure the self-narrative. This is what makes Ricoeur (1983, p. 85) say that narrative activity transforms the episodic into a logic.

He assumes the existence of different "narrative regimes", based on a principle of co-determination between the duration of lived experience as grasped during the narrative activity and the processes used for the composition of the narrative. The main difference between these regimes is the duration of experience grasped by the narrative activity. In fact, the narrative investigation of sensitive life would privilege description over experience: the narrator will seize

Lived experience
Previous experience
Date, place, extent of time

Narrative situation: temporal distance between
the moment of the lived experience and that of
the narrated experience

Narrative of the experience
compression or expansion of time in the narrative
Text or discourse: number of characters
or time available for the expression

FIGURE 3.1   Time lived and time told during the self-narrative activity

a short moment to examine it in detail. Conversely, the biographical account would be characterised by the long duration of the experience captured by the narrative activity. Ricoeur's theory, however, is the subject of heated discussion, especially in narratological studies (Adam, 2012), where description is usually considered as a suspension of duration. If this may hold for an object's description, it seems to me more problematic when it comes to describing lived experience, which appears as "naturally" taking place over time, if with different degrees of graininess

If a relationship can be established between the time lived and the time told, a third factor must also be taken into account: time to say. Its consideration makes it possible to define and interrogate the notion of "speed of the narrative text", as producing effects that can be distinguished according to whether the experience is described in detail (for example, by choosing a short moment of life) or narrated "en bloc" (for example, a period of ten years of life).

The diagram in Figure 3.1 distinguishes "lived" and "narrated" experience, presenting a dialectical tension between duration and narrative forms. This relationship generates effects regarding the detail in wording some aspects of experience, thus the possibility itself of telling. The variation of the relationship between "time lived" and "time told" may explain those effects. In the following sections, I will consider how the emphasis placed on short-term experiences, during the narrative activity, leads to microphenomenological description, that makes it possible to explores the embodied dimensions of existence, while the understanding of a longer period of time directs towards biographical narratives, hence highlighting the social and historical dimensions of life.

3   Ecology of the Sensitive World and Embodiment of the Lived World

While working on my computer, sitting in my favourite café in the morning, a situation comes to my mind, and reminds me of another café, six months ago. It is ten o'clock, I am in New York and the rather vast, very bright space where I am sitting resonates of movements and discussions, all around me. My workspace is very narrow, and I can hardly find room for my computer, on the same table where three businessmen are having a meeting and discussing aloud. I start sipping my coffee, which is awfully weak. New York's coffee ... It reminds me of other coffees, drunk in a previous trip to Quebec ... Gradually, my thoughts gather, and orient themselves towards the text that I am writing about "narrative regimes". Now, noises are fading around me. Even the coffee has become more flavourful, and I feel its necessity, as a fuel for the activity that is about to start. Now, I feel compelled to write ... and here I am, in a state of absorption ...

The first-person microphenomenological description (Depraz, 2013) focused on a short moment (or instant) of life, as in the story here above, provides access and expression to the sensitive and experiential aspects of lived experience and to the "sensory strata of the experience" (Petitmengin, 2010, p. 168). Attention to details ("qualia") offers a specific learning opportunity, that is linked to feeling and understanding the sensitive qualities of the specific lived experience, by grasping the atmosphere, listening to the lived body, and expressing the structure of perception. These sensitive dimensions of experience manifest themselves in presentational form: "Rather than saying that we have the experience of representations, it would be better to say that our experiences are presentational and that they present the world as having certain characteristics" (Zahavi, 2015, p. 91). In other words, the sensorial is the way in which the "world of life" is given to consciousness and, by extension, the way by which we live and inhabit the world. Before being represented or imaginable, the world is experienced.

This "first and immediate" dimension of experience has the effect of overlaying the underlying models of ecological relationships that govern our interactions with the environment. We forget that our perception is itself the outcome of interaction (enactment). Thus, the recognition of the ecological dimensions of existence demands that we become attentive to what constitutes the nearest and most obvious part of existence: our sensations in relationships with objects and matters, perception of atmospheres, affordances (Gibson, 1979) and enaction processes (Varela et al., 1993). To access these sensitive dimensions of experience, and be able to "translate" them into words, we use a specific narrative form, that moves towards detailed forms of exploration. The narrator pays attention to short moments of lived experience, and proceeds by careful examination of each strata.

In fact, micro-phenomenological description can distinguish and put in word different strata of the sensitive experience, the as follows:

- The stratum of affordances: action is described here from an ecological point of view, illuminating the narrator's interaction and reciprocity with what is perceived in the situation.
- The physical stratum of perception: here, words try to express the sensations felt by the body in contact with objects, things or living beings: tensions, relaxation, agitation, texture of materials, smell of the place, sound of voices ... The narrator's attention is focused on the proprioceptive sphere.

The identification of these strata may be helpful in clarifying how it is possible to translate into language those aspects of the experience that are not grasped by language or reasoning. The story that I used to open the paragraph illustrates these strata. I told a specific moment (an instant) in my history, that resonates with another story told by Jean-François Billeter (2012), who proposes a microphenomenological description of the atmospheres experienced in public places such as coffee shops, that appear to inspire reflection. Billeter dedicates this work published in 2012 entitled "A Paradigm" to the study of the process of incorporating gestures, whether physical or psychological, into situations. Through the phenomenological descriptions of moments and the autobiographical narration of his life's path, it allows readers to grasp the temporal character of learning processes and the forms of participation arising from the environment in the development of the individual's agentivity.

The short text that I narrated, written in the first person, was meant to grasp and present different aspects of my embodied experience in the café: sensory perception, atmosphere, and the dynamics of the place. The narrator's attention is focused both on the qualitative dimensions of the experience, and their reciprocal effects with the writing and thinking activity: the background noises fade out, absorption in the writing activity, the coffee's taste and meaning change ... At another level, the effects of composition could be examined, which, beyond each of the identified aspects, contribute as a whole to the constitution of an Umwelt which produces the propitious conditions for reflection and thought. These data are revealed by the mobilisation of a specific form of narrative, that prioritises phenomenological description, using the present tense (which is the time of lived experience). The process entails an extreme slowing down of narrative speed and and opens access to different aspects (strata) and modes of experience for the narrative activity.

4   Life Stories as a Narrative Regime in Andragogy and Lifelong
       Learning

I first became interested in the effects of time compression and dilation within the narrative activity during my master's degree at the University of Tours in 1997. In that period, I experienced Pierre Vermersch's "explicitation interview" and the training sessions with Alex Lainé, using life stories. It was then my first experience of life storytelling practice in an adult collective at the university. I was then 25 years old: I discovered the infinite diversity of possible ways life stories can exist. I then spent fifteen years doing research within two different frameworks: on one side, microphenomenology, within the framework of a research seminar led by Claire Petitmengin, Natalie Depraz and Michel Bitbol; and, on the other side, "les histoires de vie en formation", within the framework of my doctorate supervised by Gaston Pineau. This is what led me to seek to bring together two streams of narration: biographical narration, which apprehends the experience on the basis of signification and duration; and microphenomenological description, which explores the experience on the basis of its perceptive and sensitive components. This research has been reflected in various publications, gradually becoming the central theme of my work.

Detailed exploration may also occur in biographical narratives, as shown in the 192 word-text above. If the description of experiential and sensitive dimensions implies an "extension" and "slowing down" of the narrative time, in order to put in words the sensitive strata, the biographical inquiry proceeds in the opposite direction: it compresses experience in order to contain multiple events and spheres of adult life (family, social, professional ...) in one text. In other words, while description brings attention to specific moments in history, the biographical narrative apprehends whole periods of life, or phases that can last several years.

   If micro-phenomenological inquiry attempts to grasp the ecological and embodied dimensions of existence, biographical inquiry reveals its social and historical dimensions. It is not a difference in objects or content: rather, it should be emphasised that the main difference between the two narrative regimes is in the way they capture experience by the narrative activity. However, they can ally and create a more complex text. From this point of view, what Genette (1983) calls the "pause" in his study of Proust's literature could be associated with the activity of phenomenological description.

> *To illustrate this process, the narrated time should be slowed down to the extreme in order to create the possibility of an intensification of the level of detail of the description, thus creating the possibility of putting into words micro-processes revealing the forms of pre-reflective adjustments between my modes of action and the lived environment. Thus, if I return to the moment I am in New York, in the coffee shop, I can focus my attention on the instant when, in the first sip of coffee, I perceive the singular taste of that coffee that sands me light, almost too liquid. Several directions are then open to me: describe the "texture" of the liquid; describe the taste and the intensity perceived as attenuated; characterise the temperature as it is given when the liquid pours into my mouth ... However, among all these aspects of the lived experience, one dimension stands out because of my intention: that of showing that coffee participates in the constitution of my objects of thought. I am then led to examine the effect produced by coffee on my progressive immersion in the activity of writing. I then note a phenomenon that seems almost paradoxical to me: while I physically feel a kind of awakening, an intensification of the volunteer, at the same time, I feel myself surrendering myself in writing. The computer keyboard attracts my fingers, the process of absorption begins.*

The previous passage may be considered as a pause in the story. The speed of the narrated time has slowed down to the point where it only lasts a few seconds, the time needed for the first sip of coffee during the narrated moment in NYC. Baudouin (2010) has shown this dynamic in his work on the "kinetic regimes" of texts. In his examination of the configured dimensions of the autobiographical narrative – what Ricoeur (1983) calls "the framework of the plot" – Baudouin brings attention to the variations of the kinetic regimes of the narrative, that may be rich and diversified. A first modelling of these kinetic regimes has been formalised as in Figure 3.2.

Pause	Suspended action	Important slowing down factor
Scene	Action narrated	Slowdown factor
Summary	Summary action	Summary acceleration factor
Ellipse	Action omitted	Important factor of acceleration

FIGURE 3.2   Narrative processes and kinetic variations in the life story narration (from
Baudouin, 2010, p. 419)

This model distinguishes four ways of composing a life history narrative:
- the "pause", that produces a discontinuity in the development of the story, hence making it possible to describe the experience, its strata and aspects;
- the "scene", that proceeds to a detailed description while preserving the dynamics of temporal development; so, while the "pause" indicates a moment of interruption of the temporal flow in the text, the "scene" contains a dynamic of temporal expansion (or even dilatation);
- the "summary", that makes an acceleration (therefore compression of time) in narration;
- the "ellipse", which is a "hidden time" within the life narrative; it represents the maximum compression of time in the text.

The story that opened this paragraph illustrates this modelling, by presenting a part of my life using some of the kinetic variations. This second account of experience maintains the focus on the processes of constitution of ideas and thought, so it approaches the "same object" as the first account, but adopting a biographical perspective. Thus, unlike the fragment on the café in New York, whose purpose was to illustrate the effects of microphenomenological description in focusing the sensitive dimensions of a given situation, this biographical account provides chronological and logical continuity in the process of developing choice of topics and methods within significant relationships (mentors) and academic contexts.

My 192-word autobiographical narrative compresses a duration of 20 years of lived time by synthesising and aggregating many moments (summary), which would deserve to be narrated, or even described in detail, in order to clarify the relationships between these moments and the meanings that shape the story. The level of detail, in this case, is so reduced that it hardly allows to understand the dynamics that contributed to the emergence and constitution of a research object that became a life-long research project. However, the few uncovered data can be characterised as follows:
- a narrative of continuity and an associated duration;
- the identification of "training mechanisms";
- the designation of resource persons and reference authors;
- a biography of writings and research articles that contribute to the construction of the researcher's identity?

The biographical narrative, even extremely compressed, reveals the singular, collective, and social spheres of existence. In other words, putting the singularity of stories into words makes it possible to manifest both the anthropological and the ecological dimensions of human existence and different ways to learn from it (Dominicé, 2000; Formenti & West, 2018).

5   Conclusions: Connecting Description to Narrative in Adult Education and Social Science Research

At first glance, the phenomenological description and the biographical narrative seem to rely on a similar process of "translation" of lived experience into words and configuration of these words into a narrative. In fact, the process is different: in order to access a specified point in the flux of time of my life, I must make myself available for a memory to come, while, on the other hand, if I want to understand a phenomenon experienced over time, I must go back to its starting point, then adjust the wording to reflect its evolution. The narrative challenge is thus modified: during the phenomenological description activity, the narrator is confronted with the question of relevance and graininess, that is what level of detail is necessary to describe a phenomenon. This intensification of the level of detail produces the slowing down of the text and give access to the spheres of the sensitive. On the contrary, with regard to autobiographical narrative, the narrator must deliberate on the relevance of the moments grasped in relation to the whole, and on the rhythm that their temporal ordering generates in the narrative framework of the story.

However, what seems to make sense, and to bring narratives to a deeper level of understanding, is often a mix, or an oscillation between the description of experience (embodied, authentic) and the configuration of the whole narrative (meaningful, coherent, continuous). This may generate in the long run a double perspective, and a composition of different levels of experience, producing an effect of self-understanding in context, and the awareness of the relationship between one's life and the social, collective and ecological spheres of the lived worlds.

This is what I have sought to show by proposing two stories of mine, telling about experience, and focused on a common theme – the alternance between the emergence of ideas and their inclusion in shared research objects within research collectives and academic networks – and by differentiating/composing two modes of narrative investigation (narrative regimes): the first based on phenomenological description; the second on biographical narrative. Investigation via description makes it possible to explore the contribution of interactions – with the physical, natural, and social environment, with atmospheres and places – by capturing an instant, a particular moment, and exploring it by active and sensitive dynamics. This perspective offers innovative ways to understand the contribution of natural environments, places, even food and the body's experience in the construction of a researcher's identity, thought, and scientific work (Lawrence & Shapin, 1992). Investigation via biographical narrative opens up other perspectives: that of an understanding of the deployment of the processes of constitution of thought over the course of life, by identifying significant moments, by bringing out the processes of continuity because of the configurative power of the narrative (Collinot, 2012).

On the epistemological level, the powerful effects of the oscillation between two narrative regimes brings light on the processes of (self)understanding, training and research in the social sciences. We can imagine it as a step forward in the definition of an ecological narrative epistemology. Storytelling research is an important axis within the ESREA network, as shown by the recent publication of the book entitled "Discourses we live by: Personal and professional narratives of educational and social practices" coordinated by Hazel Wright and Marianne Høyen which contains several texts presented at the 25th conference in the ESREA network, Life History and Biography Network (LHBN). The opportunity to think in narrative styles that explore the pre-reflective and sensitive dimensions that connect the person to the world opens up promising research perspectives, situated at the interface of educational sciences, hermeneutics and experiential phenomenology for both the French and English-speaking networks of biographical research in adult education.

Note

1   I mention here, following an exchange with Laura Formenti, the existence of a working group within ASHIVIF dedicated to research on sensitive experience, which led to a seminar in 1994 in Montreux, Switzerland, organised by Pierre Dominicé and Christine Josso.

References

Adam, J.-M. (2012). *Les textes: Types et protypes*. Armand Colin.

Baudouin, J.-M. (2010). *De l'épreuve autobiographique*. Peter Lang.

Billeter, J.-F. (2012). *Un paradigme*. Allia.

Chalmers, D. (1995). Facing up to the problem of consciousness. *Journal of Consciousness Studies, 2/3*, 200–219.

Collinot, A. (2012). Entre vie et oeuvres scientifiques: Le chaînon manquant. *Critique, 6/7*, 781–782. https://doi.org/10.3917/criti.781.0576

Depraz, N. (2013). D'une science descriptive de l'expérience en première personne: pour une phénoménologie expérientielle. *Studia Phaenomenologica, 13*(1), 387–402. https://doi.org/10.7761/SP.13.387

Dominicé, P. (2000). *Learning from our lives. Using educational biographies with adults.* Jossey-Bass.

Formenti, L., & West, L. (2018). *Transforming perspectives in lifelong learning and adult education: A dialogue.* Palgrave Macmillan.

Gibson, J. (1979). *The ecological approach to visual perception.* Houghton Mifflin.

Genette, G. (1972). *Figures III.* Seuil.

Lainé, A. (2004). *Faire de sa vie une histoire.* Desclée de Brouwer.

Lawrence, C., & Shapin, S. (2012). *Science incarnate. Historical embodiments of natural knowledge.* The University of Chicago Press.

Merleau-Ponty, M. (1976). *Phénoménologie de la perception.* Gallimard.

Petitmengin, C. (2006). Describing one's subjective experience in the second person, an interview method for the science of consciousness. *Phenomenology and the Cognitive Sciences, 5,* 229–269. https://doi.org/10.1007/s11097-006-9022-2

Petitmengin, C. (2010). La dynamique pré-réfléchie de l'expérience vécue. *Alter, 18,* 165–182. https://doi.org/10.4000/alter.1668

Pineau, G., & Legrand, J.-L. (2019). *Les histoires de vie.* Presses Universitaires de France.

Pineau G., & Marie-Michèle. (1983/2020). *Produire sa vie: autoformation et autobiographie.* Téraèdre.

Ricœur, P. (1983). *Temps et récit. 1. L'intrigue et le récit historique.* Seuil.

Ricœur, P. (1986). *Du texte à l'action.* Seuil.

Varela, F. (2017). *Le cercle créateur. Écrits (1976–2001).* Seuil.

Varela, F., Thompson, E., & Rosch, E. (1993). *L'inscription corporelle de l'esprit.* Seuil.

Vermersch, P. (2012). *Explicitation et phénoménologie.* Presses Universitaires de France.

Zahavi, D. (2015). Intentionnalité et phénoménalité. Un regard phénoménologique sur le problème difficile. *Philosophie, 124,* 80–104. https://doi.org/10.3917/philo.124.0080

Biographical Research at the Boundary: A Careful Listening for the Micro, Meso, and Macro in End-of-Life Care

Kjetil Moen

Abstract

Death is an intrinsic part of the ecology of life. Yet in Western societies, end-of-life care has to a large degree moved out of the home and into institutions. A pressing question for educational institutions and employing healthcare organizations is how to train for and facilitate quality and resilience among those working at the boundary between life and death. Any such endeavor must rest on knowledge about how encounters with the death of others inform the self-understanding and praxis of end-of-life care professionals.

Applying a biographical narrative approach to the narrative accounts of healthcare workers from palliative care and intensive care units, the chapter undertakes a careful reading of free-associative narratives, in order to elicit the entangled relation between the subject and his or her contexts, past and present. The chapter is thus an empirically based exploration of how the individual's fear of death (micro), organizational feeling rules (meso), and societal discourse (macro) simultaneously and mutually inform the life and narrative of the end-of-life care professionals.

Keywords

death – end-of-life care – biography – free-associative telling – discourse

1   Introduction

In the ecology of life, death plays an undeniable and significant part. However, the context of death and dying has changed to a large degree in Western societies, as the initiative for care of the dying is passed from community, family, and friends to welfare institutions. Today, for most people the process of dying, and the actual moment of death, take place in hospitals, nursing homes, and hospices. End-of-life care has become a discipline within mainstream medicine and is thus predominantly the focus of professionals who deal with death as part of their work (Ariès, 1976).

This major cultural change raises pressing questions relevant to the field of adult education, one of which is how to prepare and support health professionals working in end-of-life care. As a hospital chaplain and teacher at a university offering education for both future and current health-care professionals, I can testify to the relevance and legitimacy of this question. In order to address it, we need empirically based knowledge about how this major cultural shift in the care of the dying influences both the experiences of end-of-life care professionals and the socially constructed languages (discourses) within which their experiences and narratives are embedded.

In the following, I will present one such endeavor in which a biographical narrative interpretive approach is applied in order to help elicit the relations between the societal (macro), institutional (meso), and individual (micro) in the narrative accounts of end-of-life care professionals – physicians, nurses, and hospital chaplains from palliative and intensive-care departments in Norway and the US. The rationale, philosophical underpinnings, findings, and theoretical discussions of the study are presented more comprehensively elsewhere (Moen, 2018). In line with the aim of this book, focus on the following is methodological – on how a biographical approach can make for contextual reading of the personal in the professional.

2   Allowing for Free-Associative Telling

A premise for the study is that when asked to reflect on ourselves or another, we often respond to the question of self by telling stories (Ricoeur, 1988). There is no difference in the case of health-care professionals. Yet, as self-understanding is not only expressed by what is said, but also how it is said, it takes careful listening to both the explicit and implicit, to omissions, contradictions and paradoxes, in order to identify self-understanding – the thin sense of subjectivity, the subject's characteristic way of receiving and organizing experience – making itself evident in the telling.

In order to remain open to other contexts in life being as, or even more, influential to the health professional than what is taking place at the bedside of the dying patient, it was important to let the invitation to tell be open enough so that the professionals could narrate life both from inside the clinic and beyond. Hence, a carefully designed invitation to induce a free-associative telling was as important as the later careful reading of it. Leaning on Biographical Narrative Interpretive Method (BNIM) (Wengraf, 2001), which insists on the uninterrupted telling of stories, only a single question was offered to the participants:

> As you know, I am interested in how health professionals as persons have changed, or not changed, due to working with terminally ill and dying patients. Therefore, can you please tell me your life story: all those events and experiences, which were important for you personally? Please take the time you need! I will just listen and won't interrupt you with questions. I will just take notes so that I can remember what I want to ask you about when you have finished telling me about it all. Take the time you need. Start wherever you like.

Dina, the palliative care physician, finished her first narrative after 35 minutes. Jacob, the intensive care physician, shared over 30 clinical incidents and spoke uninterrupted for two hours, while the other participants placed themselves somewhere in between. After the first un-interrupted telling there was a second session, in which I asked follow-up questions, committing to the sequence and language of the first narrative they had shared.

3   A Contextual Reading

Most participants included stories from both inside and outside the clinic. In the next paragraphs, the cases of Fiona, Eric, Dina and Herbert will serve to illustrate how a biographical approach allows for identification of how experiences outside the clinic may inform the professionals' self-understanding and impact their practice of care.

Fiona, an anesthesiologist, working in an ICU for children, very much centers her account on questions pertaining to her choice of occupation. However, she spends the first part of her account talking about how she grew up with "a steady flow of illness and death in the family", including the death of her own father when she was a toddler, and subsequently those of her grandparents and aunt. They all stayed in her home during their terminal phase. At one point, somebody even made the comment, "Gee, you are really growing up in a hospice". As an eight to nine year-old, it left her "afraid that all around me would die".

The presence of death combined with growing up with a partly non-present mother who, as a nurse, served as "the health department for the entire family", triggered strong ambivalent feelings towards healthcare: "Not something I wanted by any means ... sick people was the worst I could think of. They were everywhere and took too much time". The impatience with the sick back then may resonate in her encounters with dying patients' relatives who, here and now, rage against the injustice implied in their beloved facing death: "How can this happen to me and mine?" The physician must temper herself in order not to exclaim, "How in the name of heaven could you believe it couldn't happen to you?"

As a coping strategy in relation to her fear of those around her dying, Fiona, looking back on her life, states that she "wanted to fix most things". This desire seems to linger with her and inform her choice of pursuing critical and intensive care and the desire to master "special and difficult patients". At one point, she even makes the statement: "Being a physician, doing intensive medicine, is a way of saving my own psyche". Yet, she concludes that ending up in end-of-life care is "a coincidence", and thus she seems to be overlooking obvious clues in her biographical account, which, to the researcher at least, make her choice of vocation, and lack of patience with certain relatives, more comprehensible if not less paradoxical.

Herbert, an expert in palliative care, is similarly paradoxical, considering his biography. He tells about his anger related to how the life of his family of origin revolved around his mother's continuous complaints about her pain and sickness as he was growing up. According to Herbert, she was "too absorbed in her pain". The anger was particularly related to how this limited the life of his father. Yet, in his early clinical assignments, Herbert is, according to his own account, paradoxically, particularly drawn towards patients with pain issues: "I began to collect a group of patients that nobody wanted, they tended to have chronic pain".

A related paradox, not mentioned in his account, is related to him growing up in a context dealing with pain, emotions, and intimacy in a "stoic" manner: "To me personally it felt awkward to say something consoling, encouraging ... in our family we just didn't know how to react to that stuff". In his present marriage, he says he still finds it hard to be emotionally transparent. Yet, in his professional life he explicitly treasures the intimacy by the deathbed, as it is "those interactions with patients where we 'touch' each other that really get to me ... It fills my vessels back up to have those relationships".

Dina is a disconfirming case in that she almost steers clear of clinical experiences in her narrative. This physician has dedicated her professional life to the well-being of terminally ill and dying patients. Such a life, one may expect, would bring forth stories about life-changing encounters at the boundary between life and death. Yet, there is another selective principle for her account, for what is included, and what she leaves out.

What "first comes to mind", when Dina is invited to share the experiences most significant to her, is an emancipation process from oppressive religiosity. The quest for freedom, opposition towards any confining structure, as well as the importance of speaking one's mind, run like red threads throughout her narrative account, as she repeatedly speaks about herself in terms of "always" having been a seeker and speaker of truth. She regards being a notorious truth-seeker her most characteristic trait, one she relates to being a truth-speaker. Dina relates the urgency she felt to speak truth to an upbringing with too many lies and double standards. "[I am] never going to tell another lie in my life". This "ability" to be "open and direct", she "use[s] it a lot" in her work, even though, at times, it feels like "breaking through a wall in order for people to understand stuff".

Even though it is a concern that originated outside the clinic, the urge to be a truth-speaker informs Dina's encounters with dying patients and their families within it. In this, she sees herself as parting not only from those she regards as hypocrites in her faith community of origin, but also current colleagues who are scared of talking about death and dying.

The concern for truth-speaking eventually brings her narrative to the bedside of a terminally ill and dying patient, and fierce accusations from relatives that her truth-speaking about imminent death was neither called for nor welcomed. This could be a legitimate response on the part of the relatives, as it should largely be the patient's call to decide how and when matters of ultimate concerns are to be communicated. At the same time, the response may also speak of a more general uneasiness with death in the culture – a conspiracy of silence – I will explore this further in the last part of the chapter.

The fact that Dina, Fiona, and Herbert did not make links between their contexts of upbringing and choice of vocation may simply relate to the fact that all human beings are limited to a first-person perspective. It takes somebody else's careful listening for omissions, paradoxes, and contradictions to identify links and tensions between different parts of a biographical account. This is no less true when considering the notion of "the defended subject".

4 Exploring Individual and Social Defense

In the second session of Biographical Narrative Interpretive Method (BNIM), immediately following the first, the researcher commits to the wording and sequence of the initial account but invites the narrator through open invitation to get beyond the rehearsed narratives and closer to marginalized experiences. These may be events and experiences that have become defended parts of the biography, but which may be of key importance when trying to understand why this life is told this way. As in Anne's case, it may take several nudges before the interviewee is comfortable visiting more challenging parts of her life and story:

> When I worked at the other unit there was a man who was dying, and we had someone attending to him at all times. I remember I got in there and he had such a frantic anxiety in the eyes, horrible anxiety. I was afraid, really, and then I ran out to grab a drink and when I came back, he was dead. That I struggled with ... in hindsight, I could say almost that I ran out to grab the drink to get out of there. It was like vicarious, right. That I struggled with for a while. I remember I had to sleep with the light on afterwards. I was a brand-new nurse.

Stories that haunt health-care professionals (Rashotte, 2005) may have originated 30 years ago, as in Anne's case, but still continue to carry shame and guilt. Situations that "stick" thus have the potential to inform both the self-understanding and practice of the professional throughout his or her career. It takes another's capacity "to contain" (Bion, 1962) painful and shameful experiences in order to turn them into sources of life-long learning for the professional. Hence, a pressing question, crucial for Anne, is whether the angst in relation to her own finitude, against which she defends herself, resonates with a social defense (Menzies-Lyth, 1960) against the same basic condition established in her professional context.

Glaser and Strauss's (1965) classic grounded theory study from hospitals in the US identified that hospital units collude in varying degrees in "conspiracies of silence" in regard to death, holding back information or providing wrong information to the patient, in order to prevent awareness that death is at hand: "The patient does not recognize his impending death even though the hospital personnel have the information" (p. 29).

Jacob, the ICU physician, shares an encounter in which he is more knowledgeable about the imminence of death than the dying patient: "[I] remember one of the days before he died he took me by the hand and kind of ... felt that 'we are going to overcome this' ... and ... deep inside I knew already at that point that he is not going to make it". Herbert, similarly reflecting on an encounter with a young man who passed away just a couple of days prior to the interview, questions himself: "Did I fulfill my role? Was I honest enough? Did I short-change him in any way?"

At times, according to the participants in this study, it is patients who do not want to know, and relatives who do not want to disclose, as in Dina's case, which implies an expectation of holding back information, which can have a detrimental impact on staff (Noble, Nelson, & Finlay, 2008).

An ontology of defended subjectivity – philosophical (Heidegger, 2002) and psychoanalytical (Klein, 1959) underpinnings for, and possible methodological implications of (Hollway & Jefferson, 2000) – are accounted for in another book (Moen, 2018). Suffice it to say here that the shared existential burden implied in finitude and death is something we defend ourselves against, both as individuals (micro), groups (meso), and societies (macro) (Becker, 1973; Yalom, 2008).

Repression can serve a purpose, make life manageable, a "strange power of living in the moment and ignoring and forgetting" (Becker, 1973, p. 23), enabling the forward momentum of activity without which people may suffer psychotic breaks. Hence, we need to be tolerant of the fact that we deal with death differently. Yet, it is of existential and ethical importance, relevant to the quality of healthcare, that health professionals are willing and able to address it when called to do so. Awareness of death can keep end-of-life care professionals from unnecessary and unethical treatment, which may bring prolonged suffering to patients and moral stress to themselves.

The above considered, research methods are called for that can identify how the death of patients triggers a defensive stand in health professionals in ways that may have a profound impact on patient care. Allowing for free-associative, non-directed telling is one methodological answer to such a call. An uninterrupted telling of stories, in which the narrator gets to "choose what to tell and how to tell it" (Charmaz, 2006, p. 27), may reveal rehearsed stories and manners of speaking, but also omissions, contradictions, and paradoxes that leave hints of what is beneath the surface.

We have seen how "feeling rules" (Hochschild, 2003) residing in the contexts of the professional (meso) may inform the experience of end-of-life care. Not all of these socially constructed and agreed-upon discursive manners of speaking (Bourdieu, 1977), or not speaking, about death originate within the clinic or healthcare system though; some are shared and implicit in the culture as a whole (macro), which is where we will turn next.

5   Investigating Discourse

Eric, a chaplain in a palliative care context, finds that his experience of death contrasts profoundly with what is experienced by people outside the clinic, and that him being more at ease with death represents something "peculiar" for them, and leaves him with a sense of being different. Whenever he conveys to those who ask that "it is not so bad and difficult" to work with death and dying, he is left with the feeling that they think: "It can't be right, it is not possible to state things like that".

Carl, also a chaplain, once took it upon himself to facilitate a gathering around the open coffin of one of his own family members: "[I] was told afterwards that it was a little too much ... it wasn't totally okay". He recognized his former attitude to death in that of the other family members: "They were in the same situation as me when I was young".

Gail expresses a similar sense of being different: "When people ask me 'how do you work with dying children' ... I want to say I enjoy being with people during the death process .... That's a weird thing, you can't say that to anybody who is not a chaplain".

Considering the marginalization of death in Western society – how it is institutionalized and thus out of sight – it makes sense that there is something strange, perhaps even repulsive and "tainted" (Kessler et al., 2012) about professional end-of-life care. The interviewees' articulation of their "natural" relation to death is uttered in a society in which death is "forbidden", if we follow the argument of the French historian Phillipe Ariès (1976, p. 85), and thus anything but natural, potentially even a provocation. The end-of-life-care professional thus represents a "discredited attribute" in the ecology of life and, as such, he or she may be regarded as a social anomaly (Douglas, 2002).

Working with death and dying in a society in which death is "forbidden", thus informs the experience and self-understanding of the professional. Even though most participants conveyed similar thoughts, feelings of resembling a social anomaly seem to resonate more strongly with those in palliative care than in intensive care. Perhaps because most people associate the latter with saving lives to a greater degree than facilitating preparation for death.

Herbert and Jacob, both physicians in end-of-life care, question colleagues who refuse to acknowledge the inevitability of death, and who continue to treat the dying patient as if he or she will survive. Both expressed indignation when the belief in treatment represented a "triumph of fantasy over reality" (Levine, 2013, p. 94). Nevertheless, both had to acknowledge being caught in the same dynamics, as they also continually encounter the expectations and demands of co-workers, employers, patients, and relatives to protect the notion that death can be prevented – even when it is clearly impending. For example, in one case, Jacob and a colleague decided to stop resuscitation, and the patient's son "got furious because we had given up on his father and he jumped onto the bed and continued resuscitation".

The above may be illustrative of how in a secular age (Taylor, 2007), following the decline of meta-narratives – religious and political – there is no shared discourse on death and dying. Nothing resembling the "Ars moriendi" (Ariès, 1976, p. 34) – the culturally shared, and very much religiously informed, ways of referring to the meaning of death in the Middle Ages and later. Rather, in the current situation, there are several discourses which may compete with one another – treatment philosophies, like palliative care (Leget, 2007) and the principle of autonomy (Beauchamp & Childress, 2013), but also organizational models, like New Public Management (Hood, 2015), and finally health-care jurisdictions.

In the final part of this chapter, we will undertake a careful reading of Jacob's account, in order to show how a biographical approach may allow for the identification not only of dominant discourses (macro), but also how they may be related to, and enhanced by, personal experience (micro). One such link is made manifest in Jacob's repeated talk about the importance of "being professional":

> But anyway our unit is very professional, I think. It is important to behave in an orderly manner, be professional, that is what I think. That is a very important message ... we have to act professionally ... and do what we are supposed to in a way without mixing in too many emotions and feelings.

This, according to Jacob, is a message he makes an effort to "convey to other colleagues", thus eliciting the interrelatedness between micro and meso. He then moves on to elaborate what he understands "professional" to imply in different clinical situations: when communicating a request for autopsy, when giving out information, when responding to requests for documents from relatives, when responding to the same requests from authorities.

What is common to all these situations is that they are regulated by law. Hence, Jacob is implicitly making a case for the importance of staying on the right side of the line between professional conduct and misconduct. The degree of regulation, and thus the risk of legal consequences, increases with every new typical situation he mentions. Eventually, the free-associative telling takes Jacob to an unpleasant memory, which perhaps explains the reason for his focus on this issue:

> [I] have had unnatural deaths that have been reported to the police, and reported to the health authorities, and then a file is opened and ... one has to give out all the documents of course ... one possibly gets a feed-back that something is blameworthy. One can get a warning. That sort of thing one must be prepared for ... one gets hung up on details ... so it is very important to be orderly when it comes to such journal notes.

The methodological point to be made is that merely recording a memo about Jacob's concern with behaving in a professional manner and adding it to similar utterances in other cases, leaving the individual case unexplored, would miss a deeper understanding. On the other hand, "being faithful to the unique histories, circumstances, and meanings" (Hollway, 2013, p. 99) by taking Jacob's biography into account, not only provides insights but also explains why "being professional" is so important to him.

Another link between discourse (macro) and the psychic (micro) is identified when Jacob tells about how he suffered "soldier's heart" – chest pain without any identification of heart failure – a few months prior to the interview. He relates the incident to the "violent organizational change" that was taking place at his hospital: "You are sucked in and whirled around with it, it never stops ... feels life threatening". The focus is on making services profitable, which is stressful according to Jacob, and the dilemmas are felt in particular when "playing musical chairs" regarding who, among the patients, are to be prioritized at the intensive care unit in which he is head physician.

Jacob is thus explicating what other participants also report, and what is echoed in the literature (Hood, 2015); namely, the stress felt related to New Public Management, which has been the organizational model in Norway and other countries since the early nineties. A major critique is that professional and ethical concerns are subject to managerial imperatives. It is this, more than the demands of encountering death and dying on a daily basis, which evokes stress, according to Gail: "The death and dying is not driving me away. I want to stress that health-care politics really sealed the deal for me". Retiring early, because she does not want "to die in my job" due to "the rat race" – the ever-increasing expectation that one must do more in less time.

6   Concluding Remarks

The accounts of Jacob and Gail echo a concern, evident in the literature, about a lack of recognition for the welfare professional as an experiencing subject (Froggett, 2002; Clarke et al., 2008). In professional contexts marked by rapid change, technological development, demands for efficiency, and profitability, it is critical to make space for personal testimonies. Allowing for narratives through open invitation, a free-associative telling and a careful reading is one way of re-humanizing, and thus it is an essential, ethical, and ontological necessity to counter de-personalizing tendencies in both healthcare and research.

Another gift of biographical narrative research is that it provides "thick" descriptions (Geertz, 1973) – rich contextual data marked by "detail, complexity and contradiction" (Braun & Clarke, 2013, p. 24). Hence, it provides in-depth knowledge about complex human beings and reduces the possibility of over-simplification and one-dimensionality that can take place when "reducing complexity to single scores" (Hollway & Jefferson, 2013, p. 101). It allows one to elicit how the ecology of the life of the individual must be understood in context (micro, meso, and macro), as "the given uniqueness of every voice" (Cavarero, 2005) is interwoven with "the universe of the undisputed" (Bourdieu, 1977, p. 18) – contextual manners of being and speaking both past and present, local and global.

References

Ariès, P. (1976). *Western attitudes toward death: From the Middle Ages to the present.* Marion Boyars.

Beauchamp, T. L., & Childress, J. F. (2013). *Principles of biomedical ethics* (7th ed.). Oxford University Press.

Becker, E. (1973). *The denial of death.* Free Press.

Bion, W. R. (1962). *Learning from experience* (3rd ed.). Rowman & Littlefield Publishers, Inc.

Bourdieu, P. (1977). *Outline of a theory of practice.* Cambridge University Press.

Braun, V., & Clarke, V. (2013). *Successful qualitative research: A practical guide for beginners.* Sage.

Cavarero, A. (2005). *For more than one voice: Toward a philosophy of vocal expression.* Stanford University Press.

Charmaz, K. (2006). *Constructing grounded theory: A practical guide through qualitative analysis.* Sage Publications Ltd.

Clarke, S., Hahn, H., & Hoggett, P. (2008). *Object relations and social relations: The implications of the relational turn in psychoanalysis.* Karnac.

Douglas, M. (2002). *Purity and danger: An analysis of the concept of pollution and taboo.* Routledge Classics.

Froggett, L. (2002). *Love, hate and welfare – Psychosocial approaches to policy and practice.* The Policy Press.

Geertz, C. (1973). *The interpretation of culture.* Basic Books.

Glaser, B. G., &. Strauss, A. L. (1965). *Awareness of dying.* Aldine.

Heidegger, M. (2002). *On time and being.* University of Chicago Press.

Hochschild, A. R. (2003). *The managed heart – Commercialization of human feeling* (20th anniversary ed.). University of California Press.

Hollway, W., & Jefferson, T. (2013). *Doing qualitative research differently: Free association, narrative and the interview method.* Sage.

Hood, C., & Dixon, R. (2015). What we have to show for 30 years of new public management: Higher costs, more complaints. *Governance, 28*(3), 265–267. https://doi.org/10.1111/gove.12150

Kessler, I., Heron, P., & Dopson, S. (2012). Opening the window: Managing death in the workplace. *Human Relations, 65*(3), 291–312. https://doi.org/10.1177/0018726711430002

Klein, M. (1959). *The psycho-analysis of children*. Hogarth Press.

Leget, C. (2007). Retrieving the ars moriendi tradition. *Medicine, Healthcare and Philosophy, 10*(3), 313–319. https://doi.org/10.1007/s11019-006-9045-z

Levine, D. P. (2013). *The capacity for ethical conduct: On psychic existence and the way we relate to others*. Routledge.

Menzies-Lyth, I. (1960, May). The function of social systems as a defence against anxiety: A report on a study of the nursing service of a general hospital. *Human Relations.* https://doi.org/10.1177/001872676001300201

Moen, K. (2018). *Death at work: Existential and psychosocial perspectives on end-of-life care*. Palgrave Macmillan.

Noble, S. I. R., Nelson, A., & Finlay, I. G. (2008). Challenges faced by palliative care physicians when caring for doctors with advanced cancer. *Palliative Medicine, 22*(1), 71–76. https://doi.org/10.1177/0269216307084607

Rashotte, J. (2005). Dwelling with stories that haunt us: Building a meaningful nursing practice. *Nursing Inquiry, 12*(1), 34–42. https://doi.org/10.1111/j.1440-1800.2005.00248.x

Ricoeur, P. (1988). *Time and narrative* (Vol. 3). University of Chicago Press.

Taylor, C. (2007). *A secular age*. Belknap Press of Harvard University Press.

Wengraf, T. (2001). *Qualitative research interviewing: Biographic narrative and semi-structured methods*. Sage Publications Ltd.

Yalom, I. D. (2008). *Staring at the sun: Overcoming the terror of death*. Jossey-Bass.

CHAPTER 5

Trying to Capture the Value of the 'Live' Conference Using an Ecological Approach

Hazel R. Wright and Marianne Høyen

Abstract

With 'live' conferences challenged by global climate and health crises, Wright and Høyen, consider what might be lost if these are ultimately replaced by online meetings, drawing on the ESREA Life History and Biography Network adult education conferences, particularly the Copenhagen meeting that they organised, to contextualise their discussion. They examine the usefulness of Bronfenbrenner's Ecological Model as a way into such a complex topic, finding that its structures supported initial thinking but were too restrictive to enable a logical but linear narrative on the value of the conference to participants, how it encourages attendance and by whom, and the ways this was examinable using publicly available sources and focused 'insider' reflection.

In a moment of epiphany, the authors understood that the conference, as a series of co-relationships, can be interpreted as a meso-level interaction, positioned between the micro-systems of everyday academic life and the macro- and external structural conditions that press down on it. Enabled to discuss how these different levels interact, the chapter considers the significance of disciplinary and knowledge boundaries and how biographical research challenges and transcends them in pursuit of the human life story, reflecting, too, on the precarious nature of the academic workplace within the neoliberal economy.

Keywords

academic conferences – Bronfenbrenner's ecological model – interdisciplinarity – life history and biography – higher education

1 The Contextual Landscape

When the content of this paper was being finalised, the entire world was being held to ransom by the coronavirus, Covid-19. As we are writing, normality is

© HAZEL R. WRIGHT AND MARIANNE HØYEN, 2021 | DOI: 10.1163/9789004465916_006 on hold. Across Europe and further afield, entire countries are in lockdown, their offices, schools and entertainment centres closed. For many, even local travel is banned, and international travellers are forced to quarantine. Routine everyday activities – teaching, shopping, social contact – have to take place online or not at all for many people. These are both frightening and interesting times, the way ahead uncharted territory, the potential for radical change at a global level immense: we are repeatedly told – in the press and on social media – that life will never be the same again, that this is a 'defining historical event' (Walsh & Millard, 2020, p. 130.) We cannot accurately predict the future, but it may be that massed gatherings, which are already a concern from an environmental perspective, will remain virtual as people fear, refuse, or are simply not allowed, to meet in large numbers in any one place. In this context, at a time when face-to-face academic conferences both local and transnational have all been cancelled, it seems particularly appropriate to consider the ecology of an academic conference and what might be missed when these take place in a virtual environment. We wonder: "What is the value of the 'live' conference as a phenomenon?" "Why (and which) academics allocate time, funding and energy to travel to meet with others to discuss their work?" We aim to examine these issues within the context of ESREA's Life History and Biographic Network (LHBN) conference around its 25th anniversary, seeking answers in relational terms, considering the interaction of influences at the micro-, meso- and macro-levels, in keeping with the ecological approach that underpins this book.

We write, having met a decade ago at a LHBN conference which took place in Geneva. Over this period, our growing familiarity with the network and developing friendship enabled us to reflect on it from both outsider and insider perspectives. Initially our experience was that of the isolated attendee. We saw the LHBN conference through independent eyes, unaware of the network's aims and intentions or its connections to the broader association, ESREA; barely aware of the work that goes on behind the scenes concerning mailing lists, conference organisation and publication. In annual steps, we progressed to chairing sessions, to scrutinising abstracts and thence to organising a conference ourselves, and subsequently a publication, choosing for both a conference in Copenhagen and an edited publication to focus on the theme 'Discourses we live by'. Thus, we write as people who have attended and organised the annual LHBN conference and with a perspective that continues beyond the experience of hosting to once again attending chiefly to present a paper and meet with colleagues. Our medium-term perspective, and our separation from the overall organisation of the Network enables an element of detachment but, nevertheless, we acknowledge the subjectivity that underpins this chapter. However, we are positioned differently to the established convenors – guardians of the aims and principles on which the Network is run – and the newcomers approaching it afresh; we are *sufficiently* familiar to have an overview.

Like most of those who support the Network we are adult educators, both accustomed to working predominately with students slightly older than the typical undergraduate, often those who seek to enter the educational professions – social educators and teachers in Marianne's case, early years educators in Hazel's. We have visited each other's country many times, met colleagues and friends and looked around the educational settings, co-devised and co-taught narrative inquiry courses for MA and Doctoral students in Denmark; eventually, working collaboratively to support each other's writing and co-editing *Discourses we live by: Narratives of educational and social endeavour* (Wright & Høyen, 2020) which is both extensive and diverse in its coverage. So, we felt that we should be well-able to negotiate the creation of a shared chapter but still found the chapter hard to write, perhaps, because our initial degree subjects established different epistemological expectations – Hazel was a Geographer, Marianne a Civil Engineer – and an 'ecological approach' held specific meanings for each of us that seemed difficult to apply in other contexts as we will demonstrate later. We had both studied widely to move from semi-scientific disciplines into the humanities. Marianne embraced Sociology (making a commitment to Bourdieu) and thence to work with this within Education, Hazel moved into Education where a practical and professional route took her research into Sociology and the Humanities, always in the thrall of interdisciplinary approaches. We became interested in narrative research initially as a tool to capture what people really think and feel, and like many others, found this a position that is hard to reject once adopted and (fortuitously) a sense of community within the LHBN Network. So now we will look more closely at the Network conferences but first we start by considering what constitutes a conference.

2   What Is a Conference?

The term conference, as *conferentia* meaning conversation or talk, was in use in the 16th century but derives from the Latin *conferre*, to bring together (Lexico, Oxford online). In its main definition it involves attendance: 'A formal meeting of people with a shared interest, typically one that takes place over several days'. As yet, in its usage as: 'A linking of several telephones or computers, so that each user may communicate with the others simultaneously', it is seen as modifier; the complete phrase being 'a conference call'.

Even a brief comparison of these definitions identifies 'duration', 'live contact' and 'structures' as important aspects; foundational characteristics that shape relationships around 'conference'.

At this point we could simply launch into a reflective account of conference experiences but choose instead to adapt an ecological model as a way to establish a degree of structure for our discussion, believing that this may enable us to look more widely than the individual conference we organised in Copenhagen. Looking wider is important as our positioning is as 'insider reflectors' – not 'researchers' who negotiated ethical agreements – so we must keep the discussion broad to preserve the anonymity of attendees. To this end, too, the chapter draws on our personal viewpoints, remaining reflective, rather than using quotations from other attendees.

Bronfenbrenner's Ecological Model was used as a tool to assist our thought rather than a means to systemise our thinking, as it would facilitate the task of capturing the relationality between the different aspects of academic life. We are aware that with his model Bronfenbrenner (1977, p. 513) sought to heal the dichotomy between 'rigor' and 'social relevance' of concern in the 1970s, and we also seek to achieve both but from a different starting point as times have changed. Rather than using experiment and hypothesis to conduct our social analysis in a systematic fashion like Bronfenbrenner, we employed informal naturalistic observation, reflection and recall. This was supported by analysis of material that is in the public domain through the conference website (LHBN Copenhagen), and the model (theoretically) works as a focusing structure, at least as a way into examining a complex subject.

3   Exploring Bronfenbrenner's Model

Bronfenbrenner's model places the individual (in his case a child) at the centre of his/her world, surrounded by a set of distinctive spheres of influence or levels (Bronfenbrenner, 1981). In the model we find four systems (the micro-, meso-, exo- and macro-) relating to the individual child who is seen as an active participant in the process of development, engaged in continually adapting to the environment which is continuously changing; the notion of time conceptualised as a surrounding chronosphere. In our version of the ecosystem, the conference attendee occupied the central position and we were mindful that this was an adult whose interactions with and in the world would be constituted differently.

Our context for using Bronfenbrenner's model is the Copenhagen conference, and we worked as he did from micro- to macro-level, driven by our shared concern that each LHBN conference ends with uncertainty for the future, particularly around where we might meet the following year. This initial application was not too taxing. As Bronfenbrenner's focus is developmental, his underlying interest is in the transitions as the child moves from the micro- to other systems, his spheres are populated with centres that serve children, like preschool and day-care settings, orphanages and hospitals (Shelton, 2018). In our initial discussion we, too, follow this directional pattern needing to look at microsystems before mesosystems, and to establish the way that the exosystem influences the macrosystem. We use the spheres to identify the different layers of influence that may impinge on the conference attendees who sit at the core of our model. For our purposes, it is the specification of the different levels of influence that matters, the relationships they enable and constrain and conversely the constraints and affordances they establish. We are mindful, too, that each conference will present a unique set of affordances to those who attend it but speculate that these are diminished when a conference goes online and loses its sense of place, its tangibility, the 'colour' that emanates from belonging in the real world. But, here, we are actually working to reduce difference, for in drawing out the aspects that populate each sphere we are seeking to simplify complexity into sets of influences.

The micro-level for the attendee has two aspects: the patterns, roles and relationships relating to the home university to which s/he belongs and those that relate to the actual conference. In terms of the home university we would position colleagues and managers as important and see their relationships with the attendee in terms of practicalities: teaching schedules, willingness to provide cover for absence and to allocate elements of budgets to finance the attendance, the extent to which they view a particular conference, topic or staff member as worthy of support. Many of these are potential barriers to attendance. Within the conference there are relational issues around the location (is it attractive, is there affordable accommodation, are the organisers helpful in answering questions by email), relationships with colleagues from the home university (peers, supervisors, those of similar or different academic status) and with the other conference delegates whose names may be publicised in advance and with whom the attendee may or may not already have a relationship. Notably those who supervise doctoral students bring a steady stream of new researchers into the Network demonstrating how contact in the home university can translate into relational issues within the conference. Conversely, a conference can also represent an escape from everyday connections. It is only since Hazel became an Honorary Fellow that she has invited colleagues and students along. When she worked full time, she preferred to attend alone to meet new people. Marianne, too, came by herself prior to becoming conference host when departmental support was both useful and achievable. We wonder, does the LHBN attract academics seeking new contacts and sufficiently independent to 'come solo'? For we recognise now that, alongside those who attend with supervisors, there are many who travel alone. And looking back to those early experiences as a newcomer we recall how, despite the welcome, there was a sense that everyone knew everyone else and of an inner clique of people with years of shared experiences that bordered on the exclusionary. Seeking to belong, we were aware, too, that there were no formal structures to facilitate this, no committee to join, no posts to volunteer for, no tasks to take on short of offering to host a conference; all points we will return to later.

The meso-level holds the interrelations among two or more settings. This is a little confusing as 'settings' more commonly means physical spaces, but Bronfenbrenner's examples are conceptual – family, work and social life. The meso-level is where aspects of individuals' lives begin to mesh, forming a web of relationships that may combine or conflict, thereby supporting or constraining the individual's development and it is this personal web of connections that constitutes a unique mesosystem. If we claim that for conferences generally, groups of researchers within a network, the conference convenors, academic publication systems, and the conference hosts are examples of microsystems, then the links they make with the individual and with each other constitute the mesosystem, with them remaining discrete entities. LHBN provides a gateway to a broader meso-level for those who seek this, providing an entrée to other subject networks within the broader ESREA framework, and the parent society that offers opportunities to set up a new network, to join the central organising committee, and to access further publication opportunities in books and the *European Journal for Research on the Education and Learning of Adults* (RELA), too.

In the exosystem we find structures/settings that indirectly affect the individual attendee. Our suggestion for populating this level consists of discursive settings (discourses understood as talk and practice), namely: the political frameworks shaping research and education; funding systems; and the media as gatekeepers to success, whether as reporters of events or publishers of academic material. These arenas differ from country to country as does the extent to which they influence 'what it is to be a researcher now' and hence affect the attendee. As it is based in Western Europe, even though the emphasis varies across nations, the conference is shaped and constrained by prevalent neoliberal forces. Funding is a major consideration and also the 'pressure' for academics not only to research and publish but also to teach to higher and higher standards. LHBN members are not exempt from such expectations and can find it difficult to get their universities to recognise the value of small-scale research and 'stories' when others are solving global problems or serving the local community.

It is the macro-level, which holds the culture, value systems and underlying ideology that shapes the other spheres and although globalisation is continually challenging difference, this also varies according to country. Arenas here include the labour market (especially the academic job market), overarching disciplinary discourses, and the predominant knowledge paradigm. These arenas were once straightforward but are continually changing in today's globalised society (Lyotard, 1984; Nowotny et al., 2001) where they are increasingly affected by changes in the exosystem (the Covid-19 pandemic being an extreme example). Within a context – ours being academia – these arenas rarely function in isolation. In terms of conference attendance, attendees must navigate within these framings and position themselves within the possibilities that are available. They must cope directly with the consequences of the macro-level systems acting on the lower (meso) level, making negotiation even more complex. Academic culture is under pressure, our value systems challenged by structures in the exosystem. LHBN conference attendees annually face these challenges. For us, as authors, the challenge was more structural, one of trying to simplify real-world complexity to align with a theoretical model.

4   Working with Bronfenbrenner's Ecological Model

For then we struggled with the model. It served to support our thinking at a theoretical level, enabling us to identify different influences affecting and affected by the conference attendee, but however we approached it, working outwards or, even worse, trying inwards, it became unwieldy and restrictive as a format to shape discussion. We realised that, in part, the problem is the centring on an individual when in reality all the influencers affect each other, sometimes directly, sometimes filtering through other influences. We had followed Bronfenbrenner in actively seeking to place individuals at the centre of their own lives, to set those lives in context, and to promote agentive behaviour but this was at variance with our understanding that interactions are multiple and multi-directional. Trying to apply the model in real life clearly highlighted this conflict, identifying the model's limitations. Because of the complexity of interactions, to shape our discussion to address each level in turn would lead to much unnecessary repetition and artificially constrict the discourses.

Only at this point, about to give up on the ecological model, did we grasp an important point. In an 'aha' (Mezirow, 1975) or epiphanic moment (Denzin,

2001) we realised that a conference is a mesosystem as it only exists in the coming together of disparate elements – the interrelation of people, places, papers, plenaries, social events, in all their different ways. Our interpretation of the mesosystem and our earlier analyses had whispered this, but we hadn't listened carefully enough! Our editors alluded to it, too, but in the context of a longer trialogue on our first draft where it remained unread, lost in words. But suddenly we knew it, without knowing how. To explain thoroughly (if we could) would be to reject the notion of 'aha' moments and epiphanies for the causes of that transformative moment when you 'just know something' are essentially elusive. For Marianne the moment equates with a sense of enlightenment, for Hazel this conviction is also embodied as an inner calm, a feeling that she is fully in the present moment; for both it signifies a puzzle solved even a new understanding that was unsought but is now irreversibly known.

So, Eureka! Our discussion of actual conferences, and specifically the one in Copenhagen sits within the meso-level but our further discussion needs to follow its relevant themes, with only casual reference to levels when we bring in specific key influencers. So, with structural problems to some extent addressed, we can turn at last to our core interest in what makes going to a 'live' conference valuable?

5   Exploring the Value of the 'Live' Conference

We look now more closely at the LHBN conferences, and specifically at the Copenhagen one when detail is useful. We will look briefly at aspects that span the levels – ever mindful that hostile conditions in the exosystem (like pandemics) react on practices at the macro-level (like lock down), together creating challenges at the micro-level (like staying home) – but the main focus will be on the meso-level, particularly those things that serve to make the conference hospitable. We gave up trying to deal with levels and their content as distinctive entities – that was useful only at a theoretical level – and accepted that it is the relationality between entities and across levels that matters, mindful that Bronfenbrenner was trying to demonstrate connectivity and at least point to the complexity of causality.

Under neoliberalism (which we consider to be a facet of the exosystem), academics are increasingly expected to cope with a heavier workload, to teach more students for longer periods, and to publish regularly; all factors that potentially lead to more standardised approaches and less space for creativity. We struggle with these expectations – Hazel even moved from paid to honorary status to reduce their impact – and find they make it harder to 'get away' any-where. Yet we find the time to come to 'live' conferences and so do those others who attend. Perhaps this time pressure is even reflected in the abstracts sub-mitted to the Copenhagen conference. Researchers choose their methods to suit their projects but quite possibly the predominant use of biographical and narrative methods over full life histories is a sign that researchers have limited time available to carry out their work and need to use quicker methods in order to publish more frequently for career progression in a competitive labour mar-ket. We are not suggesting that this is 'quick and dirty' (Petre & Rugg, 2010, p. 70), only that evaluative regimes favour speed and quantity, and data that ena-bles generalisation. It may even be that biographical and narrative methods are too slow. Collecting and interpreting such data is a time-consuming pro-cess and this is reflected in the costings that accompany bids for funding and maybe makes them uncompetitive. Often funded research is required to have a social 'impact', too, but we found this to be evident in most papers whether or not the research was funded. Quite possibly, in educational and caring disci-plines, professional and client interaction makes social impact inevitable.

Abstracts to the Copenhagen conference reflected the adult educational theme of the Network and most were found to pursue themes within the dis-ciplines of education, social work or health. These are all non-traditional dis-ciplinary areas that sit within the public services sector and themselves draw material from other disciplines (facets of the macrosystem). These are sec-tors, too, that operationalise policies devised at macro-level as services for the individual, demonstrating that biographic methods serve a useful function in establishing people's views. In talking freely, end-users provide insights that relate to 'how' rather than simple 'what' questions, revealing the shortcomings or benefits of social provision for those to whom it matters.

Most contributors had an affiliation to a specific disciplinary area, whether traditional or more recent, and would have encountered its inherent value sys-tems as exemplified by our difficulties in reinterpreting 'ecological approaches'. However, it is likely that they had also looked beyond disciplinary boundaries to achieve the broader understanding of the human required for work with life stories. In this way, biographical research serves to disrupt traditional knowl-edge boundaries, to avoid 'fragmentation' (West, 1996) of lives by disciplinary boundaries. In conversation, attendees appeared to privilege inter- or trans-disciplinarity as a more compelling and inclusive way of researching. In this way, the LHBN conference could be seen as innovative, and this is self-perpet-uating as its 'live' nature provides opportunities to learn from colleagues in other disciplines, to work co-operatively with them and to make the first steps beyond the security of the disciplinary boundary. Thus, it follows ecological principles of constant and harmonious adaptation. Attendees may not fully anticipate this, but it is clear from chatting to them at this and subsequent conferences that once they have experienced it, they appreciate the chance to meet with others who also work across disciplines. This sense of shared values is not always easily found within the traditional disciplinary structures of the university; in education we are privileged to have some learning in common but may still reside in separate subject silos, utilising a previously acquired qualification set.

The conference abstracts also drew attention to value systems through their content. Many dealt with the consequences of external constraints on working life – cuts in educational budgets, the narrowing possibilities to care properly for those for whom we are professionally responsible, the effects of external evaluation criteria of various sorts. Harking to the exosystem, the label neoliberalism appeared in several titles as well as within abstracts. That many attendees were insider researchers showed clear links between what is happening externally and concerns for how this affects individual sectors in education, social care and health. Abstracts also reflected significant events in the real world, migration, for example. This was a commonly studied topic, individually but also within larger funded projects, demonstrating the importance attached to this issue at higher levels but also the significance of funding (part of the exosystem) in shaping what happens elsewhere. There are definite linkages confirming that the component elements in a system affect each other, supporting an ecological interpretation.

Examining the abstracts as a group, also provided a snapshot of 'who' attends the conference. At a number of conferences, we have been part of discussions about the nature of the membership and whether it is sufficiently diverse, again a reflection of the conferences' values. Our records for Copenhagen enable us to comment on this but we recognise that the picture may be very different in other places in other years. In Copenhagen, the majority of the abstracts were from the English-language world (47%), with a high percentage from women (71%). It was also clear that although many of the researchers had a university affiliation a considerable number were either at an early stage of their academic career or the opposite, close to retiring officially (61%). The largest national group were from the UK (35%), followed by Italy (11%) and then Denmark (6%), the home of the conference this year, demonstrating that the network still has work to do in extending its geographical cover and participant range. The remainder were individuals from other European countries and a number of regular attendees from further afield who often extend their visit to include holiday, maybe with their partner. We have no means of accurately establishing class or ethnicity but know from the conference itself that some openly claim working class (or other) origins as a 'badge of honour', yet very few identified as, or were identifiable as, belonging to an ethnic minority. There was a significant gender imbalance, a marked Anglocentric skew for a society purporting to be pan-European, and attendees were predominantly white, socially mobile working-, if not yet middle-, class. More unusually, the age of attendees was polarised, early career researchers and a significant proportion of elder academics. Overall, the attendees did not represent the diverse group that we, as that year's organisers, were keen to attract.

The abstracts fitted into one of four categories and it is tempting to speculate that these related to career stages. Many were personal projects pursued as part of a higher education qualification, usually a doctorate, and these clearly aligned with early career researchers. Others were personal projects discussing work that the individual had pursued over a considerable period of time, and here the timeframe suggests mid-career status. In a third category were a small number of larger projects with groups of researchers working together over a number of years, usually supported by external funding from the EU or other official establishments or administrative bodies, for example within health. We have seen that it is often the experienced academics with established contacts who manage to acquire such funding. The last category comprised a significant number of small-scale individual projects possibly devised and carried out to provide material specifically for the intended conference presentation; others were retrospective reflections on projects carried out earlier. Some of these we know to be the work of retired individuals who no longer command the resources to undertake larger-scale projects.

Despite its lack of refinement, our overview of the content of abstracts may partly explain a problem that the Network regularly faces but so far has managed to overcome, namely a shortage of conference hosts (and consequently, but of secondary importance, difficulty in finding new locations). The neoliberal expectation that members of educational establishments will be directly charged to use their own premises and facilities has surely exacerbated matters but the polarised membership in terms of age and career status may also play a part. We wonder why the Network attracts so few mid-career researchers or lecturers, those with established positions who might be able to host new conferences? Perhaps they judge a bigger conference to better meet their needs. Maybe they are forced to pursue more quantifiable topics – biographical and narrative research, being interdisciplinary but at a personal rather than team level, may be difficult to submit to national evaluations. Perhaps they are too busy teaching or working on externally funded projects to get to conferences not held during the long vacation, constrained by fixed budgets that restrict international travel or make it more difficult. It is also possible that they are being replaced by cheaper, digitally, competent, more malleable(?) younger staff in line with the neoliberal agenda. We can only speculate but see this last fear reflected in Standing's (2011) claim that the precariat (those with unstable working conditions, such as hourly paid lecturers) now dominate the academic labour market. Finance features significantly in the issues raised here and certainly at the micro-level it had a direct influence on attendance. Some 25% of people who submitted abstracts later cancelled and many cited lack of funding as the reason for doing this, but, inherently, their withdrawal prevented further explication.

As adult educators, we wonder whether higher-level value judgements about useful methodologies are at play here. Despite the very different circumstances, are there echoes of the nineteenth century call for 'really useful knowledge' (Johnson, 1988)? We also question whether the conference could do more to support its own continuity. Earlier we talked about the lack of structures to enable a newcomer to find a niche (another term appropriated from ecology) but finding ways to do that whilst respecting the central role of the convenors may be a challenge. To threaten the Network's established practices could be counter-productive, and the fluidity of the 'gatherings' we hold in place of 'meetings' is important. But the convenors have now *started* to invite people to volunteer to take on specific tasks to spread the workload beyond themselves, and a prudent formalisation of such roles, could afford opportunities to those who want to commit. Such volunteers might also share the work of organising a conference with sensitivity, so that people who attend alone and lack a ready-made network of colleagues with insider knowledge to support this task, could be assured of useful assistance. At present, it is possible that the mid-career researchers keen to broaden their external influence and enhance their CVs, more easily find a niche elsewhere. Perhaps we need to find ways to harness the energy of those who can 'do more' to support the network practically. These are suggestions but not answers, and we should continually probe for hidden discourses and question whether the appearance of equality, the lack of other roles, masks a reluctance to share power?

To return to conference hosts, we have to hope that the shortage is a temporary problem, just a case of waiting for some of these early career researchers to become established, for our observations show that most of those who do attend value the biographic method highly and we know that this is a method increasingly acknowledged to be important (O'Neill et al., 2015), despite its time demands and costliness. As an icebreaker at the Copenhagen conference, we invited attendees to form small groups to discuss why they favour narrative research methods and how they came to use them. Unfortunately, we did not seek permission to quote their comments directly, but we did note the depth of their commitment and, often, the passion with which they talked about this. Clearly the methodology itself, working with biographical materials, is an intrinsic reason for attending the LHBN conference, but so is the chance to hold such informal and personal conversations around a shared interest.

To specifically address our main question about the value of the 'live' conference, it is self-evident that for people to attend a conference the benefits and attractions of doing this must outweigh the reasons not to bother and no doubt motivators differ. Some conferences are hierarchical with elite committees keeping themselves apart from the masses, setting aside significant funds to attract eminent keynote speakers. Attendance at these is prestigious and there is always the possibility that your work may be noticed by someone important. In contrast, LHBN eschews displays of status, deliberately avoiding the use of academic titles on name badges and documentation, avoiding expensive keynote speakers and striving for a semblance of equality even though we usually know the professors from the doctoral students. Other conferences attract attendees through their choice of venues, visiting a new 'place of interest' each year. Hazel used to attend a significant conference that never fails to locate in a popular tourist location, until she became disenchanted by its size, the consequent difficulty in finding proximate accommodation and, finally, a decision to offer many established presenters a poster slot in order to accommodate the numerous new participants. Neoliberal values with regard to finance and status resonate here but also, disciplinarity: those colleagues for whom the focus is more 'central' continue to attend.

In contrast, the locations of LHBN conferences are determined by which members are able to access suitable but non-costly venues and willing to be hosts. To encourage attendance LHBN tries to minimise conference costs, offering reduced rates for doctoral students, advising on low-cost accommodation and providing as many meals as possible. Often, especially in more expensive locations, the academics and their colleagues themselves manage the catering. In Geneva, members brought in food, in Magdeburg and Turin we were fed informally on campus, in Bergen we were invited in small groups into colleagues' homes for a meal '*en famille*'. Similarly, conference dinners are held in interesting places rather than formal restaurants: in the old bath's changing huts on Lake Geneva, at the communal diner in the hippy colony of Christiania in Copenhagen, in a historic boathouse in Bergen. Pre-conference events are informal and low cost too, walking or bus trips around the city we are in, visits to local landmarks – to the ruined abbey and cathedral archives in Canterbury, for example.

By popular request we now build 'free time' into the programme so that there is time to shop, to visit galleries or museums, to attend local events (a concert in Bergen, evensong in Canterbury cathedral), to socialise in small groups or go to a pub or café in a big one, to meet and plan shared ventures with colleagues whose interests overlap with your own. This informality enables people to relax and make friends, creating a sense of community within the Network that would be difficult to establish in an online conference. In turn, genuine friendships lead to working relationships that really 'work', making it possible to survive the ups and downs of collaborations later managed at a distance. In contrast, we all know other conferences where the papers are presented continually from an early hour until late into the evening. Last year Marianne and Hazel arranged to meet up at a different European conference. This was much larger than LHBN's, catering for a single-discipline, and aspiration and inspiration were clearly focal. It attracted many mid-career researchers suggesting, as might be expected, that for them perceived career opportunities influence conference attendance. It was an interesting and stimulating event but very intense. We found it did not even schedule a lunch break, one had to decide which event to miss to eat at mid-day. It is hard even to find your existing friends at such an event, even harder to make new ones, but this can be an important step in developing a collaborative partnership for future work, making all conference attendance potentially valuable – an insight that management may find hard to grasp!

A Network with a 'live' conference like LHBN, in creating a safe space for sharing and co-operation, may also serve as a site of resistance. The social contact of the 'live' conference offers opportunities to find others to support your cause or find a cause you wish to join, the chance to co-publish material rather than stand alone, to petition collectively for policy or other change. Not least it offers chances to 'test the water', to find out discretely if the problems you are encountering are commonplace or exceptional, to share solutions or ways to ameliorate the undesirable, perhaps simply to empathise. We remember the relief in finding that other academic colleagues were struggling with overwork; the sense of perspective gained from finding that Iberian colleagues were even worse off, facing pay cuts as well as increased workloads. We hope they found some benefit in our sympathy and doubt that a digital meeting would offer such opportunities to 'share' and reflect on the realities of academic life. Yet this is important for an academic's sense of wellbeing.

Thus, through valuing equality, informality, sociability and, importantly, by promoting a methodology that is intrinsically attractive, the LHBN conferences encourage attendance. Structurally – by offering free time, safe spaces and shared experiences, chances to get to know people properly and make friends, alongside the normative agenda of papers, plenaries, workshops and a dinner – our conferences are relaxed and welcoming even for newcomers.

There is a dark side to this – informality can leave people unsure what to do, close relationships can mean that people disagree and fall out (and we have some experience of picking up the pieces here), built in free time can leave some people wondering whether they are getting their money's worth – but we deal with it as individuals and as a collective. By setting out our values we open the conference to criticisms that we fail to practice what we preach – but short-term challenges, if addressed, can ultimately strengthen the Network. Twenty-five years on, it is still flourishing and attracting new members to its 'live' conferences. Many return year after year; confirmation that they deem the conference to have value. Whether this will continue under the post-pandemic 'new normality' remains to be seen.

References

Bronfenbrenner, U. (1977). Toward an experimental ecology of human development. *American Psychologist*, July, 513–531. https://psycnet.apa.org/doi/10.1037/0003-066X.32.7.513

Bronfenbrenner, U. (1981). *The ecology of human development: Experiments by nature and design.* Harvard University Press.

Denzin, N. K. (2001). *Interpretive interactionism* (2nd ed.). Sage. https://dx.doi.org/10.4135/9781412984591

Johnson, R. (1988). 'Really useful knowledge' 1790–1850: Memories for education in the 1980s. In T. Lovett (Ed.), *Radical approaches to adult education: A reader* (pp. 3–34). Routledge.

LHBN (Copenhagen). (2017, March 2–5). *Discourses we live by.* ESREA/LHBN Conference, Copenhagen. Retrieved June 6, 2019, from http://conferences.au.dk/esrealhbn2017/

Lyotard, J.-F. (1984). *The postmodern condition: A report on knowledge.* Manchester University Press.

Mezirow, J. (1975). *Education for perspective transformation: Women's reentry programs in community colleges.* Center for Adult Education, Teachers College, Columbia University.

Nowotny, H., Scott, P., & Gibbons, M. (2001). *Re-thinking science: Knowledge and the public in an age of uncertainty.* Polity Press.

O'Neill, M., Roberts, B., & Sparkes, A. C. (2015). *Advances in biographical methods: Creative applications.* Routledge.

Petre, M., & Rugg, G. (2010). *The unwritten rules of PhD research* (2nd ed.). Open University Press.

Shelton, L. (2018). *The Bronfenbrenner primer. A guide to develecology.* Routledge. https://doi.org/10.4324/9781315136066

Standing, G. (2011). *The precariat: The new dangerous class.* Bloomsbury Academic.

Walsh, Fergus talking with Rosie Millard. (2020, May 9–15). I got in my car and cried. *Radio Times.*

West, L. (1996). *Beyond fragments: Adults, motivation and higher education, a biographical analysis.* Taylor & Francis.

Wright, H. R., & Høyen, M. (2020). *Discourses we live by: Narratives of educational and social endeavour.* Open Book Publishers. https://www.openbookpublishers.com/product/1110

PART 2

Dialogue in Learning Together, and Its Distress

∵

Dynamic Ecologies of Person and Place: Dialogic Ethnographies as Public Engagement

Richard D. Sawyer

Abstract

In this chapter I explore the intersectional ecology (both physical and discursive) of dialogic ethnographic research and place. I suggest that agency is not located entirely within individual action, but is generated within an intertwined material/collective relationship within a lived ecology. For my theoretical framework I draw from Bourdieu's notion of habitus and place, Barad's theory of posthumanist performativity, and finally my and Norris's conception of duoethnography. I provide one illustrative example, a duoethnography (more specifically a trioethnography) of place walking around a college campus. Vonzell Agosto, Travis Marn, and Rica Ramirez conducted their trioethnography as they "place walked" around their college campus, encountering a landscape actively imbued with symbolic power. Through conversation and movement, they explored the symbolic codes mediating thought and action within their space. Their study made the invisible, visible and the symbolic, concrete. Furthermore, their study was a meaningful context for their own growth: it facilitated a reflexive change in their stance and engagement on their campus. And finally, I suggest that their study itself became a public pedagogy of resistance.

Keywords

embodied inquiry – duoethnography – multi-cultural inquiry – life history inquiry

1 Introduction

Examining relationships between humans and larger socio/cultural/political/ environmental/and historical contexts, life history research has long focused, often implicitly, on ecologies of human living within a complex world. Recent examples about the examination of the interdependence of life (human and otherwise) and ecological justice include studies by Chan (2017) on land and

Indigenous postcolonialism in Canada, Bainbridge and Del Negro (2020) on human transformation in relation to ecological biodiversity, and West and Carlson (2006) on autobiography and the claiming and sustaining of space.

These contexts for life history research expand knowledge systems in relation to language, culture, and power. Being culturally constructed, they may be culturally deconstructed and then reconstructed. While obviously there is a focus on human epistemologies, new forms of life history research are beginning to not just examine the relationship between human life and ecology, but much more: they seek to explore how such inquiry may decenter and replace discourses of eco-injustice with discourses of ecological wellness.

In this chapter I discuss the intersectional ecology (both physical and discursive) of dialogic ethnographic research and place. For my theoretical framework I draw from Bourdieu's notion of habitus and place (1983), Barad's (2003) theory of posthumanist performativity, and finally my and Norris's conception of duoethnography (Norris & Sawyer, 2020; Sawyer & Norris, 2013). As part of this discussion, I provide one illustrative example, a duoethnography (more specifically a trioethnography) of place walking around a college campus.

2   Theoretical Framing

Duoethnography is a collaborative and dialogic form of autoethnography (Sawyer & Norris, 2013). Working with a research partner, duoethnographers critique and question their positionality in relation to critical issues and constructs and reconceptualize their own narrative constructions in the face of the other person. Foucault (1990) and others have theorized how individuals are socialized into discursive genealogies – scripts which direct how people live their lives. It is these scripts and inscribed discourses, running through their lives, that duoethnographers often examine.

For their inquiries, duoethnographers are guided by central tenets. These tenets include an engagement in currere, the examination of difference as a heuristic, and the separation of voices within the produced text. I view currere (Pinar, 1975, 1994, 2012; Sawyer, 2017) as life-history curriculum with which people (e.g., teachers, students) engage in an embodied deconstruction of the past to reconstruct the future through engagement in the present.

Duoethnography is not focused on concrete research questions, but rather on cultural translations created within a third space (Bhabha, 1994; Sawyer et al., 2016; Wang, 2006). It is focused on the contingent, relational, emic, interdisciplinary, critical, phenomenological, and generative movements within these spaces (Norris & Sawyer, 2015; Sawyer & Norris, 2013). Duoethnographers do not record what was; rather, they reimagine and transform views of the past, framed by the inquiry topic. Finally, as researchers engage in duoethnography, they use language in an intentional yet playful way. They set up the page as a script from a play, with the different speakers indicated by name. The goal is to not blend the voices together into a monolithic text, but rather to emphasize difference and voice.

Bourdieu (1983) is frequently used as a theoretical frame for duoethnography. A central concept that Bourdieu explored is that of habitus. Habitus is the "socially constituted system of cognitive and motivating structures" (Bourdieu, 1977, p. 76), the codes embedded within situations and places (Lefebvre, 1991). Habitus creates a mutually mediating field, with the setting itself relaying social structures that guide thought and practice, and with individuals interpreting these internalized codes. Seemingly normative, the guided thoughts, motivations, and practices appear taken-for-granted and may even operate at an unconscious level.

One aspect of habitus is its symbolic power, the often taken-for-granted interpretation of codes by people within specific spaces. Within duoethnography, researchers attempt to excavate the codes related to "that invisible power which can be exercised only with the complicity of those who do not want to know that they are subject to it, or even that they themselves exercise it" (Bourdieu, 1991, p. 164). Within Bourdieu's theory, space becomes place by way of this mutual activation of codes and meaning structures. These structures, part of the representational space, are embedded in the history of the place (Lefebvre, 1991). In this way "social life is materially grounded and conditioned, but material conditions affect behavior in large part through the mediation of individuals, dispositions, and experiences" (Brubaker, 1985, p. 750).

Another theorist who examines space, specifically in relation to materiality, is Barad (2003). She ascribes a much greater independence and agency to material spaces. She suggests that agency is not located entirely within individual action, but is generated within the intertwined material/collective relationship. The material space is inhabited by humans, non-humans, and objects. It is not a representation of human culture or language, but rather aspects of matter, of which the human body is part. Material space and the human mind are not separate, but rather entangled in a dynamic and mutually constitutive relationship.

3   Placewalking on Campus: A Trioethnography of Person and Place

In *Biracial Place Walkers on Campus*, Vonzell Agosto, Travis Marn, and Rica Ramirez (2015) conducted a trioethnography in which they "physically and dialogically revisited locations on the campus (primarily within a college of education) at a large, urban research university to share past and current experiences at the intersection of race, place and power" (Agosto et al., 2015, p. 113). While some of the description and analysis in their study were conducted after the campus exploration during moments of individual and collaborative reflection, much of it took place in "real time" as they walked through different buildings, offices, hallways, and classrooms on their campus. They call their approach in their trioethnography "place walking" (p. 109).

In their study, they used currere both in a regressive way in order to consider earlier experiences and in a progress way to reconceptualize those perceptions: Here they discussed their use of currere:

> Currere guides our walk around the curriculum of our lives (the past, present, imagined future, and integration of all) and how we go about "laying down a path in walking". (Varela, Thompson, & Rosch, 1991, p. 236)

> ... [with] the questions we often confront: What inhibits or inspires our sense of belonging or isolation on campus? What can we learn in the interactions between us and the place (epistemological, social, and physical)? (p. 110)

In the above quote, they first emphasized how they were exploring the integration of self, society, and subject matter together. Their statement suggests that a critical part of this process is the transtemporal process of currere, with the analytical and synthetic phases related to their conceptions/movements within the past, present, and future. By using the word "interactions", they acknowledge the agency of place. They added that,

> Place walking brings a literal re-visitation to sites where our past, present, and imagined futures converge through dialogue. Through place walking we were able to explore how our biracial identities are expressed in connection and disconnection from the cultural environment and consider how our sense of membership is strengthened or diminished. (p. 113)

Place walking, they immersed themselves into the material environment and described aspects of the physical space that caught their eye. Their descriptions included the thin, brightly colored walls separating small offices, the hospital-like ambience, and the lack of art. Here they described entering a classroom where Marn and Ramirez had taken classes. The classroom is empty "and the only adornment was the American flag" (p. 116). They examined how the space became animated during class with racial and cultural meanings: "This classroom [with the flag] is significant in Travis and Rica's memory for how the topic of race has come up during courses" (p. 116). Later, they told a story about a class discussion that took place in this room:

> Our professor ... always tries to get us to think about different things, and race is included. But it was so interesting because there are a couple of Hispanic students in the class and the professor is Hispanic so I don't feel like there have been a lot of racist things that have been said about them. But there is not one Black person in there. And we were talking about African American English or Black English Vernacular and they were doing a presentation that was based upon how they talked, they would say it out loud and make fun of it – sort of. They would laugh after every example like, "Ain't got no job". And they would all laugh. I looked back and said to a friend, "I wonder if we would be speaking like this and laughing after every single example about how they talk if there was a Black person in here?" She said, "Oh no, we wouldn't be". (p. 117)

As can be seen, their situated analyses were sometimes expressed as reactions to practices found in the different locations. In this classroom, with the American flag perhaps visually underscoring the classroom banter, they described how one student actually admitted to feeling safe enough in class to take a racist stance. Marn and Ramirez's comments suggest a question of the level of congruence between the discourses within the classroom and discussion and their classmates' personal narratives.

Their descriptions of enclosed spaces contrast with more open spaces as they walked around the campus. In one of these walks they encountered both an explicit and implicit (null) ecology of space. In the following passage, Agosto described a liminal awareness of how space both foreclosed some aspects of identity, while opening up others:

> This sentiment surfaced as I walked with Rica and Travis through stairwells in the College of Education that I did not know existed. They showed me routes that left me asking: Where are we? I grew painfully aware there were places I had not traveled because there were few invitations for me to know the landscape more thoroughly and therefore few opportunities to develop a deep sense of belonging. In conversation, Rica reminded me of the adage in Spanish, *mi casa es su casa*. Although I knew this phrase well from childhood it seemed to be archaic when it came up in our conversation. It helped me to pin down the hidden curriculum,

the cultural norms of the institution that conflicted with what I believe learning environments should provide: a welcoming climate character-ized by invitations, tours, and hospitality. (p. 124)

As seen in the above quotes, space communicated diverse cultural messages to the researchers. These messages were communicated on institutional, class-room, group, and individual levels. At times these levels appear to reinforce and possibly even to amplify each other; at other times the discursive intersections clashed, as counter narratives hit more institutional and dominate ones.

Part of the actual (material) structure of the paper itself presented a dia-logue of contrasting spaces. As part of this spatial dialogue, they entered and discussed their own offices (and included photos):

3.1   *Agosto's Office*
Of all the places to which they walked, her office was the place they spent the least amount of time and spoke in the quietest of voices.

Scene Direction:	As they exited the office, the door nicked the lavender wind chime hanging from the ceiling. The chimes remind Dr. Agosto to seek evenness of temperament, or equanimity. They also work as an alarm to alert her/others that someone has entered or exited the office.
Agosto:	So I worried about doing even this walk today because I feel like even talking with my door open now with people around they can hear. I don't know why I feel kind of protective. And maybe I don't feel really trustful of my colleagues.
Rica:	Would you like to close the door?
Agosto:	No we can walk out of here.

3.2   *Marn's Office*

Scene Description:	A newspaper clipping is taped to the wall in Travis' office between two bookcases. It reads, "What they didn't tell you in graduate school".
Agosto:	[It is] hidden out of the way.
Travis:	So no one sees it. To that's the extent of my decorating. I have students coming in and most of them are white female. The students don't usually

	spend longer than two minutes in here. I don't have any personal relationships or connections with them. It's a functional relationship. The walls are for the most part undecorated. [...] My office has two pieces of academic art. I share an office and worry about [how] others might react. What would I say?
Agosto:	You would say: What is it that about this that bothers you – [what do] you want to talk about? [Laughter]
Travis:	[Laughter]. Yes, but I depend on these people. I only exist here with the support of as many people as possible.
Agosto:	I think that is true for many of us. We [faculty] have a contract but we serve at their leisure, until we get tenure. But even then there are other ways to push us out – withholding support. (p. 122)

3.3   *Ramirez's Office*

Interestingly, they provided little verbal description of Ramirez's office but did include a photo. Examining this photo I found it compelling that they shifted (perhaps unintentionally) from verbal to visual representation, allowing me to give my own analysis. The photo shows a cluttered space. No windows appear on the three visible walls and the office furniture displays a stylistic hodge-podge. Full boxes are stacked around the space, suggesting a storeroom office. No decorations appear on the walls. The room is devoid of individual personality, communicating a message of institutional, secondhand space.

Their discussion of their offices suggested that the larger campus discourses frame meanings within their own spaces. The drab institutional nature of the offices became a dominant narrative, filtering their own individual and collective narratives. The dominant narrative, perhaps acting as a form of institutional bullying, engendered reactions of apprehension and powerlessness (the institutional power expressed in processes related to faculty tenure, student funding, and student assistantships/teaching positions) within the trioethnographers.

The structure of contrasting spaces within their paper also promoted a form of praxis within the study. This approach may be found in their exploration of the progressive stage of currere. They encountered one of these spaces serendipitously. Walking through their campus they found themselves looking into the open door of an inviting and culturally inclusive office. The occupant of the office, Professor X, invited them into his office. They see a postcard of Gloria Anzaldúa on the door and decorative wall hangings covering blandly colored walls. They tell Professor X about the study and he introduces himself and mentions that he teaches courses about race, class, ethnicity, and sexuality. He then makes a subtle parallel between discourses and meanings within his classes and the appearance of his office:

> **Professor X:** I came to this career knowing that I wanted to create this kind of environment for my students and for my teaching. So it's not just for my pleasure but it also has a pedagogical point too.
>
> **Agosto:** I get it. It carries over into what you do and how you teach. It's not just for show. (pp. 119–120)

This particular conversation mirrors a pedagogy of hope embodied within Professor X's office. Within this study of a dehumanizing environment, even as they identified a sense of oppression, they did so in a way that showed and even built solidarity, a reimagined narrative of hope. They stated in their conclusion: "We came to this trioethnography talking from a victim's stance but have learned from one another's stories how to talk back from a survivor's stance" (p. 125). They concluded their study on a hopeful, artful (and witty) note, using a metaphor that referenced an American television show, *The Walking Dead*, about zombies trying to survive:

> ... we act as place walkers searching for feeding grounds to share and nourish our cultural selves through a relationship to the campus that is symbiotic rather than parasitic. Rather than be deadened into walkers by an institutional culture and climate that breeds alienation, intolerance, and neglect of cultural difference we seek places and people that imbibe the campus with social, epistemological, and physical hybridity, intersectionality, and eclecticism. We are place walkers eating (away/our way out of) cultural starvation. (p. 125)

Remarkably, as they suggested possibilities for a more inclusive and culturally equitable future – replacing normative with inclusive discourses – they constructed these possibilities partly from places they visited during their study. Later, when they reflected on the situation, their thoughts moved them to an ideological analysis and a greater sense of hope and connectedness outside the actual space. Laying down a path in walking and research itself shows agency, altering the material world.

4 Discussion

Agosto, Marn, and Ramirez's (2015) study suggests that agency is not located entirely within individual action, but is generated within an intertwined material/collective relationship. Conducting a trioethnography as they "placed walked" around their college campus, they encountered a landscape actively imbued with symbolic power (Bourdieu, 1983). Through conversation and movement, they explored the codes mediating thought and action within their space. They observed "traditional" discourses related, for example, to patriotism, acceptable knowledge, entitlement, voice, and art. However, this symbolic and lived ecology was not closed and defined. Instead, they destabilized narrow, normative meanings related to identity through their discussions of intersectionality, subversive art, and tolerance and acceptance of difference. When Agosto used the expression "*mi casa es su casa*" as a metaphor for a new way to think about and experience their campus, they reimagined the space.

Their research illustrates the words of Barad (2003), who stated that "particular possibilities for acting exist at every moment, and these changing possibilities entail a responsibility to intervene in the world's becoming, to contest and rework what matters and what is excluded from mattering" (Barad, 2003, p. 827). These possibilities for acting are entangled in and partly generated by multiple tensions. The authors revealed tensions between their agency in their local, specific place and their unwilling reproduction of regulatory ideology and discourses related to race and privilege that actively stretch across time and place.

Ironically, they generated their possibilities for greater liberation within a relatively hegemonic space. A number of years ago, Massey (1984), exploring feminist geographies, suggested that the experience of oppression within settings that constrict and marginalize might ultimately produce a reimagination of those settings. Rose (1993) called this tension and conflict paradoxical, acting both to regulate but also to highlight problems. This latter action may thus provide a context for critique and imagination, releasing an awareness of new possibilities. For example, Professor X's office, holding a more inclusive message of equity for all, became an embodiment of new possibilities and ways of being in time, space, and place. Valorizing difference, Bondi and Davidson (2005) wrote,

> The challenge we all face entails using the tension of our contradictory positionings to critique and undermine hegemonic space, and to reveal what lies beyond it, elsewhere. By speaking out about the complex and multiple spaces in which we live, and about the ways in which we experience space differently from each other, all of us can seek to disrupt,

rupture, and perhaps partially transform the masculinist and heterosex-
ist status quo. (p. 25)

As they explored spaces containing normative discourses of privilege and
possibility, their physical presence problematized these spaces.

In terms of the material space's agency, Agosto, Marn, and Ramirez acknowledged the active messages of place by contrasting spaces with both positive
and negative meanings. They focused on the meanings and codes within Professor X's office, for example, scaffolding their newer views of self and environment. Part of this process was consistent with Bourdieu's (1983) notion of
habitus in that their mediation animated and activated codes and meanings
embedded within the places they explored. At the same time, consistent with
Barad (2003), their inquiry and dialogue were shaped by the agency of the
material places they visited.

Critically, Agosto, Marn, and Ramirez deconstructed their place-based
dynamics of inequity with a goal of restorying their and the location's narratives
in a more inclusive and equitable way. They decentered deeply engrained normative views that they encountered. They also surfaced and began to delineate
counter-narratives – tracing and contrasting their positionality in relation to
these normative structures and discourses. As Barad (2003) mentioned, "Discourse is not what is said; it is that which constrains and enables what can
be said" (p. 819). In this sense, their trioethnography was an exploration and
reconfiguring of the discursive web they experienced in different locations.
They also traced the convergences and connections of these discourses across
different places on their campus (Webb et al., 2002).

In their study, they surfaced discourses that were important to the researchers but missing from the places they visited. These discourses centered on culture, ethnicity, power, and even educational equity. The null curriculum they
described was, on one level, about inclusion – discourses that were evident due
to their absence. On another level, it was about how place can operate in a larger
and more beneficial pedagogical way. Unfortunately, as they show, in this case
it did not. They were aware that the different places they visited created a larger
interlocking system that failed as the pedagogical space it could have been.

The researchers' use of space also created a context for their engagement of
the regressive stage of currere – their examination of past memories in the light
of present meanings and associations. The layers of ideology they encountered
on their walk told a meta-story about how they should act and see themselves.
However, as they told each other their stories about their lives and experiences
and as they in turn heard new stories from each other, they developed a new
collective story that reframed the narrative chauvinism of their campus. In this

process they did not so much construct "counter-narratives", as engage in a reimagining of the present – based on healthy memories that contrasted with their "real time" experiences with their physical campus.

In many ways, theirs was a ground-breaking study. Their descriptions made the invisible, visible and the symbolic, concrete. They used a methodology that helped them to surface the mediating codes in their lived environment. Second, their study was a meaningful context for their own growth: it facilitated a reflexive change in their stance and engagement on their campus. And finally, their study itself became a public pedagogy of resistance.

5 Conclusion

In the face of ecological disaster, research that claims to be neutral and value free will no longer suffice. New questions and approaches to life history inquiry are taking up the challenge of examining intertwined relationships within diverse ecological contexts. In this chapter I have tried to raise both possibilities and questions about how to examine the ecology of person and place.

As we engage in ecological life history research, we attempt to intertwine and create synergy among a number of academic fields, including environmental education, place based education, curriculum theory, and popular culture. We attempt to create a praxis-based ecological/life history research, changing its boundaries as its boundaries change us. This research has a goal of praxis, operating, in a complex way, as a form of pedagogy. Agosto, Marn, and Ramirez's work suggests that inquiry may be situated within and interact with place: as place may hold discursive symbolic power, so too may inquiry. As their study suggests, a dialogic engagement of inquiry and place may engender a sense of praxis, a transformative pedagogy of hope.

References

Agosto, V., Marn, T., & Ramirez, R. (2015). Biracial place walkers on campus. *International Review of Qualitative Research, 8*(1), 109–126. https://doi.org/10.1525/irqr.2015.8.1.109

Bainbridge, A., & Del Negro, G. (2020). An ecology of transformative learning: A shift from the ego to the eco. *Journal of Transformative Education, 18*(1), 41–58. https://doi.org/10.1177/1541344619864670

Barad, K. (2003). Post humanist performativity: Toward an understanding of how matter comes to matter. *Signs: Journal of Women in Culture and Society, 28*(3), 801–831.

Bhabha, H. K. (1994). *The location of culture*. Routledge.

Bourdieu, P. (1977). *Outline of a theory of practice* (R. Nice, Trans). Cambridge University Press. (Original work published in 1972)

Bourdieu, P. (1983). The field of cultural production, or the economic world reversed. *Poetics, 12*(5–6), 311–356.

Bourdieu, P. (1991). On symbolic power. In J. B. Thompson (Ed.). *Language and symbolic power* (G. Raymond & M. Adamson, Trans.) (pp. 163–170). Harvard University Press. (Original work published 1979)

Brubaker, R. (1985). Rethinking classical theory: The sociological vision of Pierre Bourdieu. *Theory and Society, 14*(6), 745–775.

Chan, A. (2017, March 2–5). *The decolonizing and the indigenizing discourse* [Conference presentation]. European Society for Research on the Education of Adults, Copenhagen, Denmark.

Foucault, M. (1990). *The history of sexuality* (Vol. I). (R. Hurley, Trans.). Vintage.

Greene, M. (1978). *Landscapes of learning*. Teachers College Press.

Norris, J., & Sawyer, R. D. (2015). Duoethnography. *International Review of Qualitative Research, 8*(1), 1–5. https://doi.org/10.1525/irqr.2015.8.1.1

Norris, J., & Sawyer, R. D. (2020). Duoethnography: A polytheoretical approach to (re) storying, (re)storying the meanings that one gives. In P. Leavy (Ed.), *The Oxford handbook of qualitative research* (2nd ed., pp. 397–423). Oxford University Press.

Pinar, W. F. (1975). Curerre: Toward reconceptualization. In W. F. Pinar (Ed.), *Curriculum theorizing. The reconceptualists* (pp. 396–414). McCutchan Publishing Corporation.

Pinar, W. F. (1994). The method of currere. In W. F. Pinar (Ed.), *Autobiography, politics and sexuality: Essays in curriculum theory 1972–1992* (pp. 19–27). Peter Lang.

Pinar, W. F. (2012). *What is curriculum theory?* Routledge.

Sawyer, R. D. (2017). Tracing dimensions of aesthetic currere: Critical transactions between person, place, and art. *Currere Exchange Journal, 1*(1), 89–100. https://www.currereexchange.com/uploads/9/5/8/7/9587563/14sawyercejv1i1.pdf

Sawyer, R. D., Neel, M. A., & Coulter, M. (2016). At the crossroads of clinical practice and teacher leadership: A changing paradigm for professional practice. *International Journal of Teacher Leadership, 7*(1), 17–36. https://www.cpp.edu/~ceis/education/international-journal-teacher-leadership/documents/Sawyer_IJTL.pdf

Sawyer, R. D., & Norris, J. (2013). *Duoethnography: Understanding qualitative research*. Oxford University Press.

Wang, H. (2006). Speaking as an alien: Is a curriculum in a third space possible? *Journal of Curriculum Theorizing, 22*(1), 111–126.

Webb, J., Schiratom T., & Danaher, G. (2002). *Understanding Bourdieu*. Sage.

West, L., & Carlson, A. (2006). Claiming and sustaining space? Sure Start and the auto/ biographical imagination. *Auto/Biography, 14*(4), 359–380.

CHAPTER 7

Beyond Truth: A Pragmatist Approach to Narrative Pedagogy in Professional Learning for Healthcare Practitioners

Laura Mazzoli Smith

Abstract

This chapter is focused on adult professional learning in healthcare by focusing on an innovative narrative-based training platform for seniors that uses transformative learning theory to better support person-centered healthcare. It is suggested that adopting the theoretical framing of pragmatism can support professionals to move beyond dualistic thinking with respect to medical knowledge and the lived experiences of patients. Adopting a pragmatist perspective in this sense can therefore have practical consequences that supports the over-arching aims of the training, which is to move professionals from categorical to cognizant thinking.

It is suggested that the tenets of pragmatism offer adult learners a highly practical set of concepts that could support interpretive, narrative-based learning and more particularly the likelihood of transformative learning. Considering knowledge in action and for use, dialogue based on a pragmatist approach can facilitate the opportunity for narrative knowledge that broadens the conception of what knowledge itself it. This is reassuring the healthcare practitioner in how connected meaning frames are with many aspects of lived experience, and how complex, drawing on multiple levels of micro, meso and macro. Such a connection between research, theory and practice can facilitate a better ecology of learning in this area.

Keywords

narrative – pedagogy – healthcare – transformative learning – pragmatism

1 Introduction

This chapter presents an overview of how pragmatism, alongside narrative pedagogy and transformative learning theory, can benefit adult professional learning in healthcare and support a better ecology of learning. It is suggested that adopting a particular theoretical frame – that of pragmatism – for professional learning in healthcare, has practical consequences, in helping to break down, rather than reinforce, disparate bodies of knowledge and avoid dualistic thinking amongst professionals. This chapter therefore explicitly addresses the section's aim of considering the interaction between research and practice and how this links to ecologies of learning and living. The professional learning referred to here is developed as part of a European Union (EIT Health) funded project involving a multi-disciplinary consortium of researchers. The aim of the project is to develop professional learning for healthcare practitioners working with seniors, utilizing the narratives of seniors, to better support person-centered healthcare.[1] This chapter reflects on how the methodology, or learning framework, for the training was developed. It considers particularly how a pragmatist approach facilitates the over-arching aim of the training, which is to move professionals in healthcare from categorical, to cognizant thinking, as discussed further below. Early feedback from learners suggests that a pragmatist approach, alongside the narrative content, can support and potentially transform practice through a better ecology of learning for healthcare practitioners.

There has long been a concern that healthcare practitioners are not adequately trained to be self-reflexive interpreters of meaning systems, but rather naïve realists (Kleinman, 1988). Fragmented and overly scientific and universal views of patients are said to be at the root of the problem (Marini, 2015). This can be described as a 'difference between biomedical understandings of pathophysiological processes of a medical condition and the individual patient's subjective experience of living with the condition' (Powell et al., 2013). As Charon (2006) has pointed out in her seminal work on narrative medicine, patients' explanatory models and their families' understandings of the illness have clinical significance. However, '… it is charged that doctors' innate empathy, respect for the suffering of others, and ethical discernment diminish in the course of medical training and that doctors become hardened against the suffering they witness through their education' (Charon, 2006, p. 8). Charon's work underpins the development and aims of this professional learning and her reflections on the role of narrative are worth quoting at length:

> To know what patients endure at the hands of illness and therefore to be of clinical help requires that doctors enter the worlds of their patients, if only imaginatively, and to see and interpret these worlds from the patients' point of view … To accomplish all these goals – empathic and effective care of individual patients, candid reflection, professional idealism, and

responsible societal discourse about health policy – requires a unified set of skills. To do all these things requires what psychologists and literary scholars call narrative knowledge ... Narrative knowledge provides one person with a rich, resonant grasp of another person's situation as it unfolds in time ... Unlike scientific knowledge or epidemiological knowledge, which tries to discover things about the natural world that are universally true or at least appear true to any observer, narrative knowledge enables one individual to understand particular events befalling another individual not as an instance of something that is universally true but as a singular and meaningful situation. (Charon, 2006, p. 9)

What is significant here for the development of the learning framework being discussed in this chapter is how to foster narrative knowledge and a 'unified' set of skills if this can be seen to stand in opposition to scientific or epidemiological knowledge. As an interdisciplinary project team we therefore drew on research in the development of a methodology that we felt would best enable learners to think across these dualisms in practice, or, attempt not to think of them as dualisms at all.

What we take as narrative determines its use in practice. Narrative is often said to be purposive, moving towards endings and aiming for closure (Andrews et al., 2002), idiographic and culturally dependent (Goodson, 2012), therefore context is essential for meaning and understanding. Drawing on MacIntyre (1987) and Ricoeur (1992), life is seen as meaningful, but the meaning is implicit and can become explicit in narratives. Thereby narratives can (but need not always) construct coherence and continuity (Taylor, 1989). Narrative-based learning can therefore foreground questions about how individuals endow experience with meaning in their own contexts (Rorty, 2009). An interpretivist framing demands that any phenomenon has to be contextualized in order to be understood: 'Differences of interpretation proceed, in large part, from differences in how we contextualize the matter at hand' (Charon, 2006, p. 26).

Unlike a more realist use of narratives in healthcare, whereby stories are seen to give an account of events and experiences from which better diagnosis can ensue, narratives are here conceived of interpretively. From this perspective, narratives are not realist reflections on the truth, but create the events they reflect upon. This differs from the long tradition in medicine and healthcare that utilizes narratives in a realist and largely content-based way, to support the professional knowledge of the practitioner in further ascertaining generalizable properties of individuals, rather than interpretively in accessing individual meaning-frames. As Hurwitz and Bates point out, 'case reports are terse outsider views of a person's situation recounted from a distinctively medical or psychiatric standpoint, rendered in detached, depersonalized and factual terms' (2016, p. 568), although these different approaches to using narrative are not mutually exclusive. In the case of our project however, the narrative content of the training was oriented towards taking the trainee into the lifeworld of the teller, rather than viewing the narrative from the outside.

Professionals in the field of healthcare have a formalized knowledge-base that will, in large part, shape how narratives are heard. This professional knowledge contributes to the structuring of the world through our expectancies (Bruner, 2009) and because this primarily positivist medical and health-related knowledge holds true in a general way, it is largely context-independent. This links to the concern that both learning and human experience can be theorized in an overly rational, functional and logo-centric way, a criticism sometimes levelled against medicine and healthcare practice too (Charon, 2006). Countering this is the belief that life should be conceived of in a more fluid and unbounded way and the call not to view learning as solely cognitive and logo-centric (Formenti et al., 2014). This is also associated with the desire to challenge the common binaries of mind/body, person/nature, individual/collective, for instance. Whilst the constructivist paradigm clearly frames much narrative-based learning and professional training oriented to interpretive processes, it is suggested here that the tenets of pragmatism offer adult learners in this area a highly practical set of concepts that could also support interpretive, narrative-based learning and more particularly the likelihood of transformative learning.

2   Pragmatism

In order to demonstrate the interaction of research and practice in the development of the learning framework for this training, and its links to ecological learning, it is necessary to explore some of the key theoretical tenets of pragmatism. Pragmatism is best understood as standing in opposition to a correspondence theory of truth, that is, that language, and philosophy, are about reflecting the truth of an objective, real world. For the pragmatist, the question of truth, or an innate essence of things, is supplanted by the question of which vocabularies and cultures produce new and better ways of thinking and acting. In this sense, pragmatism is anti-essentialist and opposed to the idea that there is any intrinsic nature to things. Rorty, a key contemporary proponent of American Pragmatism, refers to this as the development of a new intellectual tradition (1982). Malachowski, writing about Rorty, says that what makes him 'so provocatively 'interesting' is that he maintains we can do this without thereby having to lose our grip on effective standards of inquiry, useful norms of behavior and so on' (2002, p. 4). Ontological and epistemological traditions are just that – traditions;

> [Pragmatism] views science as one genre of literature – or, put another way around, literature and the arts as inquiries, on the same footing as scientific inquiries .... Some of these inquiries come up with propositions, some with narratives, some with paintings. (Rorty, 1982, p. xliii)

The criteria that one uses to assess knowledge-claims cannot therefore be universal criteria about validity for instance, in terms of some conception of truth as would be the norm for scientific – and hence medical – knowledge. Rather, utilitarian criteria have specific ends in specific cases: 'On the pragmatist account, a criterion ... is a criterion because some particular social practice needs to block the road of inquiry, halt the regress of interpretations, in order to get something done' (Rorty, 1982, p. xli). What is interesting here in terms of narrative learning is that narrative interpretation is not then perceived as infinite and unbounded, but there can be criteria of use about interpretations in practice and how to assess the utility of these. This link to practice is worked out in dialogue and the development of our learning framework drew on this specific sense of criteria for use as having a particular appeal to the adult professional learner. The learners discuss the usefulness of particular interpretations of seniors' narratives in the context of their practice, taking into account multiple levels; the micro of the individual in their own orientation – and their own narrative(s), the meso of the relationships which structure lives, and the macro of the wider structured system of healthcare knowledge and their institutions. The learning framework is structured to commence with exercises based on learner's own narratives and it was interesting that in the stakeholder feedback collected to support design of the training this aspect was never mentioned. Most (but not all) stakeholders consulted could appreciate the value in working with the narratives of seniors, but did not consider a link to their own to be relevant.

As Rorty suggests, the question of whether the pragmatist view of truth is itself true is rather a question about whether a pragmatist position is useful and worthwhile adopting. For the adult professional learner in healthcare, the question is not about whether such learning gets at alternate truths, likely to fall in with subjective/objective, positivist/interpretive dualisms, but rather what usefulness there is in incorporating more and wider forms of interpretation into the repertoire of healthcare knowledge. 'When the notion of knowledge as representation goes, then the notion of inquiry as split into discrete sectors with discrete subject matters goes' (1982, p. 203). So, the point here is that a pragmatist framing can enable the healthcare trainee to consider the usefulness of differing interpretations, positioning different ways of knowing – medical and narrative – as closer together and more commensurate by unsettling foundational and dualistic thinking. The pragmatist approach does not suggest either/or – that narrative knowledge invalidates scientific knowledge, or vice versa – but rather that by considering knowledge in action and for use, dialogue based on a pragmatist approach can facilitate the opportunity for narrative knowledge that broadens the conception of what knowledge itself it, facilitating a better ecology of learning.

Put another way, pragmatism can help professional learners to move away from the normative disposition that there is a choice of methodologies on offer with allegiance to something either more positivist, or subjective/constructivist, in terms of understanding human beings as the only epistemological route. In Rorty's terms, what is normatively construed as a difference of epistemology and methodology (the positivist versus the interpretive understanding of human illness and wellbeing for instance), is better conceived as a difference in vocabularies. Of particular relevance is Rorty's point that we fall too easily into thinking 'that the irreducibility of one vocabulary to another implies something ontological' (1982, p. 201). The implications of this, if we are to adopt Rorty's pragmatism fully, are profound. In not being about the accurate representation of reality, language – and the mind from which it springs – is not mysterious or numinous. Our awareness of the numinous is in fact awareness of our membership of a moral community of fellow humans, so potentially an orientation to unity rather than the epistemic threat of division if one's knowledge as a learner – i.e. scientific knowledge – cannot be embraced alongside that of another epistemic orientation, in this case narrative knowledge. The lack of a universal human nature or set of natural laws to which we all link, is not the same as the lack of a universal human solidarity therefore. In terms of an ecology of learning, foregrounding narratives that take account of the micro, meso and macro in complex ways, and using dialogue as a primary mode through which interpretations are framed on this pragmatist account, helps towards an ecology of adult learning. This is elaborated further in relation to narrative pedagogy and transformative learning, which are also core aspects of the learning framework and how it was created to support an ecology of learning.

3   Narrative Pedagogy and Transformative Learning

Goodson and Gill refer to narrative pedagogy as 'the facilitation of an educative journey through which learning takes place in profound encounters, and by engaging in meaning-making and deep dialogue and exchange' (2011, p. 123).

As discussed, narratives are widely used in healthcare, the narrative case study being the most notable form, and in nursing, for instance, Diekelmann describing narrative pedagogy as 'a new approach to schooling, learning, and teaching identified in the content of interpretive research in nursing education' (2001, p. 69). There is also much focus on use of patient narratives in professional learning in healthcare (e.g. Walsh, 2011; Sherlin & Quinn, 2016; Johnston et al., 2017) where it is common to find narratives presented primarily as content-based learning opportunities with respect to better clinical interpretation. Notwithstanding the fact that narrative pedagogy is commonly used to refer to learning for the narrator (Goodson & Gill, 2011), or such content-based learning, in the context of this project it refers to adult professional learning aimed at fostering patient-centered care through skills and dispositions that can specifically be developed through the interpretation of narratives.

Transformative learning as conceived of here involves alienation from earlier established conceptions of values and one's actions, and the reframing of new perspectives (Mezirow, 2000). Mezirow's seminal theory characterizes this as praxis and 'a dialectic in which understanding and action interact to produce an altered sense of being' (2000, p. xii). Critical self-reflection at a cognitive level is seen as the core of adult transformative learning theory, being meaning-making, since transformative learning can be 'understood as a continuous effort to negotiate contested meanings' (Mezirow, 2000, p. 3). Adult transformative learning suggests itself as useful in the facilitation of person-centered healthcare, as a process of making sense of and interpreting experience, utilizing heightened awareness and understanding, re-examining assumptions, synthesizing, justifying and creating and then being able to act upon new meaning perspectives is made possible in dialogue. This leads to what Mezirow describes as 'perspective transformation', which involves an empowered sense of self, more critical understandings of how social relationships and culture shape beliefs and feelings, and greater recourse to functional strategies and resources for taking action, all aspects of what we might also think of as an ecology of learning. The essence of transformative learning comes through critical self-reflection and active meaning-making with three main elements; critical reflection on assumptions, dialectical discourse to validate new meaning perspectives, and the context of the learning experience (Greenhill et al., 2018; Mezirow & Taylor, 2009), uniting theory and practice in dialogue.

Research demonstrates how a dialogic methodology is a positive means of supporting students' maturing self-awareness about their epistemologies and perspectives (Formenti & Joria, 2018) and as a way of enabling transformative learning to develop over a series of learning activities. Formenti and Joria find three epistemic leaps in the process of sustaining transformative learning with their adult learners in higher education, which have parallels in the learning framework developed for our training platform and which are also discussed further below. Firstly, an epistemic leap in personal reflection, which we refer to as mindset orientation at the start of our professional learning. The second leap Formenti and Joria identify is interpersonal learning, the dialogic space which they define as more than just a container for individual learning: 'Dialogic groups are forms which transform, and not only given containers for transformative learning' (2018, p. 16). This space is provided in the dialogic exercises that are designed to enable trainees to work with and through the narratives in the context of pragmatism, where epistemic orientations can conflict and meaning is seen in the context of practice. The third epistemic leap is about self-reflexive transformative learning, which entails a meta-theory of self-in-context, where students themselves re-interpret their learning experiences and which we build into the final learning activity in our professional learning to support the meta-cognitive process of interpreting and then utilizing learning in the context of everyday professional lives.

Gadamer's (1989) view that understanding starts from projection is useful here, that is individuals project meaning for the text or narrative as a whole as soon as they think they have grasped an initial meaning, based on particular expectations. This initial projection is revised and re-configured as the narrative ensues, but the extent to which this is the case depends on the listener not holding to their own initial meaning and being open to having this unsettled. For Gadamer, in order to pay attention to the meaning implicit in a narrative, and thereby achieve understanding, the criterion of questioning is very important. Goodson and Gill (2011) define this as the critically alert participant, as opposed to the critically detached observer, in direct contradistinction to how we might consider the clinical case study is often utilized in medical education. The conditions in which such epistemic leaps of the critically alert participant can best be fostered are not just important, but crucial. Rogers (1969) wrote that certain attitudinal qualities embedded in the personal relationship of narratives can lead to significant learning, through trust in the learner by the facilitator and the establishment of a space where there is a feeling of acceptance, an empathetic atmosphere and a dialogic environment.

These dialogic qualities could be seen as key criteria for enabling narrative pedagogy. Dewey (1938/1997) further supports the idea that relationships are key to establishing a trusting dialogic encounter in talking about active 'constructive listening', which underpins learning that can be achieved with conversation, dialogue, questioning, negotiating meaning and critical collaborative interpretation. Whilst these relational and contextual factors are of great importance, conversations with healthcare practitioners in the development of the professional learning discussed in this chapter revealed that framing the dialogic exercises around pragmatist tenets supported the disposition of the learner towards making such epistemic leaps. Feedback revealed this could facilitate a move from not understanding the place of narratives that were not of the case study variety and therefore directly linked to diagnosis, to seeing their potential value.

This was also linked to use of the words 'stories' or 'story-telling' rather than narratives, which was a somewhat opaque term for many. In their feedback during the initial phase of designing the training, one care home provider said that they would favor the term 'true stories', which led to a very deliberate discussion of pragmatism, albeit without use of the term, to explore what could be meant by truth here. The care home was invested in the idea of true stories as standing for one truth that objectively represents events that were open to distortion both by staff, or residents themselves, at different times. It became apparent that reflection on this concept of 'true stories', drawing on the tenets of pragmatism, was useful as a way into exploring the idea of multiple meanings of stories without threatening this foundation entirely. This is explored further below, after outlining the structure of this professional learning.

4   A Pragmatist Framing for Adult Professional Learning

A core aspect of the professional learning that has been developed, drawing on this theoretical and applied work around pragmatism, narrative pedagogy and transformative learning, is the overarching learning outcome of a move from categorical to cognizant thinking. Categorical thinking characterizes routine performance and working under pressure, being largely resistant to change, whilst cognizant, reflective thinking, which is meta-cognitive, denotes a high level of cognitive responsiveness (Ringberg & Reihlen, 2008). This is to be encouraged through enlisting the learners' inner resources; curiosities, memories, creativity, associations, interpretive faculties (Marini, 2015). The training moves through a series of exercises, commencing with an invitation to reflect on and revise basic assumptions and beliefs situated and situating one's professional body of knowledge, referred to as mindset reflection. Ryden et al. (2015) describe this as the mental models that we hold, which are both private and cultural and under-pin individual sense making in that they are viewed as the way the world works. Ryden et al. discuss how a shift from categorical to cognizant thinking depends on the reflexivity to sense dissonance between external feedback and the learners' own sense-making, through dialogue and in particular, questioning. This is, in the words of Goodson and Gill 'a dialogic approach to being and becoming critical' (2011, p. 47). In the case of the care home mentioned above, this would include questioning about not only the possibility, but the usefulness of multiple versions of one story – a not uncommon occurrence in a care home, through reflection on the kind of categorical thinking that underpins much functional training in this sector.

Subsequent activities focus on interpretation of a narrative, firstly from a structural perspective and then on content. The structural interpretation comes first, as this is not what is commonly prioritized. Usually we read and listen for content first, with an understanding of structure working at a more tacit and implicit level. These activities are followed by a systems approach to thinking about interpretations across professional groups, or departments in an institution. The main aim here is to attend to the concern that learning theories can be oriented largely to individual learning, whereas it is often at the level of the organizational learning of the workplace that meaningful transformation can occur and that we might come across the barrier of seeing multiple versions of one story, or not knowing that there could even by other versions. Theories of expansive learning and Engeström's boundary crossing exercises (2018) underpin how this activity is focused on the interconnected activity systems of an organization. Finally, there is an activity based on self-reflection of the learning that has taken place at a meta-cognitive level, with a specific focus on the embedding of new skills and insights in professional life and renewed mind set reflection. This was found to be of value by the learners because it acknowledges the importance of the task and process-oriented nature of much work in healthcare and hence the importance of exploring new narrative knowledge in the context of such practice.

The challenge of a self-sustaining training building on the above, is that in a relatively short space of time – given the demands on healthcare practitioners and the practicability of releasing staff for professional learning – holistic learning based on transformation is the aim. This professional training is aimed at fostering practitioners' awareness not only of the meaning frames of the seniors they care for and how to better access these through increased interpretive, dialogic and listening skills, but also of their own personal meaning frames by increasing critical reflexivity and awareness of language and imagery. Reflecting on the centrality of narrative pedagogy and transformative learning theory in the development of this healthcare training, it is arguable that a pragmatist orientation can support both methodological and contextual aspects.

The provocation of pragmatism, which could in turn function as a provocation for other professional learning courses such as this, where transformation of mindset and a shift from categorical to cognizant learning is the aim, is the question of what would a neutral standpoint, from which first principles could be evaluated, look and feel like (Rorty, 2009). Pragmatism critiques the very idea of meta-practice, or meta-theory, from which vantage point all other social practices and theories are then assessed. The possibility of opening up a non-foundationalist position from which adult learners might re-imagine their own normative associations could be prompted precisely through the evocation of such meta-level thinking. Rorty's profound scepticism about methodology is a useful starting point from which to begin to disorient the professional adult learner whose methodology may well be largely taken for granted in the support of their epistemology. In the context of a learning activity delivered within a supportive environment, there is the potential to see this as playful with respect to one's philosophical commitments and to inhabit, as an exercise in imagination, the possibility that there are no foundations or criteria from which to make particular kinds of epistemological claims about truth. Instead, there is the richness of interpretation and questioning arrived at through dialogue, and the openness of inquiry in engaging with a range of commensurate methods and the knowledge claims based upon them, at micro, meso and macro levels of understanding. The challenge and hope of pragmatism is in the dismantling of constraints on knowing and what counts as knowledge, but in an unthreatening way and in this sense we might think of this approach as promoting an ecology of learning.

Rorty describes the efficacy of narrative as the medium through which to effect this transformative learning in being able to 'induce the Gestalt-like switches that are needed to view philosophical commitments in a fresh light – one that reveals, for instance, that they are 'optional" (Malachowski, 2002, p. 55). This last point, about the optional status of philosophical commitments, could arguably function as a disorienting dilemma, as posited by Mezirow. A disorienting dilemma is usually a life event that causes an adult to question their frame of reference and their reaction to this pushes them towards dialogue (Taylor & Cranton, 2012). It is sometimes commented that not a lot has been written about disorienting dilemmas (Taylor & Cranton, 2012) and it may be that for some adult learners a life event is necessary to function in this way. However, conversations with healthcare professionals in the development of this professional training point to the fact that there is also the possibility that the specifically applied nature of pragmatist tenets – the focus being knowledge in action – can facilitate a disorienting dilemma itself if introduced at the outset of professional learning as an explicit provocation and through the use of narrative to explain such an approach.

Rather than presenting narrative-based training such as this as occupying a different epistemic space to usual medical/healthcare knowledge, the subjective or idiographic frame can be presented as a way of disorienting such foundationalism. Professional learners are introduced to the tenets of pragmatism in the context of being introduced to the training and to narrative, to support openness and confidence in discussing meta-theories in this way (notwithstanding the fact that academic terminology need not be used and is likely to be unhelpful).

5   Concluding Comments

Charon draws a distinction between listening for stories and listening to them, the latter being important for more healthcare practitioners to be skilled in; '… only this kind of narrative listening will hear the connections among body, mind, and self, and disease recognition and treatment cannot proceed, we are beginning to believe, without simultaneous attention to all three' (Charon, 2006, p. 67). The focus on pragmatism, not only as a paradigmatic positioning, but also as a pedagogical resource that unifies research and practice, could be introduced in an explicit way to orient professional learners to a context in which epistemological understandings are unsettled, and binaries lose their hold, as they become detached from particular essentialist realities to which they are supposed to refer. In adopting an approach in which 'There is nothing to be known about an object except what sentences are true of it' (Rorty, 2009, p. 55), we meet directly the idea that no-one but us, in what we say and how we choose to engage with each other, is responsible for meaning making. Learners previously unfamiliar with narrative pedagogy, or even working with narratives – or stories, appear to be aided by a pragmatist approach to narrative knowledge if this is presented through the idea of a narrative that can have more than one truth. The anti-foundationalism of pragmatism offers reassurance against the stark dualism, and hence epistemic (and perhaps even ontological) threat, of a divide between scientific knowledge and narrative knowing. Working with narrative content can reassure the healthcare practitioner in how connected meaning frames are with many aspects of lived experience, and how complex, drawing on multiple levels of micro, meso and macro. In the development of this learning framework, narratives, and pragmatism as a wider framing approach, can help to foster a better ecology of learning.

Note

1   Further details on this project are available at www.eithealth.eu/ccentre and the training platform is available at www.caringstories.eu

References

Andrews, M., Day Sclater, S., Squire C., & Treacher, A. (Eds.). (2002). *Lines of narrative: Psychosocial perspectives*. Routledge.

Bruner, J. S. (2009). *Actual minds, possible worlds*. Harvard University Press.

Charon, R. (2006). *Narrative medicine: Honoring the stories of illness*. Oxford University Press.

Diekelmann, N. (2001). Narrative pedagogy: Heideggerian hermeneutical analyses of lived experiences of students, teachers, and clinicians. *Advances in Nursing Science, 23*(3), 53–71.

Dewey, J. (1997). *Experience and education*. Touchstone. (Original work published 1938)

Engeström, Y. (2018). Expansive learning: Towards an activity-theoretical reconceptualization. In K. Illeris (Ed.), *Contemporary theories of learning: Learning theorists in their own words* (pp. 46–65). Routledge.

Formenti, L., & Jorio, F. (2018). Multiple visions, multiple voices: A dialogic methodology for teaching in higher education. *Journal of Transformative Education, 17*(3), 208–227. https://doi.org/10.1177%2F1541344618796761

Formenti, L., West, L., & Horsdal, M. (2014). *Embodied narratives. Connecting stories, bodies, cultures and ecologies*. University Press of Southern Denmark.

Gadamer, H. G. (1989). *Truth and method* (J. Weinsheimer & D. G. Marshall, Trans.). Continuum.

Goodson, I. F. (2012). *Developing narrative theory: Life histories and personal representation*. Routledge.

Goodson, I. F., & Gill, S. R. (2011). *Narrative pedagogy: Life history and learning*. Peter Lang.

Greenhill, J., Richards, J. N., Mahoney, S., Campbell, N., & Walters, L. (2018). Transformative learning in medical education: Context matters, a South Australian longitudinal study. *Journal of Transformative Education, 16*(1), 58–75. https://doi.org/10.1177%2F1541344617715710

Hurwitz, B., & Bates, V. (2016). The roots and ramifications of narrative in modern medicine. In A. Whitehead & A. Woods, (Eds.), *The Edinburgh companion to the critical medical humanities* (pp. 559–576). Edinburgh University Press.

Johnston, S., Parker, C. N., & Fox, A. (2017). Impact of audio-visual storytelling in simulation learning experiences of undergraduate nursing students. *Nurse Education Today, 56*, 52–56. https://doi.org/10.1016/j.nedt.2017.06.011

Kleinman, A. (1988). *The illness narratives: Suffering, healing, and the human condition*. Basic Books.

MacIntyre, A. (1987). *After virtue*. Duckworth.

Malachowski, A. (2002). *Richard Rorty*. Acumen.

Marini, M. G. (2015). *Narrative medicine: Bridging the gap between evidence-based care and medical humanities*. Springer.

Mezirow, J. (2000). *Learning as transformation: Critical perspectives on a theory in progress.* Jossey-Bass.

Mezirow, J., & Taylor, E. W. (2009). *Transformative learning in action: A handbook for practice.* Jossey-Bass.

Powell, S., Scott, J., Scott, L., & Jones, D. (2013). An online narrative archive of patient experiences to support the education of physiotherapy and social work students in north east England: An evaluation study. *Education for Health, 26*(1), 25. https://doi.org/10.4103/1357-6283.112797

Ricoeur, P. (1992). *Oneself as another.* University of Chicago Press.

Ringberg, T., & Reihlen, M. (2008). Towards a socio-cognitive approach to knowledge transfer. *Journal of Management Studies, 45*(5), 912–935.

Rogers, C. R. (1969). *Freedom to learn: A view of what education might become* (Vol. 69). Merrill.

Rorty, R. (1982). *Consequences of pragmatism: Essays, 1972–1980.* University of Minnesota Press.

Rorty, R. (2009). *Philosophy and the mirror of nature.* Princeton University Press.

Rydén, P., Ringberg, T., & Wilke, R. (2015). How managers' shared mental models of business–customer interactions create different sensemaking of social media. *Journal of Interactive Marketing, 31*, 1–16. https://doi.org/10.1016/j.intmar.2015.03.001

Sherlin, M. M., & Quinn, P. T. (2016). End-of-life patient simulation: Lessons learned. *Teaching and Learning in Nursing, 11*, 184–188. https://doi.org/10.1016/j.teln.2016.05.002

Taylor, C. (1989). *Sources of the self: The making of the modern identity.* Harvard University Press.

Taylor, E. W., & Cranton, P. (2012). *The handbook of transformative learning: Theory, research, and practice.* John Wiley & Sons.

Walsh, M. (2011). Narrative pedagogy and simulation: Future directions for nursing education. *Nurse Education in Practice, 11*(3), 216–219. https://doi.org/10.1016/j.nepr.2010.10.006

A Key? Conflict, and the Struggle for an Ecology of Dialogue, Learning and Peace among Israeli Jewish and Palestinian Educators

Alan Bainbridge and Linden West

Abstract

This chapter is about the potential for using auto/biographical narrative enquiry in teaching and research to build small ecologies of learning, healing, dialogue and peace across trauma, and profound difference. This as part of an educational project to encourage active citizenship and democratic values in teacher education in Israel, among Palestinian and Jewish educators. Auto/biographical narrative workshops and research were used to chronicle common experiences of trauma, hurt and insecurity within the unresolved conflict between Israel and Palestine. Here the other, for many Palestinians, is the Israeli Jewish coloniser over 70 years and more. For Israeli Jews, the other can be perceived as a would-be terrorist, uncivilised and bringing danger to the democratic, metropolitan light of Israel. The darkness of two unresolved traumas hangs over the work – the Holocaust for Jews and Al Nakba for Palestinians. The former is the murder of 6 million Jewish people in Europe during the 2nd World War. The latter, in English, means the Catastrophe: of the 1948 War with the putative state of Israel, and of dispossession and loss. How much can auto/biographical and narrative processes create small ecologies of light, hope and justice? The answer is not easy, but the effort worthwhile, if the alternative is continuing cycles of hatred and violence.

Keywords

trauma – violence – auto/biography – narrative – dialogue – learning – healing and peace

• • •

The tragedy of … so many post-colonial experiences, derives from the limitations of the attempts to deal with relationships that are polarized, radically uneven, remembered differently. The spheres, the sights of intensity, the agendas, and the constituencies in the metropolitan and ex-colonial

worlds appear to overlap only partially. The small area is perceived as common does not, at this point, provide for more than what might be called a
rhetoric of blame (original emphasis)

SAID (1994, p. 19)

∴

1   Introduction

This chapter draws on auto/biographical narrative research and forms of adult
education designed to foster empathy, risk taking, storytelling, dialogue and
hope across profound difference. We describe and illuminate the use of 'psychosocial' perspectives and auto/biographical narrative adult education and
research among groups of Israeli and Palestinian teacher educators living and
working in the State of Israel. This is against the backcloth of two profound
traumas: the Holocaust and, less well known, Al Nakba (or the Catastrophe,
the forced evacuation of many Palestinians from their lands and communities,
in the 1948 War and since). What may be colonialist oppression, intolerance,
and violence against the Palestinians continues. The word trauma is chosen
deliberately, begging questions as to its effects in the past and present, and the
conditions in which it might be transcended in struggles for peace.

Jacqueline Rose (2019) has challenged the view that the Holocaust represents history, while Al Nakba is firmly contemporary in people's lives. The
effects of past trauma, she suggests, drawing on psychoanalytic perspectives,
are visited on present and future generations, for both peoples. It is the failure,
she insists, however difficult, of Israeli Jews to process the deepest experience
of trauma that drives what is oppressively done in their name, here and now.

How much can adult education of an intensive, in-depth therapeutic kind,
address these issues is a basic question of our chapter. We sought to create
good enough, playful and experimental spaces for generating stories, and a
culture of listening to self, and the other; to move beyond a rhetoric of blame
in Said's (1994) compelling words. To create, in short, a kind of ecology of life
for some learning and healing. We were not there to smooth over difference
but to engage with it, when possible, in manageable and developmental if also
inevitably restricted ways. We wanted to identify common experience and to
use this as a site for reflexivity, dialogue and self/other recognition. But we
struggled to transcend silence and silencing. We wanted in fact to build a larger
project, to include Palestinian educators living in the Palestinian Authority

and Gaza as well as in the State of Israel. We failed. Perhaps it reflected naivety and lack of understanding of how the trauma of the oppressed is experienced and responded to at personal, institutional, national and international levels. Maybe the weight, complexity and unresolved trauma of Palestinian and Israeli peoples illustrates the limitations of adult education and struggles for peace. How much, for instance, can projects like this represent a good enough therapeutic space, with the necessary time, empathic listening and processing required? Or is there some hope in what we sought to do, given the bleak alternative of rhetorics of blame?

Our initial project included educators from Georgia, living in fragile contexts too, born, as their country was, out of the disintegration of the old Soviet Union. The spectre of Russia haunts Georgian society, with one province, South Ossetia, occupied after the 2008 War, while the integrity of the border is constantly threatened. There are ethnic tensions as Georgia seeks to modernise, giving primacy to Georgian as the national language, which is resisted by Armenian minorities in the south of the country. They of course have suffered their own massive historical traumas. But the prime focus of the present chapter is Israeli/ Palestinian/Arab Israeli dynamics and our efforts to create good enough transitional and narrative space for dialogue and mutual recognition. Elias Khoury (2019) has written that the oppressed Jew of twentieth century Europe is not simply the mirror image of the Palestinian but of every human everywhere. The Palestinian is also the mirror image of expelled and oppressed peoples in all lands. The mirror image in fact of the refugee crisis engulfing the world today. Is it possible to recognise the other – Jew or Palestinian – as traumatised, hurting, like ourselves, as a basis for dialogue? For what Bashir and Goldberg (2017) call empathic unsettlement, where our stories and assumptions are listened to and challenged, humanely, as a basis for seeing things anew.

There are of course profoundly differing perspectives on the historical and contemporary Middle Eastern situation. Both Palestinians and Jews claim the same land and arguably have valid emotional reactions to conflict, displacement and existential threat. But their personal and historical stories dramatically diverge: on the one hand, there is the narrative that in 1897 there were around half a million Arabs, Bedouins and Druze living in Palestine, with only 30,000 or so Jews. By 1935 the Jewish population comprised a quarter of the population and in 1948, Al Nakba represented, for Palestinians, ethnic cleansing of a people who were driven from their homes, land and communities in which they had lived for centuries. Here is a manifest asymmetry of power between the Israeli state, with its metropolitan pretensions, Western military guarantors, on the one hand, and displaced, stateless and colonised Palestinians on the other. Jewish people tell stories of waves of anti-Semitism, across centuries, in Europe and beyond, culminating with 2 out of 3 European Jews being exterminated in the Holocaust. Israeli Jews celebrate the 1948 War as one of liberation and finding security, while for Palestinians, as noted, it is the catastrophe (Baron-Cohen, 2019). Part of the problem however is the Holocaust tends to be cast as an historically unique event, in the dominant Jewish narrative, in effect downplaying or rejecting the significance of the Nakba altogether.

2   The Key?

We are two seasoned practitioners using auto/biographical narrative methods over a period of years, in a search to create what we call, in the spirit of Donald Winnicott, good enough transitional and even transformational space where significant and difficult life experiences can be engaged with dialogically and relationally (see Bainbridge & West, 2012; Formenti & West, 2018; Dominicé, 2000; Merrill & West, 2009; West, 1996, 2016; West, Alheit, Andersen, & Merrill, 2007). We seek to nurture deeper forms of self/other relationship, reciprocal understanding and shared commitment to social justice. Our teaching seeks to encourage empathic, reflexive listening, respectfulness, openness, dialogue, trust, playfulness, equality and learning about self and the other. But the process is often difficult as the other's presence and story challenge our own, and we, in turn, might freeze. It is not about smoothing over this difficulty rather to name and engage with it narratively, reflexively and developmentally.

We use the metaphor of the key as allegory and symbol of hope. The inspiration is an old Sufi parable from the tales of Mulla Nasrudin (Shah, 1985). Teachers from ancient times have used allegories to nurture knowledge and insight into messy, dark, and illusive aspects of experience. There are different versions of the story but in the original the traveller is walking home late at night when he sees an anxious Mulla Nasrudin crawling on hands and knees, on the road, searching, frantically, under a streetlight. 'Mulla, what have you lost?' the passer-by asks. 'I am searching for my key', Nasrudin says worriedly. 'I'll help you look', the man says, and joins Mulla Nasrudin in the search. Soon both men are on their knees, under the streetlight, searching. After a while, the traveller asks, 'Tell me Mulla, do you remember exactly where you dropped the key?' Nasrudin waves his arm back toward the darkness and says, 'Over there, in my house. I lost it there'. Shocked and exasperated, the passer-by jumps up and shouts at Mulla Nasrudin, 'Then why are you searching for the key out here in the street?' 'Because there is more light here than inside my house', Mulla Nasrudin answers nonchalantly (Shah, 1985).

Superficially, the event is nonsensical. But there are different levels of meaning. People may constantly look for the key to peace, happiness, or the good life, or for bliss, freedom and tranquility, maybe even for love, and God, in the wrong place. They may frantically attach themselves to cults or immerse themselves in particular theories because they are popular or dominant. For a while, there can be a sense of belonging but quickly followed by disappointment. Maybe the key lies deep within, in our unconscious, and or in our biographies, cultures and suffering, but the light is hidden and the search arduous. Perhaps one educational and therapeutic key is to see the other, not as identical to ourselves, in a kind of conflation of complexity, but traumatised, too, in ways we find difficult to acknowledge. For many Israeli Jews, as noted, the Holocaust allows no comparison, everything pales in its presence. Palestinians may refuse its admission in the light of colonialist oppression, and their own pain. The world is easily divided into binaries of self and other, them and us, good and bad, violent and peaceful, to cope with trauma. Reparative work can seem too difficult in the face of the depth of all this while present Israeli politics – of downgrading the status of Arabic and of encouraging illegal settlements, for example, serve to make things worse.

The allegory however is infused by Sufi belief in the importance of a poetic sensibility in relation to difficult and disturbing aspects of the human condition and the need to cultivate greater tolerance of difference. It values inner qualities above external piety. Nasrudin is often regarded as an 'Idiot', an appellation Dervishes use in describing their Divine Madness. But he represents a rebuke to the dangers and excesses of the clerical, literal or fundamentalist mind. We need to look beyond appearances or outward show, to seek common understanding across trauma, injustice and the repressed, in and through the stories we tell. We draw in doing so on our experience as psychoanalytic psychotherapists as well as educators, entering a kind of conceptual and practical border country, between research, teaching and therapy (Bainbridge & West, 2012). But the territory is challenging, and we risk getting out of our depth even though the experiment is worth trying against the darkening backcloth.

It should also be noted that the metaphor of the key is a symbol of hope among Palestinian peoples: of return to homes, communities and lost lands; in short, for justice and reparation. Both Israelis and Palestinians seek in fact a 'secure' homeland, and there have been many and varied attempts, internationally, over many years, to secure agreement, security and peace, if to little or no lasting avail

3   Fragile Democracies

Although Israel has a formal representative democracy, there are deepening socio-economic, cultural, educational and religious fragmentations, which include the noisy emergence of an extreme ultra nationalist and Zionist religious fundamentalism. One cohort study of young people in Israel (Hexel & Nathanson, 2010) illustrates how, in such a context, they experience a world lacking any security and clarity. Their attitudes and values are influenced by life in the State of Israel, after 62 years of its existence. They still fear their neighbours while the challenges of the financial crisis of 2008–2009, of climate change, (and no doubt now coronavirus) bear down on them. What, the authors ask, can young people rely on in the contemporary world? Who or what might inspire them? Where can security and stability be found? Who might be role-models? Finding a key to create secure, confident, assertive and empathic citizens, with the will to engage, constructively, with the other, appears daunting.

Stephen Sheps (2019) has reviewed a range of studies and suggests there to be a clear link between particular versions of Zionism and the manifest and latent racism in Israeli society. He argues that successive generations of Israeli citizens (and non-citizens) are exposed to a single historical and cultural narrative rather than a pluralistic one. This is intentionally designed to strengthen the emergent ethno-national character of Israeli democracy. Shep's own research engages a small sample of Jewish–Israeli teachers in reflecting on teaching in Israeli high school history and civics classrooms. He chronicles some of the institutionalised racism they encounter within textbooks and their students. The pedagogic space is riddled with dilemmas stemming from historical and structural conditions. Israeli teachers are forced to mediate the singular narratives within curricular materials; and any impetus they feel to teach counter-historical perspectives, and to creatively manage their own emotional responses, and students' reactions, can be frozen. Sheps states the problem in blunt terms:

> As long as the nation is imagined as both Jewish and democratic, Israeli teachers will have limited potential to engage with the content and their students in order to make the classroom a space for meaningful dialogue and transformative social change. However limited this potential may be, it is imperative that teachers ... continue to address these challenges, despite the precarious and emotionally vulnerable conditions that they endure. (Sheps, 2019, p. 358)

Disillusionment with government and worsening racism render the classroom deeply problematic. Government and its agencies are aware of these issues but do not prioritise forms of education to empower citizens to question and act critically. This point is especially important with regard to Teacher Education programmes, as teachers have a pivotal role in preparing the next generation of citizens. But there are no official curricula committed to the promotion of active, inclusive and practical civic, democratic and environmental education, let alone engaging imaginatively with Palestinians for peace. The only curriculum content takes a technical and legal perspective on political and state structures, as well as conflict. 'CURE' was one small experiment in trying to do something different.

4   CURE: The Workshops

The CURE project was a European Union funded programme aiming to cultivate and strengthen the teaching and learning of democratic values and active citizenship in teacher education in Israel and Georgia. It was a multi-faceted programme for curriculum reform seeking to improve the level of content, teaching and learning in various institutions, while also aiming to involve students in 'Centres of Civic Engagement'. Collaboration between five colleges and universities in each of the two countries, and five European universities, including our own, offered expertise, advice, support, evaluation, and a range of workshops, for staff and students. This included, in our case, auto/biographical narrative enquiry as a resource for building mutual recognition, dialogue and hope.

Each Israeli and Georgian institution selected 3 faculty members and students to take part in each cycle of workshops. The formal aim, for us, was to provide quality training to empower participants from the partner countries to work with diversity in the classroom or research, using auto/biographical narrative methods. Our workshops included 'Arab Israelis' (who privately identified as 'Palestinians'), Israeli Jews as well as Georgians.

4.1   Canterbury Tales: A Talking Cure?

A brief note on auto/biographical narrative research workshops, which have been developed in Canterbury over several years. The ESREA Life History and Biography Research Network was a particular inspiration, methodologically and epistemologically. The workshop methodology has been used in varied contexts, including careers counselling, early years and teacher education as well as in family support programmes in marginalised communities. The research methods have been recently used in illuminating the dynamics of racism and Islamic fundamentalism and the role of what we might call a 'democratic education' in a post-industrial, culturally divided English city (West, 2016). Pierre Dominicé's (2000) work in Geneva was an important starting point for these developments. It involved an iterative process of building educational biographies, beginning with oral accounts of significant life experience, among professionals, and then working intensively in groups, moving towards formal presentations and written accounts. The accounts combined stories of diverse experience, with critical reflexivity and a theoretical repertoire designed to enhance professional competence and creativity.

One intention in Canterbury has been to build an interdisciplinary theoretical repertoire, drawing on psychoanalysis, especially object relations theory, ideas of 'biographicity' (Alheit & Dausien, 2007), and critical theory, not least the work of Axel Honneth on self/other recognition (Honneth, 2007, 2009). An earlier EU financed study of non-traditional learners in various European universities, (RANLHE), of which CCCU was part, provided an opportunity to experiment with various theoretical psycho-social 'sensitising' frames, when interpreting the stories of diverse learners. The frames included Bourdieu's ideas on habitus, Honneth on self/other recognition, and Winnicott on transitional space (Finnegan, Merrill, & Thunborg, 2014; Formenti, West, & Horsdal, 2015). Donald Winnicott (1971) focused on the nature of transitional space and qualities of relationship, and even playfulness in self-formation, in analytic settings. For us, and Winnicott, these ideas can be applied broadly to cultural or educational experience. The latter represent an intermediate area between people, where self and narrative negotiation takes place – 'who am I, who might I be?' – if anxiety is sufficiently contained and we feel seen and legitimate in taking risks. But movement within the space, or we might call it a habitus, can be especially difficult for some – in a workshop or university seminar – as we risk exposing uncertain, vulnerable selves to the other's gaze.

Linden (West, 1996) has illustrated these processes in studies of non-traditional adult learners who enter the unfamiliar habitus of a university. At first a seminar can seem forbidding, as students wonder whether this is really for the likes of them. They worry how others might react to them, and their stories. 'Will anyone like me, or what I have to offer? Will what I do or say be liked? Maybe I don't deserve to be liked. I come from the wrong background and this will be despised'. Such feelings are psychologically primitive in the sense of being layered down in early experience; but they can be reactivated in new, anxious socio-cultural interactions where we feel exposed. Like an infant, so to speak, all over again. And yet we can find what Winnicott calls good objects – other students, a tutor or even something symbolic in a character from literature, with whom we identify and find recognition. These objects are internalised, and over time strengthen our intrapsychic dynamics, enabling us to claim space and agency. The stories we tell ourselves, and others become more assertive, legitimate, and we become less defended against others and otherness.

Winnicott wrote that 'When I look, I am seen. So, I exist. I can now afford to look and see' (Formenti & West, 2018, p. 121). This is a view of self as contingent, relational, developmental and potentially agentic, forged in our interactions with diverse others and the symbolic world. What is inter becomes intra-subjective in processes of what is termed projective identification. Reparation, of whatever kind, is possible, given the right quality of psychocultural and relational space, where we feel seen, and can see.

These processes are deeply embodied, affective, unconscious and relational as much as cognitive. They can generate deep anxiety as we move beyond normal defensive structures and open ourselves to others. Eventually, perhaps, we learn to listen to the other and their story, however disturbing. Some of the anxiety is contained by us, as facilitators, in naming what is happening and using ground rules as benchmarks to encourage respectful, reflexive practice. We seek to build trust, openness, dialogue, listening, storytelling and non-abusive relationships. Our feedback to individuals and the group is done in manageable or digestible ways, informed by therapeutic practice. The capacity to digest, and the metaphor of feeding and being fed, and resistance to it, is an important part of the psychoanalytic lexicon.

The quality of space can represent, as indicated, a kind of border country between adult education and therapy, psyche and politics, rationality and emotionality, conscious and unconscious processes, self and other (Bainbridge & West, 2012). A border country where we might begin to recognise what we have in common, which can be an important step in recognising the other. Axel Honneth supplements Winnicott by suggesting that processes of self/other recognition are important at the meso level, in seminar groups, for instance, when we feel accepted and belong; and at the macro level in wider cultural exchange when we may take on a leadership function for a group, which is essential for building stronger social solidarities (Honneth, 2007, 2009). Could we achieve some of this, at least, in our work with diverse educators? This at least was the theory.

So, a typical workshop includes an opening round in which people share an object of biographical meaning to them, like a photograph, poem, drawing, or piece of music. There is a theoretical and methodological introduction, an explanation and agreement over ground rules, followed by a role play of a narrative interview, in which one of us tells the other stories of learning to be citizens while the other models good narrative interview practice. We illustrate a nuanced respect for silence and giving time to the other. The whole group discusses the experience, agrees our interview protocol, and moves into small groups of four people, deliberately diverse in backgrounds. Participants interview each other and experiment with being interviewees, interviewers, and observers in turn. Over the course of a week, their oral material is developed into written auto/biographical accounts of becoming citizens and experiencing democratic values in lives. These written accounts are completed individually and or in small groups; everyone presents their auto/biographical writing, and finally, we consider how methods like these can be used in their own schools, colleges and universities.

The work touches the deepest sensitivities, and evoked frustration and anger among particular Palestinians. This was often expressed privately to us, as facilitators, about injustice and the difficulties of not being able to raise issues in the wider group. Power was asymmetrical, they said, and there could be negative implications back 'home' if they were seen as troublemakers. Israeli Jews held the power. The Israeli Jewish novelist, Amos Oz (Hari, 2018), likens the position of Palestinians and Israelis to two traumatised characters adrift on a piece of driftwood in a raging ocean. Each party wants the other to let go, while both desire safety and the land of ancestors, free from danger and oppression. But one party has more power to decide who lets go. The Palestinians in our groups live within the State of Israel and have learned how to remain silent, or adjust their stories to avoid danger. One Palestinian we interviewed, later, outside the programme, was born in the State of Israel. They said what we were attempting was like asking people to talk when the other held a gun to the head.

So to begin to illustrate the lived experience of the group. For ethical reasons, we have disguised aspects of small group experience and have elided and partly fictionalised material from different people in our analysis. We have sought to do justice nonetheless to the encounters, in narratively truthful ways. We want to describe, in fictionalised form, the stories of two people who were based in one small group. We observed one of them interviewing the other, and then talked to both, in depth, later and specifically interviewed two of them, auto/biographically. But the two people below represent a kind of amalgam of various experiences that we have elided to ensure, as much as we are able, confidentiality.

One of them introduced themselves as Palestinian and a Christian who worked in an Arab College of Higher Education near Nazareth. They talked about teaching and some of their own history of citizenship and activism. They and their partner held prominent positions in the community, and sought peace and reconciliation, based on justice for all. They preferred education and dialogue to hurling bombs and missiles at each other. They were active citizens, working in the field of Palestinian cultural studies, and the preservation of Palestinian history and culture mattered greatly to them. They wondered about introducing auto/biographical and narrative methods across their work to encourage agentic citizenship. The interviewer, who was Jewish, listened without interruption, despite some of the turmoil they later admitted to. They had served in the defence forces, as history, so to speak, met the present, and a difficult family story of forced expatriation was alluded to. We return to this below, in an auto/biographically more developed form: only so much was possible in this particular format, for reasons of time and trust.

Another Palestinian decided to opt out of the groups altogether, in any meaningful way. They were especially angry, they said to us, in a back and off-stage setting, using Goffman's (1956) dramaturgical metaphor. We knew things were not working, for this person and listened to his story, in private. Other Palestinians talked of how difficult it was to mention Al Nakbah or the Israeli occupation of 'their' land. Al Nakbah remained unrecognised in the wider Israeli State. Auto/biographical narrative work of this kind can touch deep and raw wounds while the group might not be good enough to deal with such trauma. This is dark, distressing territory and it was our responsibility to manage the group at any moment of time, and to decide what could and could not be handled. We erred on the side of caution, and made clear that no-one was obliged to say anything, and everyone had the right to remain silent and that we aspired, at least, to create a group where people worked respectfully and truthfully with one another. Silence might be the only legitimate option for some.

We tried to keep the dialogue going. We reminded everyone that the basic aspiration of auto/biographical narrative enquiry was to imagine the world through the others' eyes. But empathy is a difficult journey and can be disturbing. It may be easier to close things down when listening to someone we feel is racist, colonialist, or even a potential terrorist, and not open to us and our story (West, 2016). And if a week is a long time in politics, it may be far too brief to find the capacity to recognise each other's pain in a kind of common experience; let alone consider small reparative pedagogic acts for the classroom. Not to say that the weeks were insignificant, but we achieved less than we hoped for.

4.2   *Meaningful and Inspirational*

One person, however, who was Jewish Israeli, felt recognised and was motivated to work for peace:

> For me it was a meaningful and inspirational week. I realised the significance of narrative writing that reveals the writer to herself and also generates contact and closeness among the group members. I discovered that everything in my life has a narrative, a history, a meaning: hobbies, occupations, values I believe in, and even clothes I like to wear. Through narrative writing I realized that nothing is impersonal.

... I want to continue practicing this with myself and with my students, and ... in order to draw closer people with differing and even conflicting narratives. Precisely in a world that centres on individualism, I would like to become intimately familiar with the narratives of others, to participate in them, and to expand my own narrative thanks to narratives that differ from my own. I wish to find a way of creating a bridge between ethnic, ideological, and political groups with diverse narratives. In the next month I hope that I will facilitate a group of Arabs and Jews, a group of people with a left-wing narrative and with a right-wing narrative, and maybe also a group of ultra-Orthodox and secular Jews, and I will explore the practice of narrative therapy designated "definitional ceremony", which takes narrative writing even further, to investigate whether it is possible to participate in each other's narrative and open up to it. I am eager to see what will happen.

Another Israeli Jewish woman also felt recognised although her proposals to pedagogically experiment excluded any reference to peace:

I teach a course called Educators, Parents and the Community, so I am aware of the role and the importance of each, and of the effort necessary to bring these parties together, but the CURE program in Canterbury, where I was exposed to the experiences of people from different countries and cultures, enhanced my knowledge and awareness of civil engagement, of individuals and institutions ....

I feel that I have received "training", from professionals about the theoretical and more so the practical aspects of active citizenship and democratic sensibility, and I have been given the tools I need to work these into the fabric of my teaching. I taught a student whom I knew had begun a chess club at his school, one that had grown successfully and spread to a number of other schools, but I did not introduce this into my lesson, not seeing how this could be relevant to English. Upon return from Canterbury, we listened to this student's narrative about his chess club. And of course, the ways in which it was related to civil action, civic education and the teaching of English were numerous and relevant. It was a learning experience, from which we all benefited ...

... Upon returning to the college, I began collecting narrative data from my students, namely those who are new immigrants, for my own research, research that is now well underway. Our discussion about narrative method also brought me closer to solving a particular problem. I am ... requiring that students speak about their own language use.

In every class, there are guaranteed to be speakers of English, Hebrew, Arabic and Russian, as well as other languages, and I believe that there is value in recognising this diversity .... Their narratives provide me not only the necessary insight I need into their linguistic backgrounds and language practices, but enable me to get to know them better as individuals .... These narratives also apply the material covered in classes to their real-life language use, and include elements that are applicable too to their own eventual language teaching experience .... I took away from my experience in Canterbury knowledge, tools and experiences that are bound to impact my teaching for many years to come. It was a privilege to participate in such a program.

There was other positive feedback, including from the Georgians. But there was silence too. Particular Palestinians, and Jews, preferred to tell their stories in the relatively safer space of an auto/biographical narrative interview, rather than in the larger group. If the space is to be therapeutic, listening and the containment of anxiety are essential. And as Molly Andrews (2007) suggests, in the context of the South African Truth and Reconciliation Commission, traumatised individuals may take months and even years to speak of certain experiences, while support is necessary both before and after telling their story. Of course, we were operating on a much smaller scale, but our experience suggested the need for a longer, better resourced programme.

5 Moving On?

We wanted to bring other groups of Palestinian educators (from the Palestinian Territory, Gaza and Israel itself), and diverse Israeli Jewish educators, to such a programme in Canterbury, in a more substantial search for dialogue and peace, using auto/biographical narrative methods over a longer period. We would seek money for this from the European Union and other possible funders. We used contacts made in a teacher education project in the West Bank, led by our University and financed by the World Bank (CCCU, 2016). We would also exploit contacts made in the workshops, and from colleagues researching the effects of trauma, for instance, in places like Gaza (Diab, Veronese, Jamei, & Kagee, 2019). We imagined three main cycles in the developed project, modelled on the existing week-long workshop but with a longer initial phase; those participating would be expected to commit to all the cycles, including a virtual element, over two years and more. Time would be given to gathering initial auto/biographical narratives, and resources identified for providing therapeutic support, as appropriate. Eventually participants would move to consider curriculum experiment in their own institutions, and to undertake projects on local, family and community histories, across dislocation and oppression in the past and present. Attempts would be made to work in highly segregated situations, where walls of one kind or another separate peoples; maybe use could be made of festivals of diverse cultures and histories, exhibitions, theatre, music, dance, poetry a well as other forms of storytelling in the search for dialogue and peace.

Through experiences of community rituals, and teachings, *mythopoetic* or imaginal ways of knowing can serve to overcome negative images of the other and self by generating new ones (or retrieving ancient ones) derived from myth, poems and personal stories (Willis, 2005; Formenti & West, 2018). Peter Willis (2005), and Leonard and Willis (2008) have described how film and poetry may be used to provide relevant images of an event (in this context, a significant moment during a person's life, as portrayed in film) to explore wider group consciousness and difference. The pedagogy seeks to create a good enough reflexive space for learners' individual and collective contemplation, encompassing existential, imaginal, family, community, historical and contemporary experience, including trauma. We wanted to find a key to generate a little more light and hope in the present bleakness of Israeli/Palestinian relationships.

5.1   *Walls*

But we walked into a hard metaphorical wall. We imagined bringing together groups of progressive educators from diverse backgrounds, as suggested. To tell and share stories of migration, trauma, injustice, and colonialism and to build some mutual understanding in a kind of pedagogy of interruption, unsettlement and struggle for recognition; maybe to create a shared grammar by which to talk about past, present and future – including of teaching and curriculum development – in new ways in what could become both an educational and potentially therapeutic space.

We talked with colleagues from 5 Palestinian universities involved in the West Bank Teacher Education project. They listened silently as we described our idea. 'No way', the group leader said. 'If we cooperated with these people, even if we wanted to, we would be sacked in the morning'. Of course, we recognise, as Elif Shafak (2020) has recently written, the dignity of rage in the face of such injustice and oppression. But we listened to this with the noise of deteriorating relationships in the Middle East in our minds. Black (2020) suggests that this might well lead to further expropriation of Palestinian land and property, and the expulsion of individuals, families and communities from annexed territories. But who were we to challenge our Palestinian colleagues? We had known no such trauma in our lives.

A colleague researcher who works among Palestinians wrote to us:

> I was talking to you about the real absence of a dialogue between oppressed and oppressor. Perhaps, a path for change could come after a real new catastrophic event. The oppressor is trapped in a predatory narrative of denial and disqualification, looking at the indigenous people as an obstacle for realising their happiness and reparation from the crimes they experienced in their recent and ancient history as a victim. So far, the oppressor appears disgusted by an uncivilized, homophobic, and misogynistic stereotype about the oppressed; their dirty indigenous villages are disturbing the civilised white and technologically advanced world of the oppressor, they must be excluded and hidden from those civilised eyes by walls, barriers, electronically protected fences and drones that vertically (land, airspace, and underground) control the Palestinian lives. On the opposite, the oppressed envy the clean, easy and perfumed lives of the oppressor, their freedom to travel, to bathe in crystalline swimming pools, to be celebrated internationally as champions of freedom and democracy for few. The result, revivifying the Fanon metaphor, is the confrontation between two mutually excluding species – the ones of the oppressed and the oppressor. Structures of power such as settler colonialism and capitalistic agendas are making the dialogue impossible .... I guess even Paulo Freire who promoted the dialogue between oppressor and oppressed, between colonised and coloniser, black and white, man and women, will recognise that in such a condition just the monologue of violence in the confrontation between power and powerless can take place .... Listening to the mourning of the oppressed, listening to their desperation and thirst of justice, their right for self-determination and return to their land, I do think is the only way.

The message was powerful, and we pressed the pause button on the whole idea. Even Paulo Freire it was suggested, would baulk at the possibility of dialogue in a context like this. Structures of power like settler colonialism, and images of a kind of metropolitan glitter contrasting with Palestinian dirt and shabbiness, was strong language. So too was the continuing reminder of everyday violence against ordinary people in the present as well as past. But questions still nagged away: was it impossible for Israeli Jewish educators to accept that their country was engaged in violence and settler colonialism? Might they be open to the idea of an unresolved historical trauma in their own individual and collective lives played out in their own State's relationships with Palestinians? Maybe something could be achieved if their stories of family trauma, existential angst and insecurity could be acknowledged in some way by the other? Despite asymmetries of power and present privilege, both sets of stories need to be heard for progress to be made, on however small a scale.

We think it helpful to return at this point, to our two fictionalised characters above, participating in our workshops. In the auto/biographical narrative interviews we witnessed detailed, harrowing accounts of family and personal histories from Jews and Palestinians. One talked about the time, in their family's story, when the Jewish Hagenah (terrorists, in this perspective), came to their town, Haifa. Their parents had lived and worked there all their lives, including on the railways built by the British. The family now lives in Nazareth. They talked of a desolate, desperate search for safety, and of relatives lost, homes seized, and communities abandoned. Their family had fled to Nazareth alongside other relatives, who were escaping a village close by 'being ethnically cleansed'. The family imagined that Jewish forces would not enter Nazareth because it was the place of Christ's birth and there were so many churches of different denominations. Surely Jewish forces would not desecrate the place for fear of losing Western support. They were right. But in more recent times, the same Palestinian talked of a relative who lived in Gaza not been allowed to finish their degree studies in Bethlehem. In fact, they were arrested by Israeli defence forces on the way back to Gaza, handcuffed, blindfolded and left waiting for hours in a kind of ritual humiliation.

The other, an Israeli Jew, told a story of Jewish people in North Africa, from where their family had come. Zionist organisations had encouraged emigration, particularly from poorer areas to provide valuable labour. Persecution, anti-Semitism and poverty combined with an increasing identification of 'their' country with the 'Arab struggle' to provoke another kind of Jewish exodus. Security, in this instance, had an intimate face. A father was a bully, and there was constant abuse and humiliation in the family. When the family arrived in Israel, the overwhelming feeling, for one child, was 'at last there is safety'.

Later, like everyone else under compulsory conscription, they joined the military and felt recognised there and were chosen for special counter-insurgency training. They had been deployed to deal with what they saw to be 'terrorist infiltration' and might well have been responsible for the abuse of the young student from Gaza. But the new training brought abuse all over again, from sadistic authority figures, and they quit as soon as they could. What auto/biographical narrative work could achieve is to illuminate common, insecure and painful experience, where dialogue could be born through sharing stories, witnessing these and slow, maybe at times ambivalent processes of self/other recognition. We can get to a human core, as Said terms it, beyond binaries and blame, to common suffering; and the possibility of shared, fragile humanity given a narrative airing as a basis for some learning and maybe healing too.

The alternative is likely to be more violence, which of course, for some, is a solution of a kind, however hopeless. Franz Fanon wrote that 'naked violence ... only gives in when confronted with greater violence' (Fanon, (1963 p. 53). Fanon was educated in an impeccably French way, and his vision of terror, Tom Holland (2018) suggests, would have been familiar to Robespierre and the Committee of Public Safety. One of our interlocutors stated that there could never be meaningful dialogue without an Israeli admission of guilt as a colonial oppressor. How might our Israeli Jew relate to this challenge, without some recognition of their suffering and insecurity too? We are left with a conundrum about how people can profitably engage with the other, and the role of forgiveness and magnanimity. This is of course an age-old question about the potential of violent and non-violent struggle, and the place of a generosity of spirit in our humanity and quest for progress and reconciliation. In the witness of Martin Luther King, Gandhi and Nelson Mandela, a life can involve trauma but alongside determined, painful and courageous recognition of the oppressor as human too.

We are aware of other grassroots projects seeking to establish greater empathy between Israelis and Palestinians, such as the Parents Circle or Family Forum and these appear to work in good enough ways (Baron-Cohen, 2019). There are women coming together and dialoguing – even when sons have been killed by the other side – in the search for peace, reconciliation and healing. Creating space for a dialogical, auto/biographical, narrative experiment in the border country of therapeutic adult education for peace could provide another key. If, as Jaqueline Rose (2017) observes, it can be too painful to traverse the passage from trauma into words and that words are not easily formed in the face of the colonialising other, there can be nonetheless a flickering auto/biographical light in which telling and sharing stories becomes more possible, while poetry, music, dance and enactment can also humanise the gaps between people.

Moreover, not all Israelis are complicit in violence and some protest and work in places like Gaza, in early years education, for instance. We have a researcher colleague involved in such international collaboration there, with some success (D. Valkanova, private communication, 2020). There are Jewish people who do recognise the continuing Palestinian pain of the Nakba, and act politically as well as educationally for peace and justice (see Bashir & Goldberg, 2017). There could be a narrative, playful and poetic key to open a small door to small ecologies of learning and hope. It is just possible to imagine transitional space where disturbance is mutually recognised, and people feel seen, and can exist more openly and playfully together, over time; a place where shared traumas of death, forced migration and profound loss are given narrative form, and managed therapeutically as well as educationally, and where a light of peace might flicker more brightly.

References

Alheit, P., & Dausien, B. (2007). Lifelong learning and biography: A competitive dynamic between the macro and the micro-level of Education. In L. West, P. Alheit, A. S. Andersen, & B. Merrill (Eds.), *Using life history and biographical approaches in adult and lifelong learning* (pp. 57–70). Peter Lang.

Andrews, M. (2007). *Shaping history, narratives of political change.* Cambridge University Press.

Bainbridge, A., & West, L. (2012). (Eds.). *Minding the gap: Psychoanalysis and education.* Karnac.

Bashir, B., & Goldberg, A. (2017). Introduction: The Holocaust and the Nakba: A new syntax of history, memory, and political thought. In B. Bashir & A. Goldberg (Eds.), *The Holocaust and the Nakba; A new grammar of trauma and history* (pp. 1–42). Columbia University Press.

Baron-Cohen, S. (2019, January 27). Only empathy can break the cycle of violence. *The Guardian.* https://www.theguardian.com/commentisfree/2019/jan/22/empathy-cycle-violence-israel-palestine

Black, I. (2020, June 11). Israel's annexation of the West Bank will be yet another tragedy for Palestinians. *The Guardian.* https://www.theguardian.com/commentisfree/2020/jun/11/israels-annexation-of-the-west-bank-will-be-yet-another-tragedy-for-palestinians

CCCU. (2016). Website. https://www.canterbury.ac.uk/education/our-work/partnership/international/palestine.aspx

Diab, M., Veronese, G., Jamei N. A., & Kagee, A. (2019). The interplay of paradigms: Decolonising a psychology curriculum in the context of the siege of Gaza. *Nordic Psychology,* October, 183–198. https://www.tandfonline.com/doi/full/10.1080/19012276.2019.1675087

Dominicé, P. (2000). *Learning from our lives.* Jossey-Bass.

Fanon, F. (1963). *The wretched of the earth.* Grove Weidenfeld.

Finnegan, F., Merrill, B., & Thunborg, C. (Eds.). (2014). *Student voices on inequalities in European higher education.* Routledge.

Formenti, L., & West, L. (2018). *Transforming perspectives in lifelong learning and adult education: A dialogue.* Palgrave Macmillan.

Goffman, E. (1956). *The presentation of self in everyday life.* Edinburgh University Press.

Hari, J. (2018, December 31). A life in focus, Amos Oz, Israel literary colossus and lifelong advocate of a two state solution. *The Independent.* https://www.independent.co.uk/news/obituaries/amoz-oz-dead-israeli-writer-novelist-palestine-israel-tale-of-love-and-darkness-a8705681.html

Hexel, R., & Nathanson, R. (2010). *All of the above, identity paradoxes of young people in Israel. The third youth study of the Freidrich-Ebert-Stiftung Changes in National,*

Societal and Personal Attitudes. Freidrich-Ebert-Stiftung, Israel Office and Macro Center for Political Economics.

Holland, T. (2019). *Dominion. The making of the Western mind.* Little Brown.

Honneth, A. (2007). *Disrespect: The normative foundations of critical theory.* Polity Press.

Honneth, A. (2009). *Pathologies of reason: On the legacy of critical theory.* Columbia University Press.

Khoury, E. (2019). *Children of the Ghetto, my name is Adam.* Archipelago Books.

Leonard, T., & Willis, P. (Eds.). (2008). *Pedagogies of the imagination. Mythopoetic curriculum in educational practice.* Springer.

Merrill, B., & West, L. (2009). *Using biographical methods in social research.* Sage.

Rose, J. (2017). Afterword: The Holocaust and the Nakba. In B. Bashir & A. Goldberg (Eds.), *The Holocaust and the Nakba: A new grammar of trauma and history* (pp. 353–361). Columbia University Press.

Said, E. W. (1994). *Culture and imperialism.* Virago.

Shafak, E. (2020). *How to stay sane in an age of division.* Welcome Collection.

Shah, I. (1985). *The Subtleties of the inimitable Mulla Nasrudin.* Octagon Press.

Sheps, S. (2019). History and civics education in Israel; Reflections from Israeli teachers. *Critical Studies in Education, 60*(3), 358–374.

West, L. (1996). *Beyond fragments, adults, motivation and higher education, a biographical analysis.* Taylor and Francis.

West, L. (2016). *Distress in the city: Racism, fundamentalism and a democratic education.* IOE/UCL Press.

West, L., Alheit, P., Andersen, A. S., & Merrill, B. (Eds.). (2007). *Using life history and biographical approaches in adult and lifelong learning.* Peter Lang.

Willis, P. (2005, July 5–7). *Transformation and the inclusive heart. Mythopoetic pedagogy for an adult educator curriculum.* Paper presented at the 35th Annual SCUTREA Conference. http://www.leeds.ac.uk/educol/documents/142032.htm

Winnicott, D. (1971). *Playing and reality.* Routledge.

PART 3

*Diversity as a Content and as a Feature
of Biographic Enquiry*

∴

Understanding Women's Lives through Critical Feminist Perspectives: Working-Class Women Students in Higher Education

Barbara Merrill

Abstract

This chapter focuses on the relationship between critical feminist perspectives and feminist biographical methods in understanding the lives of working-class women in higher education. It explores the contribution of feminist methodology to biographical methods and its power to give 'voice' and richness to women's stories. Feminist biographical methods, stress, importantly, the subjectivity and intersubjectivity in research and the need for a humanistic and egalitarian approaches between the interviewer and interviewee. The stories told highlight the collectiveness of individual stories as well as the role of agency and structure (micro and macro) in the ecology of everyday lives. The women's stories illustrate how lives and identity are constructed and shaped by the intersection of gender and class. The women defined themselves as being working-class women. And although studying for a degree in higher education change their lives thy did not let go of their class identity.

Keywords

gender – class – women adult students – higher education – biographical methods

1   Introduction

> My interest in the women stemmed from my concern with the larger problem of how women struggle to make something of their lives ... they (students) shared a strong belief that education was a viable route by which to reach their objectives ... They hoped that a return to education would improve their status, income, conditions of employment, knowledge, autonomy and sense of well-being. (McClaren, 1985, p. 149)

© BARBARA MERRILL, 2021 | DOI: 10.1163/9789004465916_010

Feminist research has made a significant contribution to shaping our understanding of the lives of working-class women students in higher education (HE) through biographical narrative methods (Skeggs, 1997; Reay, 2003; Merrill, 2014). The engagement with biographical narrative methods in adult education research has been, and still is, dominant in Europe particularly, but also beyond (West et al., 2007), influenced not only by feminism but other perspectives such as symbolic interactionism, oral history, hermeneutics, postmodernism, and ethnography These various approaches originate from different intellectual traditions in various European countries. The popularity of biographical methods in adult education was facilitated by the 'turn' to biographical methods in the social sciences more generally (Chamberlayne et al., 2000) over the last thirty years. The work of the European Society for Research in the Education of Adults (ESREA) has been fundamental in developing and establishing biographical methods and in recognizing and encouraging diverse approaches to research from the more objective perspective of the German tradition to more subjective ones in the UK, Italy and Sweden. The ESREA Life History and Biographical Network has played a dominant role in this process although other networks such as the Access, Learning Careers and Identities and Gender Networks have also contributed. Within adult education it marked a welcome and refreshing change to the early, mostly quantitative research using surveys (Woodley et al., 1987) which reduced adult students to numbers and statistics thus dehumanizing them. In contrast biographical methods offers a humanistic and subjective approach (Plummer, 1991) enabling students to tell their own stories, revealing the complexities of individual lives in more in-depth and nuanced ways. In the UK biographical methods in adult education research have been heavily influenced by symbolic interactionism through the work of the Chicago School of Sociology and feminism.

This chapter focuses on the relationship between critical feminist perspectives and biographical methods in understanding the lives of working-class women students in UK higher education (HE). It will explore the contribution of feminist methodology to biographical methods and its power to 'give voice' and richness to women's stories, and in doing so, highlighting the collectivity of individual stories as well as the role of agency and structure in everyday lives which are situated within the interacting contexts of the micro, meso and macro worlds. To illustrate this, I will draw on my research undertaken over twenty years with working-class women students from different ethnic backgrounds within the context of a UK elite university. What is striking in all the stories I have heard is the dominance of class, gender, and for some, race and the interaction between them in their lives in the family, work, university, community and society more generally. Being working class and being proud of it and being different to the younger middle-class students and 'not wanting to be like them' as one woman said was central to their biographies. After gaining a degree the women continued to define themselves as working-class even though it did distance some of them a bit from their family, friends and community. Their identity as a woman is, therefore, related to being working-class. First, however, I will discuss the contribution of critical feminism to biographical methods and adult education research as it offers a particular and distinct stance to biographical research. Feminist research contributes to the ecology of life by highlighting the daily lives of women at the micro, meso and macro levels and how they constantly live in different spheres so that their life on campus.

2 Critical Feminism and Biographical Methods

Reinharz (1992) and other feminists asserted that feminist research is a perspective rather than a distinctive method which draws on feminist theory. For Burns and Walker (2005): "Feminist research is thus always more than a matter of method and raises philosophical issues of ontology ... and epistemology" (p. 66). However, although the research methods used by feminists are not new, they do offer a distinctive approach, for example, in the way that biographical interviews are undertaken and the relationship between the researcher and the researched. Feminist research in the academy developed in the 1970s and stemmed from the second wave feminist movement (Smith, 1987) and was primarily, but not exclusively, located within the discipline of sociology. It partly developed in response and opposition to male sociology or as feminists termed it 'malestream' as women's lives were ignored in sociological research and deemed as unimportant. This situation was challenged through studies such as *Girls, Wives, Factory Lives* (1981) by Anna Pollert and *Becoming a Mother* (1979) by Ann Oakley amongst others. Feminist research, therefore, began to challenge and question the notion of who has the power to construct knowledge and whose voices are being heard. More broadly it was also in opposition to 'traditional', positivistic research which objectifies the research participant reducing them to a statistical number. Both 'malestream' sociology and quantitative research makes women invisible and hidden from society. Quantitative research also does not take experiences, emotions, feelings, interactions and context into account. Feminist research became a powerful tool and voice for counteracting this. Such research according to Finch on reflecting about the link between qualitative research and feminism stated that:

> ... second wave feminism were incredibly potent for those of us who were young sociologists at that time, and were bound to make a huge impact on what we did and the way in which we thought about doing it ... the kind of ideas that were coming out of the feminist politics. (2007, p. 62)

For Finch (2007) the critical point in the UK in linking qualitative methods (biographical) to feminist research was the publication by Ann Oakley (1981) of her article "Interviewing women: a contradiction in terms". Understanding this historical context and influence of second wave feminism is important as it still continues to shape the epistemological and empirical approaches used by feminist researchers and feminist adult education researchers in particular. But we must not forget that feminist researchers in developing their research methods were also influenced by symbolic interactionism as well as the work of C. Wright Mills but taking it to a more critical and political level. By using biographical methods feminist researchers gave 'voice' to marginalized women and as Reinharz (1992) asserts:

> Biographical work has always been an important part of the women's movement because it draws women out of obscurity, repairs the historical record and provides an opportunity for the woman reader and writer to identify with the subject. (p. 126)

Thus "feminism encompassed a critical perspective that challenged some of the ideas of conventional research, as patriarchal and phallocentric ..." (Merrill & West, 2009, p. 29).

The concern was, and is, with highlighting women's oppression in society at the macro, meso and micro levels and challenging this through research for social change to transform women's lives. Feminist research is overtly political – encapsulated in the feminist term 'the personal is political'. As Lawthom (2004) stresses "Feminist standpoint epistemologies in research emphasize the perspectives of those whose lives are shaped and constrained (or marginalized) by the dominant social order" (p. 102). As a result of feminist research women's voices were no longer silenced as the lives of women became a focus of research. Biographical methods were central in this process. As Popadiuk (2004) explains:

> The feminist biographical method is a powerful tool. It engages in research from a unique perspective that provides depth, meaning and context to

the participants' lived experiences in light of the larger cultural matrix in which they live. (p. 395)

The second wave feminists' notion that only women can research women to obtain a full understanding of women's lives ignores the fact that women are diverse as there are cultural, class, ethnic and age differences which affects a woman's experience and position in society. So being a middle-class woman is different to being a working-class woman and being a black working-lass woman is different to being a white working-class woman, for example bell hooks (1982) argued in her book *Ain't I a Woman? Black Women and Feminism* that while women are linked by oppression the experiences are not the same for black and white women. For hooks feminism spoke for the white middle class women and stressed instead that feminism should not only be about women but also link to other forms of oppression such as class and race.

Feminist research in the UK has largely focused on working-class women thus highlighting the intersection between class and gender, recognizing that working-class women's lives were different to those of middle-class women in terms of, for example, economic, social and cultural capital. Being a woman and being working-class cannot be separated and this is illustrated in the stories of working-class women in HE I have interviewed. This is also echoed in the work of Beverley Skeggs (1997), and others, who asserts that "… the category 'woman' is always produced through processes which include class and classifying produces very real effects which are lived on a daily basis" (p. 2). She continues "The women never see themselves as just women: it is always read through class" (1997, p. 91). UK feminism, however, shifted away from its roots with second wave feminism and its focus on critical perspectives and the lives of working women from the 1990s as postmodernism took hold within the academy and particularly within sociology:

> The emergence and stronghold of postmodernism and the decline of Marxist feminism in the academy has established a discourse which is far removed from the material reality of working-class women. Academic feminism is becoming elitist, excluding 'other women' through its language and content. (Merrill & Puigvert, 2001, p. 308)

As a result, the use of biographical methods was overshadowed by the new forms of feminist approaches such as postmodernism. Research became more theoretical and abstract and no longer situated in the reality of working-class women's lives (Merrill & Puigvert, 2001). This was not the case I would argue, within the field of adult education research where it has been embraced by feminist adult educators as a way of understanding working class women's learning experiences by linking past and present lives.

3   Feminist Adult Education

Until the 1990s research on women adult students in the UK focused largely on women in non-HE settings (Thompson, 1985; McLaren, 1985; Kennedy, 1987) providing valuable insight into their learning, classed and gendered experiences. The impact of policies on widening participation and the establishment of Access programmes (courses for adults for entry into HE) changed this. Several studies began to emerge in the 1990s looking at access into higher education (Sperling, 1991), experiences in higher education (Pascall & Cox, 1993; Merrill, 1999; Reay, 2003) and on the separateness and connectedness between studying and family life (Edwards, 1993). Later research has explored the intersection between gendered and classed experiences in both further and higher education (Skeggs, 1997; Tett, 2000; Reay, 2003; Merrill, 2015).

Using biographical narrative approaches enabled feminist adult education researchers to highlight the complexities and sometimes struggles of working-class women students' lives both inside and outside the academy – something which earlier adult education quantitative research could not do. Such approaches illuminate inequalities in a woman's life around gender and class for as Jane Thompson (2000), a UK adult education researcher, asserts telling one's story is:

> ... a way of exercising critical consciousness and of producing knowledge from the inside about gender, class and education, deriving from personal, particular and shared experience. Not in the pursuit of ultimate truth but in the search for greater, more nuanced understanding. (p. 6)

4   The Distinctiveness of Feminist Methodology

Feminist biographical researchers have established a distinctive approach to undertaking biographical narrative interviews. Such interviews are a dialogical, empowering and sometimes transformative process as well as being an educational and learning experience for both interviewer and interviewee. Feminist contribution to methodology and biographical interviewing manifests itself in several ways and contrasts greatly, as stated above, with traditional approaches to research. This involves establishing a different and democratic relationship between the interviewer and interviewee (Stanley & Wise, 1993; Oakley, 1981) so that feminist researchers work with women and not on women (Oakley, 1981). It thus aims to avoid exploitation and an instrumental approach to research. It is, therefore, important to build up trust and respect and a secure environment to give women a voice to tell their story. Such an approach to research challenges by breaking down power differences as far as possible so that, as Oakley (1981) argues, the interview becomes more like a conversation with the interviewer and interviewee sharing their story in an ecology of communication and sharing. Not only does the interviewing process become subjective but also intersubjective as interviews are an interactive social process. As Stanley and Wise (1993) stress, "Personhood cannot be left out of the research process ... We see the presence of the researcher's self as central in all research" (p. 161). Biographical feminist interviewing is a collaborative interaction whereby stories are co-constructed and owned. Giving the transcript back to interviewees enables them to say whether or not the interview is an accurate representation of their story. Rebecca Lawthom (2004) takes the interviewing process and ownership of the story a step further as she states that: "The emancipatory framework ... allows the interviewee – or co-researcher – to shape the story, have full editorial control and present a first-person narrative" (p. 60).

Biographical approaches enables us to understand the role of agency and structure (two fundamental foundations in sociology) in people's lives and the inter-relationship between them as well as locating individual lives within a historical, social, political and economic context (Wright Mills, 1967; Bertaux, 1981). For critical feminist researchers such processes highlight how individual stories at the micro level are also collective ones at a macro level acted out in contexts at a meso level so that issues of inequality such as gender and class are illuminated. "Yet in constructing a biography a person relates to significant others and social contexts: a biography is, therefore, never fully individual" (Merrill, 2007, p. 7).

5   Working-Class Women Students' Voices

The voices presented here are those of working-class women adult students who I have interviewed in relation to several EU funded research projects which have focused primarily on the experiences of adult students studying in higher education and the effects which this has on the self, families and future lives. More recently my research shifted to issues on transitions and inequalities from higher education into the labour market. Their stories reveal commonalities of gendered and classed lives in relation to domesticity, education, family and work. In relation to schooling, as feminist academics have highlighted, education prepared them through the curriculum for their future roles as wife, mother, domesticity and 'female' jobs (Deem, 1978; Spender, 1982; Sharpe, 1982, 1994). The women in my studies were no exception. Lynne summarizes their experiences;

> I started school in 1969. Girls went to school, just did it, then got married. You know – had a little job and then got married so there is no encouragement whatsoever ... it was just the norm. Women just got married and had children and that was that.

Teachers had low expectations of girls' futures and this was also reinforced by the cultural attitudes of many working-class parents and illustrating how the interplay of micro, meso and macro levels shaped the women's lives. Jane felt that she had no encouragement from her teachers:

> ... fifteen with absolutely nothing. No exams sat so no exams passed. I went to work in a factory sewing lace on knickers because that was what I was told I was capable of. I was good at needlework and I still am.

Others would have liked to have continued with schooling so for them returning to learn at university was about completing their education:

> I was well behaved and got on with my work. I just feel that there was a lot of potential that I had that was totally wasted because assumptions were made about me. Too young at the time to know but I do feel it came back to my background and my family and where I lived and that influenced how they treated me and that's why college was never really mentioned. (Paula)

Engagement in learning often involves the complex interaction of several factors. One important motive, particularly for women, was self-development – wanting something better in life and 'to complete my education'.

The women followed similar life histories of entering unskilled work after leaving school until they married and had children. The family became the focus of their lives which many found stifling and unfulfilling. Time spent in the home looking after children or working in an unskilled job prompted women to reflect upon their lives and their identity, leading them to want to become someone other than a mother or wife (Merrill, 1999). They were looking for a way out of domestic life, wanting 'more to life than this' as one woman said, and used their agency to break from cultural and structural constraints:

Well I know for me just being in the house with the wee (small) ones – it's like you have no one to talk to – well you have them but no adults. You could go a bit mad. It's good to get out of the house and to do things. To keep your brain active. It's not good to be stuck in the house all the time. (Anne)

The isolation of being confined in a house with young children was a common motivating factor for wanting to return to learn; 'to get back into civilization' as one woman described it. Paula stated several times in her story that 'there has got to be more to life than this' upon reflecting about her job working in a bank where she noticed that male employees were treated better than female employers. Biographies also reveal the importance of critical incidents or epiphanies (Denzin, 1989), such as divorce, bereavement or redundancy which act as turning point moments. Some had been contemplating returning to education for a number of years but did not take any action until the experience of a critical incident pushed them into learning. For several women it was divorce as Julie explains; "I really didn't go out much when I was married so then I had to kind of force myself to start to go out". Critical incidents often act as an enabling factor:

... at that time I was in a violent relationship so it made me realize that this is not the situation that you're supposed to have in your life so you've got to overcome things and you've got to do things ... I wouldn't have done the things that I'm doing now because it's taken from then to this to do what I'm doing – yes it was a turning point. (Kate)

Often it is a configuration of circumstances that allows for the shift from non-participation to participation (and vice versa) through the exercise of human agency. It is an ecology of everyday life and a desire to change and fulfil themselves as women and a human being. Gender and class issues play an important role in these shifts. Being stuck in the home gave time for reflection about being a working-class woman and the possibilities for breaking out of their traditional role. It is the interaction of changes in the relationship between agency (micro) and structure (macro) that provides what Strauss (1953/1969) describes as 'turning point' which encourages people to 'take stock, to re-evaluate, revise, re-see and re-judge'. Change was, therefore, a common theme that reverberated throughout many of the stories of women wanting to escape from an unfulfilling life at work, in the home and/or a life of living on a low income. The meso level of education was perceived as the answer: a tool for achieving transformation and a better life.

Becoming a university student, however, for most of the women did not liberate them from their domestic and childcare tasks. Being a student was another role and responsibility they had to take on alongside their other roles, unlike the male adult students who had support from their partners and felt no guilt (Merrill, 1999). Juggling became a way of life:

> Time is one of the biggest factors with being a mature student because of fitting in with all of the home activities and different roles and trying so that everybody else does not feel left out. I keep trying to accommodate them as well as all the other work. It is difficult to handle and I wake up in the middle of the night sometimes and think 'I have been a terrible mother lately because I have not dome this or that. It is worth it on the whole though, but it is quite demanding. (Cathy)

Many found life exhausting but for Rose 'it is necessary in order for me to achieve my future goals'. For some the only time they could study at home was once the children had gone to bed until the early hours of the morning. While some were lone parents others were married and studying caused friction in their relationship and a few left their relationship as a result of studying. Kate's experience was not unusual:

> I have not particularly enjoyed the trouble I have had to encounter at home. It is hard work with the work and the children. My husband is not supportive. He has not got a degree but has professional qualifications. He has always regarded me as being thick. I think it has all come as a bit of a shock to him. I think he kept expecting people to throw me off the course. He can now see that I will be able to support myself and the children in the future and sees this as a threat. (Kate)

Despite the constant struggles to balance studying with domestic work the women were determined and motivated to keep on going and succeed (Merrill, 2015). For a minority, however, this was not the case and the struggles they faced with their self and other factors such as health, finance, learning and family became too much and they left. I interviewed some of them after they left. They did not discuss leaving and not obtaining a degree as being negative as they felt that they had learnt from the experience in different ways and changed as a result. A few others took temporary withdrawal of a term or a year before resuming their studies.

Studying at an elite university raised awareness of class, gender and age differences between themselves and the younger students. Cultural and economic differences became apparent especially in seminar discussions as Liz discovered:

They come from a very different background and that's when I found I couldn't speak. In the module Politics and Food we (the mature women students) were talking about school dinners and were saying that they had to be good because this is the only hot meal they get and they couldn't understand that at all. Daddy had bought them ponies and daddy had got them this car.

Doing a degree also distanced some women in terms of class from other women in their community as their new identity developed. Julie, a lone parent, describes it in the following way:

I couldn't talk about university to any other mums as I walked to school because I felt that they had snubbed me – 'look at you with your big briefcase. It was all really tricky to explain to people why I wanted to 'progress' myself. I withdrew from my friends on the estate because I found it hard to explain to them why I wanted something different.

Her parents could also not understand why she wanted to study and in working class terms she was seen as 'getting above herself'. This experience of distancing was emotional to her and as Hoggart (1957) asserts it is an isolating experience.

In coming to the end of their degree studies the women reflected upon their HE experiences in relation to their lives prior to studying.

I did my degree to prove something to myself. To get my degree that I should have got when I was 18 … So to prove to myself that I can get qualifications and for my children as well so that they would think it's the norm … When I reflected back on my degree it has changed my identity – it changes a lot for me personally. I think it changes everything. It changes my mindset. (Sally)

For Julie, gaining a degree was about obtaining a better life for herself and her son which in practical terms enabled her to move out of a deprived housing estate. And like Sally and others it was about self-improvement:

I can't explain that feeling of not just pride but about being part of something … I'd actually come to the end of something quite brilliant and I should feel really, really proud.

In telling their stories the women reflected upon their gendered and classed lives and how studying for a social science degree had made them more aware of these issues and what being a working-class woman means in relation to their identity and their relationship to learning, family, friends and work.

6   Summary

The women's voices above offer a brief snapshot of working-class women students' experiences of learning in HE. Being a student provided the women with a transitional space to reflect upon past biographies in terms of who they had been, what they have now become and what they may become in the future. Together the experiences of learning and using feminist biographical interviews has the potential to enable them to think critically about their lives and the inequalities they have faced as "a university education can be a powerful biographical experience" (Merrill, 2015, p. 1869). Their stories also revealed that individual experiences are also collective ones as echoed by second wave feminists as they shared similar experiences of life. Importantly the stories also highlight the dialectics of agency and structure in shaping lives. Although the women were constrained from time to time with their degree studies they were also able to be agentic and change their lives and the lives of their children in some ways. They adopted and enjoyed an academic life while also holding on to their identity as a working-class woman albeit in a more critical way. As Ryan (2002) argues education, particularly in the social sciences, is a powerful experience for women:

> ... I can get women to focus on contradictions, that is, the reasons why they want changes in their lives and came to the course in the first place, and where these desires show up the cracks in the social façade, then there is the possibility of politicisation. If I can facilitate women to see where they are powerful and resisting as well as seeing how constraining power relations work in their lives, this can help them make changes and be agentic. (pp. 126–127)

The women's stories illustrate the ecology of everyday life and how lives change through the interaction of micro, meso and macro experiences. Their learning experiences took place within an elite middle-class university: an environment which is different to their working-class family and community environments. The women had to learn to cope (although a few did not) with living in these two worlds. Studying at university enriched and changed their lives in how they view the world more critically and in terms of better employment and fulfilling lives. But one aspect of their lives remained constant

– they continued to define themselves as working-class women. Biographical research is powerful in illuminating lives and giving voice to those who tell their story as well as highlighting the important role which adult education plays in people's lives.

References

Bertaux, D. (1981). *Biography and society.* Sage.

Burns, D., & Walker, M. (2005). Feminist methodologies. In B. Somekh & C. Lewin, (Eds.), *Research methods in the social sciences* (pp. 66–72). Sage.

Chamberlayne, P., Bornat, J., & Wengraf, T. (2000). *The turn to biographical methods in social science: Comparative issues and examples.* Routledge.

Deem, R. (1978). *Women and schooling.* Routledge & Kegan Paul.

Denzin, N. (1989). *Interpretative biography.* Sage.

Finch, J. (2007). Feminism and qualitative research. *International Journal of Social Research Methodology, 7*(1), 61–64.

Hoggart, R. (1957). *The uses of literacy.* Chatto & Windus.

hooks, b. (1982). *Ain't I a woman? Black women and feminism.* Pluto Press.

Kennedy, E. (1987). Labouring to learn. In M. McNeil (Ed.), *Gender and expertise.* Free Association Books.

Lawthom, R. (2004). Doing life history research. In D. Goodley, R. Lawthom, P. Clough, & M. Moore (Eds.), *Researching life stories: Method, theory and analyses in a biographical age.* Routledge-Falmer.

McClaren, A. (1985). *Ambitions and realisations: Women in adult education.* Peter Owen.

Merrill, B. (1999). *Gender, change and identity: Mature women students in universities.* Ashgate.

Merrill, B. (2007). Recovering class and the collective in the stories of adult learners. In L. West, P. Alheit, A. S. Andersen, & B. Merrill (Eds.), *Using biographical and life history approaches in the study of adult and lifelong learning: European perspectives* (pp. 71–90). Peter Lang.

Merrill, B. (2014). Gender and age: Negotiating and experiencing higher education in England. In F. Finnegan, B. Merrill, & C. Thunborg (Eds.), *Student voices on inequalities in European higher education: Challenges for theory, policy, and practice in a time of change* (pp. 74–85). Routledge.

Merrill, B. (2015). Determined to stay or determined to leave? A tale of learner identities, biographies and non-traditional students in higher education. *Studies in Higher Education, 40*(3), 1859–1871.

Merrill, B., & Puigvert, L. (2001). *Discounting other women. Researching widening access – International perspectives.* Conference Proceedings, CRLL. Glasgow Caledonian University.

Merrill, B., & West, L. (2009). *Using biographical methods in social research.* Sage.

Oakley, A. (1979). *Becoming a mother.* Martin Robertson.

Oakley, A. (1981). Women interviewing women: A contradiction in terms. In H. Roberts (Ed.), *Doing feminist research* (pp. 30–62). Routledge.

Pascall, G., & Cox, R. (1995). *Women returning to HE.* SRHE/Open University Press.

Plummer, K. (1991). Introduction. In K. Plummer (Ed.), *Symbolic interactionism, foundations and history.* Edward Elgar.

Pollert, A. (1981). *Girls, wives, factory lives.* Macmillan.

Popaduik, N. (2004). 'The feminist biographical method in psychological research. *The Qualitative Report, 9*(3), 392–412.

Reay, D. (2003). 'A risky business': Mature working-class women students and access to higher education. *Gender and Education, 15*(3), 301–317.

Reinharz, S. (1992). *Feminist methods in social research.* MacMillan.

Ryan, A. (2001). *Feminist ways of knowing: Towards theorising the person for radical adult education.* NIACE.

Sharpe, S. (1982). *Just like a girl.* Penguin.

Skeggs, B. (1997). *Formations of class and gender.* Sage.

Smith, D. (1987). Women's perspectives as a radical critique of sociology. In S. Harding (Ed.), *Feminism and social theory* (pp. 84–96). Open University Press.

Spender, D. (1982). *Invisible women: The schooling scandal.* The Women's Press.

Sperling, L. (1991). "Can the barriers be breached?" Mature women's access to higher education. *Gender and Education, 3*(2), 199–213.

Stanley, L., & Wise, S. (1993). *Breaking out again: Feminist ontology and epistemology.* Dover Publications.

Strauss, A. (1997). *Mirrors and masks: The search for identity.* Transaction Publications.

Tett, L. (2000). 'I'm working class and proud of it' – Gendered experiences of non-traditional students in higher education. *Gender and Education, 12*(2), 183–194.

Thompson, J. (1983). *Learning liberation: Women's response to men's education.* Croon Helm.

Thompson, J. (2000). *Women, class and education.* Routledge.

West, L., Alheit, P., Andersen, A. S., & Merrill, B. (Eds.). (2007). *Using biographical and life history approaches in the study of adult and lifelong learning: European perspectives.* Peter Lang.

Woodley, A., Wagner, L., Slowey, M., Fulton, O., & Bowner, T. (Eds.). (1987). *Choosing to learn.* SRHE/Open University Press.

Wright Mills, C. (1957). *The sociological imagination.* Penguin.

CHAPTER 10

Some Reflections on the Meaning, Limits and Challenges of Critical Biographical Research

Fergal Finnegan

Abstract

This chapter offers reflections based on doing critical research using biographical methods for over a decade. It discusses how I formed a identity as a critical researcher within a wider community of research. Drawing on critical theory and critical realism it also outlines a summary of how criticality in research might be understood through a reading of these complementary but distinct traditions. It concludes with some reflections on the limits and value of biographical research in a particular context (an exploration of equality issues and non-traditional student experience in higher education in Ireland).

Keywords

Critical theory – critical realism – biographical methods – equality – reflexivity

1   Introduction

The radical adult educator Raymond Williams described keywords as "significant, binding words in certain activities and their interpretation; they are significant, indicative words in certain forms of thought" (1983, p. 15). 'Critical' is a significant and binding word for me and my understanding of the term has strongly informed how I approach my work. It has also been central to how I have puzzled through the challenges of doing biographical research mainly with 'non-traditional' students in higher education (Finnegan et al., 2014, 2019; Fleming et al., 2017) with a particular focus on working class students' experience (Finnegan & Merrill, 2017). After a decade of doing critical biographical research I want to pause and take the measure of what I have done and learnt.

My aim in writing this chapter is to make sense of "the imperceptible accumulation of the changes that were gradually imposed on me by the experiences

© FERGAL FINNEGAN, 2021 | DOI: 10.1163/9789004465916_011

of life and that I brought about through work on myself that was inseparable from the work I was doing" (Bourdieu, 2007, p. 68). As such the chapter is at once a personal and a propositional account of how I see research and contains three intertwined strands: biographical reflections on how I developed my approach; a theoretical summary of how I currently understand criticality based on my experience and my reading of critical theory and critical realism; and an assessment of the value and limits of what I have achieved through critical biographical research.

2   Criticality Is Shaped Collectively

My understanding of what it means to be critical is rooted in a wider field of practice (adult education) and specific networks and groups (most importantly the ESREA Life History and Biographical Network (LHBN) rather than something that was devised or discovered individually. This is perhaps a banal point but nevertheless worth stressing in a period in which an individualistic and competitive conception of research is enthusiastically and widely promoted within neoliberalized universities.

I want to say a little more about this. Before I became an academic researcher, I had been working as an adult education practitioner for just under ten years. Historically, adult education research and pedagogy has been defined by its focus on the collaborative exploration of experience and democratic modes of knowledge creation in support of individual, community and social emancipation. The 'good sense' of the field, elaborated through generations of experiment and collaboration, has become sedimented into practices and ideas which can be more or less taken for granted in many contexts including Ireland. This meant I absorbed a conception of criticality long before I had to articulate it explicitly as an academic researcher. I should say this 'critical habitus' also built on and amended what I had learnt through political activism. As a result, when I began doing biographical research the importance of theorizing power, acting for equality and attempting to create space for people to speak on their own terms was already more or less clear to me. From the outset I was already convinced that we are storied beings and that positivistic approaches to research were alienating and sterile and that despite all the discussion of 'robustness' of 'data collection' methods ignoring lived experience led to trivial and impoverished accounts of the world.

What was far less clear to me was how to conduct academic research in the light of these intuitions and beliefs in an appropriately reflexive way. I was hungry for methodological advice and theoretical resources to develop a more nuanced approach to interviewing and analysis. In an important sense I was also searching for some distance from my own assumptions and values. The Life History and Biography Network provided this 'distance' by providing useful advice and ideas which helped me find my feet in my new role as an academic.

Over time LHBN modified the way I saw critical research in several important respects. I became more aware of the embodied aspects of research, the complex way we hear and construct stories and learned to think more carefully about analysis. I can cite texts that were formative (e.g. Alheit, 1994, 2005; Alheit & Dausien, 2000; West, 1996; Merrill, 2007; Merrill & West, 2009) but this way of presenting things downplays the relational dimension of this process. Permission to take ownership of ideas, to bridge previous intuitions to new insights, and ultimately to draw on the accumulated history of the network and the wider field of adult education depended on encounters and dialogue with a much wider range of researchers than can be cited here.

The shared commitment to criticality within LHBN as a network has provided me with a much-valued space for elaborating my own particular understanding of critical research. In the next section I want to outline my perspective on this matter and foreground three things in particular: the importance of socio-historical framing, the necessity of working *through* theory and the centrality of the idea of praxis in critical research. My hope is that by offering a summative and reflexive account of my interpretation on this shared 'keyword' I can spark further debate and discussion in the network and beyond about the various ways we envisage criticality.

3 Drawing on Diverse Traditions to Theorize Critical Research

3.1 *Critical Theory*
In many respects my approach to biographical research is rooted in critical theory. Critical theory is now a fairly diffuse project but I have in mind a specific rich line of historical materialist inquiry which builds on Marx (1888) and runs from Horkheimer (2002) through to the contemporary work of Honneth (2007) and Fraser (2013) and also underpins the critical pedagogy of Freire (1972) and Apple (2013).

In various ways all these thinkers argue that to understand lived experience in a critical way it requires extensive historical and sociological contextualization combined with an analysis of the sources and distribution of social power. "In any society, in any particular period, there is a central system of practices, meanings and values which we can properly call dominant and effective" (Williams, 2005, p. 38). One of key tasks of critical research is to identify dominant interests and values and trace how inequalities in power are linked to unnecessary suffering and harm (Wright, 2010). This type of power analysis therefore also requires a conception of flourishing and justice.

In my experience conceptions of flourishing are often implied rather than stated in critical research. This tendency limits and even forecloses a full discussion about the role of values and politics in research. With that in mind I should briefly say my own perspective is strongly influenced by socialist feminism. Nancy Fraser (2013) has persuasively argued for theory of justice based on greater equality in distribution of goods and resources as well as more egalitarian patterns of social recognition linked to the principle of participatory parity. I am convinced that human flourishing depends on fostering love, care and solidarity (Baker et al., 2009). To achieve this means reimagining how we make and act upon decisions in communities, workplaces and social institutions of all sorts including education.

As the scope of these claims indicates my position differs from a good deal of critical research influenced by postmodernism and post-structuralism. I do not see 'grand-narratives' of collective solidarity and emancipation as necessarily oppressive (Lyotard, 1979) and to my mind critical research which uncovers the ruses of power without any clarity about alternative political and social goals is deeply problematic. Without this the ultimate purpose of critical research is hazy and can easily degenerate into a scholastic performance of criticality. I believe this is rooted in deeper problem – an inability to deal productively with epistemological relativism in research, an issue which I will return to below.

The purpose of this broad framing is to reflect on where and how emancipation is being, or can be, acted upon (Wainwright, 2009; Wright, 2010, *inter alia*). If the point, as Marx (1888) famously argued, is 'to change things' then criticality requires an *orientation to emancipatory praxis* which in turn necessitates an analysis of the history and current state of emancipatory social movements as an integral element in the framing of any piece of research.

From my perspective, thorough socio-political analysis, an explicit theory of justice and a clear praxis orientation are fundamental components of critical research and these need to be theorized as a dynamic totality. It is worth noting in this regard that a good deal of critical theory does not do this and is highly scholastic and shows only a faint interest in radical praxis or everyday social practices (Anderson, 1976). Significantly for the present discussion, a great deal of critical theory is 'voiceless'. The terrain of culture and politics is traversed and surveyed but without any sense of the complex ways oppression, inequality and praxis are lived and storied. How people adapt, respond, subvert and resist dominant social logic is often overlooked or assumed to be already understood. This underestimates the importance of emergence which is at the heart of the complexities and contradictions of critical biographical research.

These gaps in critical theory reflect wider epistemological problems about what it means to build critical theory through dialogue and the precise role of normative and political commitments in research. Critical theory does not resolve these fully and these issues are addressed far more systematically within critical realism. To return to a point made earlier, critical realists also offer a generative way of understanding epistemological relativism.

3.2   *Critical Realism*

Critical realism (CR) emerged first in the 1970s primarily through the work of the Indian-British philosopher Roy Bhaskar who was studying the history of science and scientific discovery as well as the development of emancipatory knowledge. Over three decades Bhaskar's CR went through several iterations which are quite distinct. My perspective has been mainly influenced by his early work (1979, 2008) what is now termed 'original critical realism' (for a general overview of Bhaskar see Collier, 1994). Bhaskar's work led to the foundation of an *International Association for Critical Realism*, regular conferences, a book series and the *Journal of Critical Realism*. This influence has been most significant in the social sciences (for a summary of general methodological implications see Danermark et al., 1997; Sayer, 1992). This includes a network of CR researchers using biographical and life history methods (an edited collection emerged from this see Archer, 2010) and some work dealing with education following Bhaskar's move to the *Institute of Education* in London (e.g. Barnett, 2013; Scott, 2010 *inter alia*).

CR offers a distinct way of thinking about the relationship between ontology and epistemology which is rooted in a critique of positivism but frames this differently than hermeneutic, post-structuralist and post-modern thinkers. Put simply CR argues that world exists independently of our descriptions of it and what we know and say does not exhaust or ever fully capture what exists. More formally Bhaskar's (2008) project reasserts the *importance of ontology* and treats ontology as distinct and irreducible to epistemology. Further, he argues that *the world has 'depth' and is stratified and differentiated.* He posits the existence of three ontological domains: the empirical, which is the level of phenomenological awareness; the actual, the level of perceived and unperceived events; and the real, the level of activated and unactivated powers. These domains overlap but should not be conflated and part of the work of critical research is to explore patterns of relationship and non-relationship between them. Further, apart from very unusual, tightly controlled circumstances – such as in a laboratory – we should *anticipate high levels of complexity and emergence due to the unpredictable way various agents, things, events and powers combine.*

If we want to comprehend, to pick some examples, the feudal system in England, working class students' experiences in higher education, photosynthesis or the act of lighting a fire we necessarily need to trace the relation between these domains. *Being critical depends on seeking explanatory depth by* moving from surface descriptions to an analysis of mechanisms, powers and structures. This is true of both natural and social science but according to Bhaskar (1979) the social world differs from the natural world because it is mediated, theory laden and human agents possess specific powers. This has implications for how we understand structure and agency: social structures enable and constrain agency and depend on ongoing intentional and non-intentional actions. Crucially for biographical research, reasons have causal power (Harré & Secord, 1972) and therefore *self-understanding and self-monitoring are fundamental to understand the interplay of structure and agency.* We understand very little about the social world if we fail to attend to how people think, feel and act and disregard the highly complex ways this occurs. Open, largely spontaneous accounts of biographical experience are immensely rich, even necessary, resources in tracing how what Archer (2002, 2007) calls "the internal conversation" which shapes patterns of action and emergence within structured contexts.

From a critical realist perspective, the 'flat' ontologies of empiricism and positivism are completely inadequate for thinking about, researching and acting in a complex, layered social world. Identifying correspondences and then ascribing the operation of 'law-like regularities' overlooks both what is specific about human agency and the complexity and depth of social structures. Positivism also misrepresents and obscures what natural science and social science have in common – the search for explanatory depth. These interlinked claims offer a distinct path for thinking about emancipatory social science which is strongly critical of positivism but *does not treat natural science and positivism as identical and thus avoids familiar oppositions and dualisms which often hamper critical research* (idiographic, particular, subjective versus nomothetic, universal and objective and so forth). This clears the ground for embracing *methodological pluralism* rather than getting stuck in reified, and reifying, debates about the so-called 'paradigms' of quantitative and qualitative research.

The emphasis realists put on the existence of structures and mechanisms in the social world which typically lie outside, or are at least not prominent, in phenomenological awareness is also significant. If these arguments are correct, they point to *the necessity as well as the limits of biographical research for critical social science* as a project. This brings us back to the earlier argument about the importance of grasping the socio-historical context in critical research.

Crucially in terms of contemporary humanities and social science this realist ontology is grounded in *epistemic relativism* but Bhaskar (1979) argues this *does not entail judgmental relativism*. While all explanations of feudalism, working class students' experiences in higher education, photosynthesis and fire starting are contingent, fallible and context bound they are not all equally accurate and valuable. Identifying what has appropriate depth and complexity and real explanatory power is certainly contestable, but it is not entirely arbitrary and *can* be assessed on rational and emancipatory grounds (Bhaskar, 2008).[1]

4   Fieldwork and Analysis in Critical Biographical Research

Critical theory and critical realism argue that attention to the research process needs to be complemented with a clear focus on the social context and goals of critical research. This praxis orientation requires extensive socio-historical framing and a theory of justice which addresses in whose interests, and on what terms, research is being done. Besides this, based on a reading of CR, I have suggested that criticality is linked to being able to identify and work with complexity and emergence and move towards explanatory depth as the research advances.

These are essentially 'framing' remarks. The conduct of field research follows from this but throws up other challenges for critical research. Interviews are embodied, emotional, relational encounters which depend on being present and open to another human being in a meaningful way. This means working through your own fantasies, compulsions and interests on an ongoing basis. This aspect of critical research has a personal dimension and an institutional dimension. As West (1996) points out, drawing on object relations we cannot make sense of the outer world without reflexive exploration of our inner world, and that we need be cognizant of and explore our own biography and positioning to grasp how this influences the joint construction of meaning in research. As Bourdieu (2007) argues, reflexivity also requires a type of sociological imagination; we need concepts and practices which allow us to trace how an embodied intersubjective encounter in an interview is mediated by the field in which it takes place. However distantly and subtly an interview which is undertaken as part of a university research project is marked and influenced by the rituals, structures and struggles of the academic field. I take from this that conducting interviews requires a type of double reflexivity which is attentive to the dynamic intersubjective process of making stories and the way the researcher is situated in social space.

Analysis is a delicate process too, which can easily be flattened into atheoretical and trivial redescription or abstract and disconnected explanation. Criticality for me entails holding on to the integrity of a given story – the fullness, complexity and particularity of any individual's life – during thematic and narrative analysis. To do this I ground myself in the stories by listening and relistening to them as well as coding the transcripts. As general themes emerge through analysis, I return to the audio or a clean transcript to connect me to what a particular person said as a whole. Throughout the analysis I try to keep in view the sort of assumptions and experiences I am bringing to the interpretative process mainly by reviewing fieldwork notes and through reflective and biographical writing.

It also follows from the remarks made about the specificities of the social world, including the theory laden nature of social relations and the importance of explanatory depth, that theory is worked through in light of what is learnt through interviews. Using theory to match or 'contain' findings and/or explicitly or tacitly express normative commitments limits or voids criticality. It is on a basic level irrealistic. *Criticality therefore depends on making a substantive attempt to rethink concepts through research in the light of an open process of inquiry.* The aim is to work through a "double hermeneutic" (Giddens cited in Sayer, 1992) in which everyday and scientific accounts are analyzed in relation to each other and what this then discloses about the structuring of the research context. This entails close attention to how a particular phenomenon is constructed in the scientific field (for example, in my case the various ways social class and inequality have been researched in empirical and theoretical terms). Cultivating what Bourdieu has called "radical doubt" about the adequacy of existing frameworks (Bourdieu & Wacquant, 1992, p. 235), especially the ones which fit your own initial assumptions, is an important part of deepening the explanatory depth of a piece of research. On a practical level, I have found the selection of a number of 'sensitizing concepts' (Blumer, 1954) a useful way of making sense of the field and your own initial understanding of a phenomenon. Criticality then depends on the recursive movement between interviewees' accounts, ongoing reflection on the research context and questions, and the creative exploration of possible theoretical explanations for what is learnt through this (retroduction). The aim here is to examine the precise way structures and agency interact and identify the powers behind them. This is necessarily iterative but if pursued systematically is a key source of empirical and theoretical discoveries in critical research.

5   Critical Reflections on the Impact of Praxis Orientated Research

What has changed as a result of the research? I am fairly certain that deep immersion in biographical stories has altered the shape of my own 'internal conversation' and made it more multi-voiced. As a result, I see my experience as a community educator, activist and academic differently. I relate in a new way to my own family stories – especially my father's biography. A number of people whom I interviewed have spoken about the impact and benefits of having space to tell their story and be heard and for these participants it been useful, perhaps transformative in small ways to 'name their world'.

The research has also enhanced the social scientific understanding of education, access and social class in an Irish context. It indicates something about how under-researched these topics are in the Republic of Ireland that this mixed methods research (with biographical research at its heart) is to date the most substantive and sustained body of qualitative research on non-traditional and working-class experience in Irish higher education (Finnegan et al., 2014; Finnegan & Merrill 2017; Fleming & Finnegan, 2016; Fleming et al., 2017; Finnegan, 2019; Merrill et al., 2020; O'Neill et al., 2018). In writing reports, articles, books, and doing workshops, and in public advocacy I have tried hard to hold on to the truth of what people said in all its richness and diversity and situate this accurately in the wider socio-political context. I have found when we put life stories at the heart of critical research it shifts the center of gravity in educational discourse in a way that challenges many of the tidy and trim assumptions of policy and 'top-down' research. It has also led to some theoretical innovation in Irish class analysis (specifically in terms of the vital importance of everyday experience and culture in an area of scholarship which has been mainly concerned with either social mobility or political mobilization) and led to the creation of a network of like-minded researchers in other HEIs. This body of work has also had some impact on my institution.

However, my small attempts to use the research to effect changes more widely through discussion with policymakers and employers has had very little effect. Overall, I think I can say the research has explanatory power and has resulted in changes which are not completely insignificant but are fairly modest.

6   Imposed and Avoidable Constraints: Reflecting on the Rhythms of the Academy

These modest results did not surprise me as I see academic research as an exercise in 'clearing the ground' and 'praxis orientated' rather than directly emancipatory. Nevertheless, there are things that could be done differently, and I think it is important to be clear about my mistakes and blindspots because I think they disclose something important about power and research. Despite being aware of the structure and demands of the academic field (Bourdieu, 2007), I underestimated the extent to which the logic of this field of practice and its rhythms influenced the way I planned the sequence and prioritisation of various tasks and also subtly informed the way I imagined the 'afterlife' of my research. Specifically, while I gave careful attention to power issues in the conduct and analysis and was concerned with how voices were 'heard' in text, I now think I did not plan carefully enough around non-academic modes of engagement and dissemination. I want to draw on Alhadeff-Jones' (2017) very suggestive work on temporalities here and suggest that I have been set, and to an extent have chosen, to adapt to the rhythm of an accelerated university that leaves little time for 'secondary' goals and almost none for unscheduled or unplanned activity. Speaking to students and other researchers and writing for small academic audiences was the main priority and while this was valuable, I now question if I should have spent more time working with social movements and community groups during various research projects as well as exploring other forms of public dissemination besides academic books, articles and presentations. Duckworth and Smith (2017), who have done exemplary work using multiple media platforms alongside academic articles, offer a more clearly *praxis orientated strategy of engagement, communication and dissemination.* I think the key difference with my own efforts is that they developed a fully integrated dissemination strategy at the outset of their project while I saw this as something that would 'follow' the research once the research was 'mature'.

This rhythm has not only been set by the university. I am very conscious of how *funding modalities of external agencies* impact, sometimes in quite hidden ways, on research. Michael Rustin (2016) observes that the EU funded SOSTRIS project, which used biographical interviews, was critical in intent but foundered somewhat because it was simply too large. The SOSTRIS researchers did not conflate 'validity' with scale but nonetheless they took on too many interviews because of the funders' criteria. Most of my research has been funded by the EU and this is how I initially met researchers from LHBN (see Finnegan et al., 2014). We encountered similar problems in relation to the critical analysis of biographical research, in deepening participation with participants and, for me at least, in terms of non-academic engagement and dissemination.

From my perspective the rhythms of the accelerated academy and the demands of funders blunted the critical edge of research. The constraints of university life and funded research cannot be avoided but can be responded to effectively if given some forethought. Yet I think there is a knottier and deeper problem beneath this which deserves consideration. As Bourdieu (2007) never tires of pointing out, distance from practice is both necessary and dangerous. *The epistemic breaks which are a precondition of critical research are also a source of alienation.* Reflecting on this, I think it is not something that can be really 'solved' individually, rather it takes sustained dialogue within research networks on how to link critical research to collective work and social action. The individualized nature of academic research means that *unless we explicitly make alliances with groups and movements with emancipatory interests the likelihood is that research will be driven by the traditional expectations and dominant rhythm of the university.*[2]

7   In Place of a Conclusion

Critical research is, by definition, always incomplete, and these reflections are offered in the hope that I can learn from these experiences and perhaps also spark debate within the network and further afield about what critical research means. I have made a case that it involves being personally and politically reflexive, as well as cultivating sensitivity to complexity and emergence. It calls for extensive socio-historical contextualization and consciously seeking explanatory depth. Working through theory and biographical accounts in a recursive way is fundamental for arriving at this depth without overlooking complexity. But it also means exploring what praxis orientated research is and can do. It means knowing how to take distance to see more clearly and critically but also having some sense of how to collaborate with participants, communities and social movements so that research makes a difference.

Notes

1   Bhaskar's links emancipation, explanatory depth and rationality too tightly together to my mind, but this is complex and cannot be explored in this chapter.
2   In this regard it is worth noting that Duckworth and Smith (2017) were partly funded by a UK Trade Union: the University College Union.

References

Alhadeff-Jones, M. (2017). *Time and the rhythms of emancipatory education. Rethinking the temporal complexity of self and society.* Routledge.

Alheit, P. (1994). The "biographical question" as a challenge to adult education. *International Review of Education/Internationale Zeitschrift für Erziehungswissenschaft/ Revue internationale l'éducation, 40*(3), 283–298.

Alheit, P. (2005). Stories and structures: An essay on historical times, narratives and their hidden impact on adult learning. *Studies in the Education of Adults, 37*(2), 201–212.

Alheit, P., & Dausien, B. (2000). Biographicity as a basic resource of lifelong learning. In P. Alheit, J. Beck, E. Kammler, R. Taylor, & H. S. Olesen (Eds.), *Lifelong learning inside and outside schools: Collected papers of the European conference on lifelong learning* (pp. 400–422). Roskilde University.

Anderson, P. (1979). *Considerations on western Marxism*. Verso.

Apple, M. (2013). *Can education change society?* Routledge.

Archer, M. S. (2003). *Structure, agency and the internal conversation*. Cambridge University Press.

Archer, M. S. (2007). *Making our way through the world: Human reflexivity and social mobility*. Cambridge University Press.

Baker, J., Lynch, K., Cantillon, S., & Walsh, J. (2009). *Equality: From theory to action* (2nd ed.). Palgrave Macmillan

Barnett, R. (2013). *Imagining the university*. Routledge.

Bhaskar, R. (1979). *The possibility of naturalism: A philosophical critique of the contemporary human sciences*. Humanities Press.

Bhaskar, R. (2008). *A realist theory of science*. Verso.

Blumer, H. (1954). What is wrong with social theory? *American Sociological Review, 18*, 3–10.

Bourdieu, P. (2007). *Sketch for self-analysis*. University of Chicago Press.

Bourdieu, P., & Wacquant, L. J. D. (1992). *An invitation to reflexive sociology*. University of Chicago Press.

Collier, A. (1994). *Critical realism: An introduction to Roy Bhaskar's philosophy*. Verso.

Danermark, B., Ekström, M., Jakobsen, L., & Karlsson, J. C. (1997). *Explaining society: Critical realism in the social sciences*. Routledge.

Duckworth, V., & Smith, R. (2017). *Further education in England – Transforming lives and communities: Interim report*. UCU.

Finnegan, F. (2019). Opening up the 'Black box': Biographical research on working-class students' experiences and higher education in Ireland. In L. Atkins & V. Duckworth (Eds.), *Research methods for social justice and equity in education* (pp. 180–184). Bloomsbury Academic.

Finnegan, F., & Merrill, B. (2017). 'We're as good as anybody else': A comparative study of working-class university students' experiences in England and Ireland. *British Journal of Sociology of Education, 38*(3), 307–324. doi:10.1080/01425692.2015.1081054

Finnegan, F., Merrill, B., & Thunborg, C. (Eds.). (2014). *Student voices on inequalities in European higher education: Challenges for policy and practice in a time of change*. Routledge.

Fleming, T., & Finnegan, F. (2014). A critical journey towards lifelong learning: Including non-traditional students in university. In A. Loxley, J. Walsh, & A. Seery (Eds.), *Higher education in Ireland: Practices, policies and possibilities* (pp. 146–158). Palgrave Macmillan.

Fleming, T., Loxley, A., & Finnegan, F. (2017). *Access and participation in Irish higher education*. Palgrave.

Fraser, N. (2013). *Fortunes of feminism: From state-managed capitalism to neoliberal crisis*. Verso.

Freire, P. (1972). *Pedagogy of the oppressed*. Penguin.

Harré, R., & Secord, P. F. (1972). *The explanation of social behaviour*. Blackwell.

Honneth, A. (2007). *Disrespect: The normative foundations of critical theory*. Polity Press.

Horkheimer, M. (2002). *Critical theory: Selected essays*. Continuum.

Lyotard, J. F. (1979). *The postmodern condition: A report on knowledge*. Manchester University Press.

Marx, K. (1888). *Theses of Feuerbach*. https://www.marxists.org/archive/marx/works/1845/theses/theses.htm

Merrill, B. (1999). *Gender, change and identity: Mature women students in universities*. Ashgate Publishing.

Merrill, B., Finnegan, F., O'Neill, J., & Revers, S. (2020). "When it comes to what employers are looking for, I don't think I'm it for a lot of them': Class and capitals in, and after, higher education. *Studies in Higher Education, 45*(1), 163–175.

Merrill, B., & West, L. (2009). *Using biographical methods in social research*. Sage.

O'Neill, J., Merrill, B., Finnegan, F., & Revers, S. (2018). Intersecção das desigualdades no ensino superior: teorização de classe e género através de uma perspetiva feminista e o olhar de Bourdieu. In A. Fragoso (Ed.), *Estudantes Não-tradicionais no Ensino Superior* (pp. 160–180). CINEP.

Rustin, M. (2016, March 2–5). *What are the objects of biographical and narrative research? Are we really generating resources of hope?* Keynote presented at ESREA LHBN Conference Resources of Hope.

Sayer, R. A. (1992). *Method in social science: A realist approach* (2nd ed.). Routledge.

Scott, D. (2010). *Education, epistemology and critical realism*. Routledge.

Wainwright, H. (2009). *Reclaim the state: Experiments in popular democracy* (rev. ed.). Seagull Books.

West, L. (1996). *Beyond fragments: Adults, motivation, and higher education: A biographical analysis*. Taylor & Francis.

Williams, R. (1983). *Keywords: A vocabulary of culture and society*. Oxford University Press.

Williams, R. (2005). *Culture and materialism*. Verso.

Wright, E. O. (2010). *Envisioning real utopias*. Verso.

CHAPTER 11

Storytelling, Culture, and Indigenous Methodology

Adrienne S. Chan

Abstract

This chapter examines the role of Indigenous storytelling as a method and an episte-mology, with an explicit connection to land-based work, community, and a sustained a process for healing with Indigenous peoples. The chapter describes important personal insights for the researcher, and the development of a better understanding of relationships with youth and young adults within the context of the storytelling process. Storytelling can be a way of reclaiming identity and reclaiming one's own stories, rather than being defined and storied by hegemonic forces.

Storytelling has been valued in traditional ways of knowing in Indigenous cultures and is seen as a primary means to pass on knowledge over generations. Through research on the resilience of Indigenous youth and their relationship to culture, identity, and land, there are stories created and recreated. The research *is* the story and it makes a difference to how Indigenous youth and adults learn experience their lives. The particular focus of this work is with Indigenous youth, young adults, and their ability to remain healthy and hopeful, rather than despairing, and at a loss regarding identity and belonging.

Keywords

Indigenous peoples – storytelling – land-based – identity – healing

1 Introduction

I am very proud to be Indigenous. You know, when I was growing up, I was not very proud, because I thought being First Nations, you had no culture and no language. And I grew up with that because my parents were descendants of Residential Schools, so I struggled with that. So, I was a woman who lived off the land. I had to learn to hunt and fish and grow food for my family .... I learned at a very young age what it took to live off the land .... (YCP07)

In Canada, Indigenous peoples have valued storytelling for centuries, as a way of conveying history and knowledge through their families and communities. The young woman, quoted above, shared her thoughts on culture and living off the land – which was common to the narratives that we heard in our research with communities. Storytelling was, and is, foundational to a way of life and has occurred over many generations as a way of sharing.

In this chapter, I describe a project working with Indigenous youth and young adults, whereby storytelling was an element of regaining a sense of belonging and identity, connection to the land, and a sustained a process for healing. I also describe Indigenous methodologies and how working with stories brought important personal insights and fostered my own development as a researcher working within a community.

Storytelling is a process of reclaiming the story, to own the story, rather than be defined or storied by others. Colonisers have historically told and shaped the stories of Indigenous peoples. The young woman, quoted above, tells her story, in her own terms, as a point of reclaiming her pride in being an Indigenous woman. As researchers, working with Indigenous youth and young adults, our task is facilitating the process of stories, and how individuals shape new narratives in their own way, based on their sense of culture. This also means that, as researchers, we learn about the storytelling process. As researchers, we do not own these stories, they are owned by the narrators. Storytelling, in this way, is a cultural and political act.

2   The Storyteller and I

My father was a great storyteller, but I was unable to think about the meaning of his stories until I was an adult; then I began to understand that his stories were about life learning. He used metaphors where meanings were not immediately apparent to me. For example, he used to talk about a bundle of chopsticks that could not be broken if they were held together. This story was about strength in numbers and unity. The chopstick is thin, often made of bamboo, and fragile. This type of metaphor is used to shape values and cultural learning in familiar places, everyday discourse, at home, and in the community.

Metaphors are ways of understanding social and educational contexts and help us to understand lived experiences, when the "existing language is not capable of adequately describing the topic term or the listener does not possess the necessary language to understand the topic term" (Jensen, 2006, p. 9). With the image of the chopsticks in a bundle, my father was, in his own way, using a metaphoric pedagogy, because we knew what he meant as family unity.

When I started this journey, I thought that I was not a natural storyteller, and yet I was surrounded by stories from my family. The process of storytelling was a path of discovery and learning activated during my doctoral studies, when I was asked: "What was the journey that brought you here?" In order to articulate the story, I had to trust that I could find the words, and work with the knowledge that storytelling already had a place in my history. In this process, I found that sense of the story through the support of my family, mentors, and colleagues. This connection is about the relationships of past, present, and future. Relationships are always there, in the research process and in storytelling. My understanding of storytelling has expanded through my current research, where stories are about experiences and learning, and also the place to teach a living history, about lived lives, and to make "ancestral and contemporary connections to place" (Corntassel, Chaw-win-is, & T'lakwadzi, 2009, p. 137), which may include cultural, community, land, and historical sites.

In this chapter, I describe how my thinking evolved about storytelling, and how the research team engaged in storytelling from our different backgrounds. We consider our relationships working with Indigenous youth, young adults, their stories, and their identity. These relationships with story are different starting points in the research process and a place to re-imagine open ways to relate to culture and belonging. One of the lessons learned was to incorporate the spirit and the heart while telling a story (Archibald, 2018), being aware that the process of telling engages us in connection to family, to heart, and to what matters. This makes the story alive and true. A fragment of such an embodied story is enough to trigger another story because of this connection to the whole and the feelings it evokes. The process is an ongoing one; there is no necessary logic, coherence, or ending to a story. It is there to teach something; it is more than recounting events or feelings to another person. The process touches others, in their bodies and souls, and it transforms the narrator as well.

Moreover, the storytelling process can be a way of reclaiming identity and the story, rather than being defined and storied by hegemonic forces. Colonialism dispossessed the Indigenous peoples of their culture and disconnected them from their ecologies: land, language, and community (Alfred, 2009). The result was social and political alienation and turmoil. Therefore, storytelling is part of healing and a means for renewed engagement with one's own roots.

For the purposes of the chapter, I use the term Indigenous; some of the narrators refer to themselves as First Nations or Aboriginal. The chapter is limited by the complexity and broad description of the storytelling process, and the important context of Indigenous peoples and storytelling. Furthermore, the chapter is written keeping the Indigenous youth and community at the forefront. From my positionality, I am aware of the potential coloniality and power dynamics of myself as the researcher.

3   Indigenous Methodology and Storytelling

> Indigenous storytelling is connected to our homelands and is crucial to
> the cultural and political resurgence of Indigenous nations. (Corntassel,
> Chaw-win-is, & T'lakwadzi, 2009, p. 137)

The purpose of the research was to understand and build resilience with Indigenous youth as a means of suicide prevention. A key element to the research
was sharing and storytelling. The research documents what interventions were
useful in keeping youth, and young adults, healthy, while keeping the integrity of Indigenous perspectives and principles. The research team, comprising
Indigenous and non-Indigenous researchers and community collaborators,
worked with land-based activities in the Indigenous communities. Youth suicide, health and mental health issues are indicators. At the same time, the project meant thinking differently about suicide, health, resilience, and mental
wellness by engaging in Indigenous perspectives. Ultimately the research team
worked towards fostering and maintaining wellness in a cultural context, with
the explicit understanding that community health agencies and Indigenous
elders and chiefs will participate fully as partners. Indeed, Indigenous communities set priorities for us.

This research is grounded in Indigenous methods (Kovach, 2009; Smith,
2012; Wilson, 2008), which means we are working with Indigenous peoples
rather than on them. We are aware of orientalism (Said, 1978) and the danger
of exoticising Indigenous cultures or claiming objectivity. Kovach (2009) suggests two principles in taking Indigenous methods: first, the approach cannot
be seen as taking something away from Indigenous peoples, and is meant to be
"accountable to Indigenous community standards on research so as to honour
the tribal worldview" (Kovach, 2009, p. 29); second, researchers recognise that
Western and Indigenous epistemologies are different in philosophy, ideology,
and method. These differences challenge both Indigenous and non-Indigenous scholars and researchers to find a balance and work with insider-outsider
relationships to the research.

Storytelling is part of Indigenous methodology: "Stories hold within them
knowledges while simultaneously signifying relationships. In oral tradition,
stories can never be decontextualised from the teller" (Kovach, 2009, p. 94).
Smith situates this within learning: "stories, values, practices and ways of
knowing continue to inform Indigenous pedagogies" (2012, p. 15).

To understand and use Indigenous methods, we are aware of our colonial
history, the need to decolonise ourselves as researchers (McAslin, 2005; Smith,
2012), and to engage in re-learning and new learning. This means our assumptions and values are challenged. It has been troubling and powerful for me to

learn more about myself, my challenges, and what I need to do in order to work with integrity as a researcher (Chan, 2017). An example of this, is with the struggle I have when some Indigenous researchers welcome me as an ally, while others reject me, as bearing colonialism and hegemony. As a non-Indigenous person, I must own the part I play, between colonialism and efforts to decolonise.

Indigenous epistemologies are relational and ecological; there is no single individual, or mind, self-determined, separated, and autonomous from its ecology, which for us means land, community, and ancestors. A recognition of these relationships is key to research work, which is about relationships, ceremony, and forms of cultural practice (Wilson, 2008). Therefore, by working with Indigenous peoples we are challenged in our deepest presuppositions, as we were educated in Western countries and traditions. Using Indigenous research methods, we intend to make a difference in people's lives and communities; we are not merely extracting or analysing information, but we work with the members of the community on community driven issues. We aim to decolonise the past and address the future. The development of trusting relationships with elders and youth requires us to meet regularly to work through and discuss the aims of our work together.

4   Indigenous Youth, Ecology, and Story

> I was just thinking, what is not a connection to the land? Because everything that we are, is the land, and that's who we are. Whatever food is there, wherever we are, is the food that's there for us; whatever medicine is there, is the medicines that we use. (YCP08)

This young man speaks of the land and the connection to living. Most of our youths live in what is known as Stó:lō Nation territory, and they entered the project through our communication with community members. Stó:lō people are the 'people of the river', and storytelling is a tradition. Storytelling was used to document the impact of our land-based activities. Over more than three years, we are actively engaging with young adults and youth; many of them were part of youth groups in their community. They may also be invited to participate by elders, parents, or youth workers, who work regularly with youth. The young people were not necessarily 'at risk', although their communities had been affected by youth suicide. The research team proposed to explore with them the cultural narratives and forces that shaped their lives. The young people shared with us what they wanted to do, in order to reconnect with the land, their culture, and the elders.

Youth and young adults participated in many activities, with ongoing learning. We saw changes in them as they grew more comfortable with certain land activities, and more open to talk and tell their stories. We came to understand that storytelling was pivotal to the process and felt a need to ascribe value to it. So, we engaged as a team in understanding storytelling and the nature of story (Archibald, 2008).

As a team, we were going on hikes and 'on land' activities with youths, learning about such things as the importance of the cedar tree, or Indigenous medicines and plants, and the meaning of cultural practices and heritage. All the activities were led by community partners and youth workers rather than researchers. In this regard, we were co-learners with the youth. Activities later expanded to drum making, drumming, working with cedar wood, storytelling from elders, and ceremonies regarding fishing. There is, for example, a salmon ceremony that involves a freshly caught salmon. This represents the harvest (in Western terms) and is considered a recognition of the gift of salmon from the river. Fishing is fundamental to the survival of Indigenous communities in the Pacific Northwest of North America.

Youths would often reflect on the activities they participated in, offering their thoughts about the land and their relationship to it:

> I, too, am getting better at being connected with the land, in the sense of learning the oral history, and the teachings that are connected with the land, because I don't know it. I've been told those stories many times, listened to an elder, and heard the stories. (YCP14)

These reflections came out regularly during our talking circles, a traditional oral practice. The circle is a cultural element that the youth are familiar with and participate in at their home communities. In working with the youths, they were aware of our need to 'document' the process. However, no notes were taken in these meetings. After our meetings and activities, the research team would journal our reflections.

We document in a reflective way since we are aware that after colonialism, fears of cultural appropriation are real. Stories are owned by the youths. We did not take the stories from them; they were shared with their permission. This was discussed at the outset of our work with the youth. Even when they shared their stories with us, they had to decide and state if they wanted to share them beyond the group. As well, the discussions were led by an Indigenous facilitator, recognised as part of the community, and with an established trusting relationship. It is common in Indigenous communities to have someone who has established relationships to work with youth. This is part of the collective value that is given to elders and youth workers who are already known by families.

We gathered many stories told by the youths while engaged in hiking, camping, and being on the land. The anecdotes and stories were mainly oral and recounted in memory, while some of them were documented in video and transcribed, with permission. In the third year of the project, we decided to engage in digital storytelling, working with a specific group of youths and adults on a voluntary basis.

Over the whole project, we came to identify some aspects that seem to have a role in building strength and resilience in these youths and in the larger group. For example, learning about traditional cultural practices sensitised all of us to take care of each other in our relationships as co-researchers, and youths to take care of each other in their shared activities.

5   Culture and Wellness

> I think the culture and everything is so beautiful, and how we're all working together in a collective. And the other thing I like too ... what matters is what you do, and the First Nations way is who are you, where are you from. (YCP04)

Culture is viewed as a fundamental resource for Indigenous communities. While the notion of cultural continuity and identity is debated by some, a number of scholars see it as valuable, in the effort to revive and preserve the connection between past, present, and future. More specifically, Chandler and Lalonde (2009) connect cultural continuity, (i.e. the preservation of traditions, the land, beliefs, and language) with suicide prevention. The premise of this work is that knowing and practicing one's culture is connected to wellness and this is the basis of cultural continuity and suicide prevention. Retaining and strengthening cultural roots and practices is viewed as a means to maintaining community culture and strength.

Carlson (2010) and Chandler and Lalonde (1998) suggest that cultural connection and continuity are key in preventing self-harm among Indigenous youths; other studies highlight the importance of self determination (Kirmayer, Gone, & Moses, 2014) and self-governance, use of traditional/original language, and re-discovering everyday customs that may have been lost due to cultural annihilation and genocide. Re-learning customs and culture receive concerted efforts by Indigenous communities, by investing in elders and cultural facilitators to promote the acknowledgement of a shared history and develop individual and collective identities (Kirmayer, MacDonald, & Brass, 2001; Kulis, Robbins, Baker, Denetsosie, & Deschine Parkhust, 2016). In this framework, cultural continuity is connected to a sense of belonging (Lieben-berg, Ikeda, & Wood, 2015), which is intended to contrast centuries of oppression and degradation.

Many elders in the communities we work with, are survivors of residential schools; where they were placed, as children, into schools for the purpose of eliminating their language and culture. The government of the time (1870s to 1990s in Canada, depending on the provinces) intended on completing assimilation through policy, and to punish individuals, families, and communities who practiced their cultural rituals and traditions (Dorrell, 2009; Truth and Reconciliation Commission of Canada, 2015). This was 'cultural genocide' for Indigenous peoples (Crichlow, 2002; Davidson, 2012). In order for healing to take place, it is widely accepted among the Indigenous communities that we engage in learning about culture and the land as a part of reclaiming Indigenous community, identity, and strength. It may be a complex and disputed truth, but our experience has revealed this is part of an understanding of cultural continuity.

The youth in our program live on reserve and therefore are mainly in contact with their Indigenous peers and friends. They talk about culture as they have participated in our project, and they sometimes state a lack of connection to the culture of their Nation; for example, a boy told us he had never spent time with an elder before, nor understood the role of ancestors. In the context of land-based activities, continuity means to re-discover and reinterpret the traditional notion of the land. Land is viewed as a primary connection, because the land provides food, water, housing, the idea of spirit, and connection to our own spirituality. This is how – in the traditional view – land provides culture; as such, it is a fundamental part of the traditional teachings of Indigenous peoples.

6   Understanding the Storytelling Process

Archibald (2018) recounts a pedagogical story for us to hear and begin new ways to see. In a story work workshop, we prepared to think differently about stories in the context of culture. Archibald (2008, 2018) tells us of Mr. Magpie and Mr. Crow, a children's story, where each bird seeks something for their community, but for different reasons, hence with different results. The lesson is about intentions, expectations, jealousy, and learning respect and rules. Stories can evoke different memories, ideas, and emotions. They would be told by elders to convey a lesson, so listeners can make sense of the story and use it in their own lives. The significance of the story is rooted in its origins, as it was told by the ancestors. In order to learn anything from it, we must be ready to listen, attend to our feelings, thoughts, and responses. Archibald (2008) also reminds us that the story is not a tidy narrative with a beginning, middle, and end.

Storytelling is situated within Indigenous epistemology and pedagogy, where knowledge has been passed on through oral traditions for centuries. For a non-Indigenous person, it is almost impossible to understand what this means, until we work on this aspect ourselves, in concrete relationships with the Indigenous peoples. The use of metaphors, animal stories, and pictures means that stories are told and understood quite differently than in Western pedagogy. I learned to accept stories as evolving, meant to help us developing our hearts, minds, and open ourselves to different ways of knowing. Storytelling sustains learning, remembering, understanding our selves, understanding others and the world: a reflexive, embodied, slow paced process that requires persistence and caring (Archibald, 2008).

As a research team, we prepared ourselves for this task by reading and taking workshops on storytelling and training on digital storytelling. We were challenged to think about, tell stories, and make sense of stories differently. I had some personal work to do. I considered my fears about telling a truthful story: would I be judged or believed? Preparation is as much a part of the journey as the storytelling itself, an activity extending beyond our thoughts or intellect. This includes developing trust, empathy, and self-understanding.

The nature of the story is grounded in a reflective ongoing space which is iterative. Past events become salient in the present when remembered. There is a flow of interaction and reconsideration; the process of discovery is key to the story work (West, 2001) and subjectivity takes precedence over objectivity. Discovery is neither Western nor Indigenous: it is a term that researchers might use to mark the human capacity to reconnect to knowledge, recognise and remember.

Indigenous principles of working with Indigenous peoples and storytelling typically refer to respect, reverence, responsibility, and reciprocity (Kovach, 2009), which are foundational to many Indigenous peoples (Carlson et al., 2018). Acknowledgment means taking time for valuing relationships which are a result of our work and the narrative. Indigenous story work is explicitly grounded in family, generations, community, nation, as well as the connection between the intellectual, spiritual, physical, and emotional (Archibald, 2008, 2018). This may be compatible with some forms of Western storytelling, when narratives are embodied and contextualised in cultural history, such as in the feminist tradition of exploring women's everyday lives (e.g. Last, 2009; Steedman, 1987).

The historic, oppressive, and colonial context has led to the annihilation of Indigenous peoples' cultures in Canada (Truth and Reconciliation Commission, 2015). This history suggests that the new generations have limited ways to connect with the past. Some elders say that knowledge was 'put to sleep' when North American laws established residential schools for Indigenous children and placed them in care away from their families. Indigenous languages were eliminated, but some survivors of residential schools were able to reconstruct their memories and work with stories (Archibald, 2018).

A powerful reconnection occurs in relationships, when young people can access memories through elders and knowledge keepers who are familiar with the community history (Archibald, 2008) and the land. Indigenous stories rely on the collective as well as individual, the method is contextual and based on stimulating other stories, asking questions, and discussing issues. No story is isolated from the whole. Translation from traditional languages (e.g. Halq'eméylem, the language of the Stó:lō Peoples) is another key to rebuilding culture and making connections to the past. Language carries memories and history (Treuer, 2008).

Hence, Indigenous storytelling often begins with stories from elders and parents (Archibald, 2018). As with my father, it may be an everyday experience, but some parents may have to regain the ability to tell, if this was lost in the process of forced assimilation. The lessons from these stories are, like my father's story, not always obvious, as they use metaphors. We heard a cultural story of Coyote, a kind of trickster, enchanter, and magician, whose symbolism refers to an alchemic way of interpretation and making sense of the world (Archibald, 2008, 2018). By 'alchemic', I mean to signify that knowledge is more than material: it is also about the spirit, mind, and heart, that combine to create something new. The story of Coyote is also about seeing: he loses his eyes and has to find new ways of seeing (my interpretation) through grief and struggle. This metaphor of seeing is a meaningful lesson within Indigenous culture.

In our group gatherings with youth, we often started by talking about the land and what it means to us. Some participants began to recognise their connection to the land and its influence on them. In hikes and camps, most storytelling took place in groups, during and after an activity, such as working with cedar wood or walking by the river. These occasional and spontaneous stories took place throughout the project and are still ongoing. We were always ready to ask and listen about their connection to the land, and they responded in various ways, as in these three examples:

> ... I wasn't that much connected to the land until they got me singing and drumming. That's how I met all my friends and started connecting to the land even more. (CBP01)

> ... I feel connected to the land by canoe pulling, being involved with smokehouse and stuff like travelling, singing for the new ones, and always living there. I think there is many more stuff to learn about the land. I

don't think I've learned very much about the trees, ancestral land and the history. I feel connected with it by being out on the river fishing, catching a lot of fish, and I enjoy having fish and giving back to the river. When I was in school, I liked to carve, make carvings, paint onto the carvings. (CBP02)

... I think I, too, am getting better at being connected with the land, in the sense of learning the oral history and the teachings that are connected with the land because I don't know it. I've been told those stories so many times, listened to an elder and hear the stories but it's not being retained. But I just think that having an open mind, like ___ said, going to an elder and learning from their teachings, values that each elder brings .... (YCP15)

These narratives make explicit connections to their thoughts while they are engaged in activities. The narrators are generating their own interpretations of their experiences. Occasionally stories are not only told through words or oral history; they can be told by songs or drumming, carving or weaving. They teach us about our kinship with the mountains, trees, and the land.

7   Digital Stories of Belonging

Our workshop on digital storytelling was aimed at producing a digital story and led by an Indigenous facilitator. We started each day in a talking circle, considering a reflexive question, as is common to Indigenous ways of sharing. We then chose a story of our own and worked individually to record it, composing music, adding images, pictures, and words. Finally, the story was converted to a short video. All the participants, nine youth and four adults developed their work individually at first. Youth worked along side of each other. Some worked together in pairs or as a group after their initial work. Digital storytelling is intentionally built through a personal and interactive process, using technology to engage and assist participants in learning differently (Behmer, 2005).

Four youth completed their stories for sharing; one of them played his own guitar music for the soundtrack. The adults who attended the session also produced and shared their digital story, including myself. Youth and adults commented on the value of the workshop and added that they would have benefited from elders participating and modeling storytelling in the workshop. To enforce the principle that the stories belong entirely to the participants, we asked permission to share them, and all of the four youth participants who completed the video, gave their permission. The videos are three minutes long, so the written material is short and evocative; to understand it, we need to connect words with the audio-visual parts.

An example: One young man recounted how he spent his time on the reserve. This story is about celebrating togetherness and reconnecting to the community. It gives an idea of 'relational ecology', which is consistent with Indigenous epistemology. This young man lives on a small reserve of 300 people, a land occupied and owned solely by Indigenous peoples, which is referred to as the "rez".

> ... Community events – you get to hang out with your cousins and do any of the activities. Enjoy their company while it lasts. House gathering – this category is for the cousins you consider – like they are almost siblings. You go to their house and watch tv and play video games ... [we can] find remote locations for fort building. This is fun when you are able to make plans with your favourite rez friends or cousins. (DST PA)

Telling the story, this young man celebrates enlarged family (collective) bonds: the cousins are "almost siblings". By choosing these simple and normal activities for his digital story, he signals that they are important. Most of his narrative refers to an ecology of relationships. He refers to being in the woodlands, the sounds of nature, and the modern sounds of rap music – all part of his living on the reserve.

The second example is about a young man and intergenerational family support and protection, as well as fears and vulnerability:

> ... I was laying on the couch one night and I was crying .... I said that I was afraid of being homeless. She (my Mom) reassured me that I would never be homeless .... It was only a few months after this that she told me I would be living with my Dad. My dad had just moved back in with my grandpa after my grandma passed away. So I would be living with him too. I loved this idea. I love my grandpa to death so that was awesome. (DST PJ)

Intergenerational bonds between family men are palpable here. His story began with his mother but evolved into talking about his father and grandfather. His sense of belonging is connected with a feeling of solace and not being alone. The visual for this part of the story is a photo of the young man, his father and grandfather, wearing fatigues (i.e. green-brown camouflage wear), sitting on a log, and holding their rifles. They would go hunting together as a family activity. The story of this young man resonated with others in the workshop, who thought about their parents and grandparents, about historical loss of family members (e.g. mother in this case), and how support evolved from the 'doing' activities together. This evoked tears in some of the participants.

All of the shared stories in the workshop are resonant with ecological land based, and potentially healing, connections to family, community, and friends. The workshop did this in two ways, by working on the stories in the workshop individually and together, and by completing the story. Their writing, thinking and oral process was talked about at the end of the day. The completion of the digital story was a source of pride, by doing something in a new way.

In the final reflective circle, we talked about how the workshop affected all of us. The young adults and youth said that it was good to share their story, making connections among us, and being able to take their own story away with them, to share with others. This gave them control over their own story. One youth posted his story on YouTube. Another was going to share it with his family immediately. We believe that the workshop was a shared giving, where the participants went away with a sense of their own power, ability to learn, and express themselves uniquely.

8   Concluding Thoughts

Storytelling can be a way of reclaiming the self and a decolonising process. Storytelling allowed us to enforce a shared, intergenerational, and culture-bond process among the youth, with adults, elders, and within the larger community. In this chapter, I have described how working with culture obliges the researcher to interrogate herself and that the process was informed by Indigenous epistemologies. I believe that in this project, storytellers took ownership of their words in the creation of narratives. The process seemed to change self-perceptions, or at least the capacity of participants to share and reflect. Based on what we experienced ourselves in the training, land activities, and workshops, we started to feel a building sense of connection to each other and to the community.

A relevant issue in cultural work is that we academics are not experts in any way. Instead, the real expertise lies with the youth and their elders in the community. Academics are knowledge seekers, so can bring a difference, especially if we do this with the permission and agreement of Indigenous communities. This kind of dialogue requires searching for a respectful, reciprocal, and collaborative relationship. Relationships are key in the work that we are engaged in, while becoming and working in Indigenous communities. Relationships are the reality and the fundament of lived experience of Indigenous peoples (Wilson, 2008). Thus, the story could only be created as a result of the relationships we have with elders, other youth, and the research team. Elders represent the roots of the storytelling process because they model how and why to tell the stories, by telling stories in circle, by using generative metaphors and symbols, like in using animal stories. In the process described, researchers also influence the storytelling, because of their positionality and by their active presence in the room or land where the stories are told. They are not neutral spectators, they tell stories too, and by suggesting new ways of doing – for example, using technology in the digital storytelling workshop – they bring discontinuity in the process.

This project and the storytelling process remains ongoing. As it has evolved, we have changed our expectations and interpretation of our work with these youth, their culture and sense of belonging. The premise at the centre of this work is that (re)connecting to our environment is part of our identity and belonging. Stories about the land and family bonds can support a stronger sense of belonging and wellbeing within the cultural context. Hopefully, this will also strengthen a sense of freedom: when you have real roots, you know that you always know where home is.

I respectfully acknowledge that these descriptors, perspectives of meaning, and interpretations are mine, as a researcher, and these may not be the ways in which the participants would describe the same process. Central to the work here described is an Indigenous methodology which means acting to decolonise rather than colonise. I am aware of the work I had to do, to set aside my cultural and biographical roots and habits, to be able to learn from another epistemological perspective. The researcher's words and interpretations of a story, or situation, might be given to the participants in order to bring the cultural dialogues to another level. However, this would only be done with a trusting communication relationship that would allow for such feedback or interpretation. Metalevel communication occurred, but was not part of the explicit project goals or analysis. It is important for us to maintain relationships over analysis. The struggle to avoid colonisation is not an easy one.

I conclude by writing "all my relations", a traditional Indigenous phrase used to acknowledge the connections we have with each other, as parts of universal relationships, and having reciprocal responsibility (King, 1990). The phrase suggests the ecology of our interactions.

Acknowledgement

This research was made possible by funding from the Canadian Institutes Health Research Grant #33785.

References

Alfred, G. T. (2009). Colonialism and state dependency. *Journal of Aboriginal Health,* *5*(2), 42–60.

Archibald, J. (2008). *Indigenous storywork: Educating the heart, mind, body, and spirit.* University of British Columbia Press.

Archibald, J. (2018, January 15). *Storyworks, storytelling.* Workshop at Stó:lō Nation, Chilliwack, B.C., Canada.

Behmer, S. (2005). *Literature review: Digital storytelling: Examining the process with middle school students* [Unpublished literature review]. Iowa State University. http://citeseerx.ist.psu.edu/viewdoc/download?doi=10.1.1.452.6410&rep= rep1&type=pdf

Carlson, K. T. (2010). *The power of place, the problem of time: Aboriginal identity and historical consciousness in the cauldron of colonialism* (2nd ed.). University of Toronto Press.

Carlson, K. T., Lutz, J. S., Schaepe, D. M., & Naxaxalhts'i (McHalsie, A. S.) (Eds.). (2018). *Towards a new ethnohistory.* University of Manitoba Press.

Chan, A. S. (2017, March). *The decolonizing and the Indigenizing discourse* [Paper presentation]. European Society for Research on the Education of Adults Conference, Aarhus University, Copenhagen, Denmark.

Chandler, M. J., & Lalonde, C. (1998). Cultural continuity as a hedge against suicide in Canada's First Nations. *Transcultural Psychiatry, 35*(2), 191–219.

Chandler, M. J., & Lalonde, C. (2008). Cultural continuity as a protective factor against suicide in First Nations youth. *Horizons – A Special Issue on Aboriginal Youth, Hope or Heartbreak: Aboriginal Youth and Canada's* Future, 10(1), 68–72.

Corntassel, J., Chaw-win-is, & T'lakwadzi. (2009). Indigenous storytelling, truth-telling, and community approaches to reconciliation. *English Studies in Canada, 35*(1), 137–159.

Crichlow, W. (2002). Western colonization as disease: Native adoption & cultural genocide. *Critical Social Work, 3*(1), 1–14.

Davidson, L. (2012). *Cultural genocide.* Rutgers University Press.

Dorrell, M. (2009). From reconciliation to reconciling: Reading what "we now recognize" in the Government of Canada's 2008 residential schools apology. *English Studies in Canada, 35*(1), 27–45. doi:10.1353/esc.0/0165

Jensen, D. F. N. (2006). Metaphors as a bridge to understanding educational and social contexts. *International Journal of Qualitative Methods, 5*(1), 2–17.

King, T. (1990). *All my relations.* McClellend & Stewart.

Kirmayer, L. J., Brass, G. M., Holton, T., Paul, K., Simpson, C., & Tait, C. (2007). *Suicide among Aboriginal people in Canada.* Aboriginal Healing Foundation.

Kirmayer, L. J., Gone, J. P., & Moses, J. (2014). Rethinking historical trauma. *Transcultural Psychiatry, 51*(3), 299–319.

Kirmayer, L. J., MacDonald, M. E., & Brass, G. M. (Eds.). (2001). *The mental health of Indigenous people.* McGill University.

Kovach, M. (2009). *Indigenous methodologies.* University of Toronto Press.

Kulis, S. S., Robbins, D. E., Baker, T. M., Denetsosie, S., & Deschine Parkhurst, N. A. (2016). A latent class analysis of urban American Indian youth identities. *Cultural Diversity and Ethnic Minority Psychology, 22*(2), 215–228.

Last, N. (2009). *Nella Last's war: The Second World War diaries of housewife 49* (R. Broad & S. Fleming, Eds.). Profile Books.

Liebenberg, L., Ikeda, J., & Wood, M. (2015). "It's just part of my culture": Understanding language and land in the resilience processes of Aboriginal youth. In L. L. Theron & M. Ungar (Eds.), *Youth resilience and culture: Commonalities and complexities* (pp. 105–116). Springer Netherlands.

McAslin, W. D. (2005). *Justice as healing: Indigenous ways.* Living Justice Press.

Said, E. W. (1978). *Orientalism.* Pantheon Books.

Smith, L. T. (2012). *Decolonizing methodologies* (2nd ed.). Zed Press.

Steedman, C. K. (1987). *Landscape for a good woman.* Rutgers University Press.

Treuer, A. (2008). *Living our language: Ojibwe tales and oral histories.* Minnesota Historical Society Press.

Truth and Reconciliation Commission of Canada. (2015). *Calls to action.* Government of Canada.

West, L. (2001). *Doctors on the edge.* Free Association Books.

Wilson, S. (2008). *Research is ceremony.* Fernwood Press.

CHAPTER 12

Profession Reimagined: Tackling Adult Educators' Alienation through Multimodal Ways of Knowing

Gaia Del Negro

Abstract

How can an auto/biographical approach be used in a group setting to bring about more holistic and complex ways of knowing for professionals in education?

Originating from a PhD study, the chapter presents my own journey of non/learning about professional knowing and becoming. Ideas of alienation from knowing are contrasted with feminist approaches and psychoanalysis that bring a more relational perspective and celebrate messiness in our learning lives, not least as professionals supporting others to learn.

A relational aesthetic auto/biographical imagination is proposed as the epistemological framework – emerging, recursively, from doing the research – as my personal take on Gregory Bateson's ecology of mind (1972) applied to biographical formative research with adults. I present the story of Federico, a teacher trainer and researcher, in a dialogue with my own, to illuminate the epistemological and affective learning, albeit as a struggle, I gained from the experience.

I invite others to draw on artful languages, and dialogue, to enrich research and education practice with professionals to develop different ways of knowing. I propose that crossing binaries, between conscious and unconscious, body and mind, cognitive and emotional knowledge, self and the world may help adult educators to draw on their whole personality, and flourish.

Keywords

adult educators – knowing – alienation – auto/biography – multimodality

Tangled Clump

We don't know when
We don't know why
We don't know where

Regular rivulets: 14066
Infernal skein, non-direction
The swallowing swamp that hides it from sight

It fakes, abstracting me
Illusory, the white

Knowledge?
Placate anxiety and then disperse it.
(Del Negro, 2018)

1 A Research Project and a Quest

Bringing the researcher's own life and orientation into the research framework
has become a key methodological focus for biographical approaches to social
research, informed in the 1980s by feminist critiques of positivistic claims of
objectivity (Merrill & West, 2009). Feminist scholars rejected assumptions
of emotional detachment and political neutrality, to be attained by means of
abstract theories and objective methods, in favour of a different set of presuppositions that include recognition of the researcher's interests and power
(Maynard & Purvis, 2013). Self-disclosure is both ethically and politically motivated: the personal is political, in feminist terms. It is also a measure against
alienation, as I argue in these pages. In biographical studies, it is now acknowledged that our choice of topic as researchers, and our ways of posing questions
tend to be deeply rooted in the fabric of ourselves. This awareness forms what
we might call an auto/biographical imagination (Miller, 2007).

My own auto/biographical imagination, initially quite stiff, developed
throughout my PhD participatory research (Del Negro, 2018) about professional knowing and becoming. This chapter is a story about my own non/learn-
ing journey. My main finding is that connecting knowing to our lives through
multimodal knowing and intersemiotic translation (Campbell & Vidal, 2019),
may be an antidote to dis-attention, dis-embodiment, and anaesthetisation,
the main symptoms of alienation in adult and professional lives, not least the
researcher's. I want to show how a method of auto/biographically informed
cooperative inquiry, can nurture the capacity to think in stories (Bateson, 1976),
connecting cognition to feeling, emotion, sensation, and to bring all of our
selves, and senses, reflexively, into the picture. I will outline how I learned this,
together with my participants, and how this framework might be enhanced by
multimodal knowing.

The prequel to this doctoral journey sees me as a performative student in organisational studies, and a successful young professional in adult training in Italy. There is a theme of distancing from knowing and idealising knowledge, linked with class issues and fragmentations in my family. I initially set out to conduct a more traditionally detached study, but as my research unfolded it also became a quest for meaning and for my own sense of self as a professional researcher, adult educator, and learner. Radical constructivism and operative epistemology (Fabbri & Munari, 1990; Maturana, 1990) posit knower and known as parts of the same circular ongoing process, suggesting that both are constructed and "revealed" by action and inter-action in one and the same hermeneutic circle of knowing and becoming. In this light, the "/" (slash) in the auto/biographical approach (Merrill & West, 2009) points in the direction of a constructivist posture of knowing as living, life as research. The chapter is also grounded in ecological assumptions (Bateson, 1972) locating "mind" in nature, in interdependencies, most of which are not accessed by consciousness. Artistic mediation can help illuminate "the systemic nature of mind" (Bateson, 1972, p. 145), skill and performance, offering professionals a wider view.

This constructivist/systemic epistemological framework and the encounter with auto/biography as practiced in Canterbury, UK, pushed me to increasingly put myself into the picture, and take a more relational stance, while struggling to be changed in the process (Maturana, 1990). I will start by offering some theoretical concepts around alienation, relational aesthetics, and how the relationship to knowing shapes adult learning. I then argue that alienation can be healed by artful and multiple languages in a participatory setting, as underpinned by my study. I will provide some insights from Federico's journey within the research, to show how artful languages worked for him. In the conclusion, I sum up what I learned, with my participants, about using a multimodal auto/biographical imagination to connect our knowing to our lives.

2   Are Professionals in Education Alienated Knowers?

I claim that professionals in education are too often alienated from their emotions, intuition, and imagination; to ensure professional status they learn to disconnect from authentic participation to their context and relationships. This also means that they find it difficult to own their knowing, or even to recognise their position in the process of learning. Participatory research can be a learning space where they can integrate multiple aspects of themselves via holistic knowing.

Sociologist Bernard Charlot (1997) proposed that knowledge makes sense to the subject if it is significantly related to their individual stories, imbued with desire linked to the possibilities or inhibitions for their self-construction. Since

1987, his team has researched students' relationships with school subjects, with a particular focus on clarifying how high school students from different social classes, in the suburbs of Paris, acquired or failed knowledge. Charlot's (1997) psychic-relational model is expressed in the idea that

> The relationship with knowledge (rapport au savoir) is the relationship with the world, the other and the self of a subject who is faced with the need to learn. (p. 93, author's translation)

This can be usefully applied beyond school settings, to professional knowing and self-making processes. In the learning process, conative and imaginative dimensions need to be considered; knowing is subjectively wired into a biographical trajectory, as we already "occupy a place" (Charlot, 1997, p. 60) from which we engage in cultural, material, and social interaction with others. To learn is to be engaged in individuation, a subjective process, as well as socialisation, which is deeply relational. Knowledge places us in the world. So, professional becoming can be understood as a non-linear, and stratified process, influenced by our webs of affiliation (families, workplaces, personal relations) (Bainbridge, 2015) and by the wider context: from the local to the global interacting eco-, socio-, cultural, political, economic, technological systems and discourses. When this complexity – in simple words, the interplay between multiple dimensions of life and interactive cycle between thinking and experience, self and world, knower and known – is lost, there is a risk of alienation.

A glowing example is to be found in the teaching professions. Gewirtz et al. (2009), among others, signal the issues raised by increasing performativity and decreasing autonomy due to teachers' professionalism. In higher education, Ronald Barnett (2011) wrote about a loss of "mystery" in how learning and knowing are understood, since neoliberal discourses rule out all that is not explicit or "evidence based". Feelings of inadequacy arise among professionals under multiple competing pressures to be accountable to a variety of stakeholders (Barnett, 2008). This tendency within education mirrors a wider culture of competition among perfectible individuals which is increasing across all sectors of our market-based societies: "from science and education to health care and the media" (Verhaeghe, 2012/2014, p. 113).

We could have seen it coming: psychiatrist R. D. Laing (1967/1977) pointed out from a humanistic perspective the condition of alienation affecting contemporary Western societies, which splits experience into "inner" and "outer" worlds,

> [...] but perception, imagination, phantasy, reverie, dreams, memory, are simply different modalities of experience, no more "inner" or "outer" than any others. (Laing, 1967/1977, p. 18)

When we separate the knower from the known and think that our grasp of reality is independent from who we are, we start to lose our humanity. Both subjectivity and objectivity need to be challenged, when we search for the whole.

A relevant contribution came from feminist studies: the seminal research study on Women's Ways of Knowing conducted in 1986 by Mary Field Belenky and colleagues explored women's knowing, which had previously gone "unheard and unimagined" (Belenky et al., 1986, p. 11), because leading studies on intellectual development usually generalised from findings obtained with male subjects, thus "using male experience to define the human experience" (Belenky et al., 1986, p. 7). Belenky and co-researchers analysed interviews to 135 women about their ways of knowing, and found that – in women's lives and narratives – "the development of voice, mind, and self were intricately intertwined" (Belenky et al., 1986, p. 18). They identified five epistemological strategies, ideally locating women learners on a developmental continuum from silenced, to objectivist, to subjectivist, towards more constructivist positions.

Constructivist knowers can draw on both subjective (personal) and objective (sociocultural) sources of knowledge: they learn to "move beyond systems" and "make connections that help tie together pockets of knowledge. There is a new excitement about learning and the power of the mind" (Belenky et al., 1986, p. 140). This is not a strict categorisation: epistemological development is not linear or cumulative, but different positions can be taken at specific times and places by the knower. Becoming is contingent, relational, and contextual. Belenky and colleagues shed light on complementarity of subjective and objective ways of knowing, and on how "the words of male authority [and abstract reason]" (Belenky et al., 1986, p. 146) can silence other ways of knowing.

Feminism joined anticolonialism in a struggle to make "other" voices audible, not least by exploring indigenous epistemologies or mental "illness" as demonstrations of a panoply of possibilities. This throws up issues of inclusivity in education and the need to invent new settings and languages to support the subject's quest for self, voice and mind beyond any reductionism (Belenky & Stanton, 2000).

3   Artful Knowledge

Since the 70s, feminist movements in Italy and elsewhere have drawn on the arts to illuminate and subvert social norms restricting knowledge, creativity, sexuality, and identity by way of developing embodied, performative and relational practices (Scotini & Perna, 2019). Women artists uncovered spoken, propositional language as biased by patriarchal categories, so they claimed a space to speak in their own voices as "unexpected subjects" (Lonzi, 1970/2010) via the exploration of multiple, expressive and creative languages. Literature, poetry, photography, abstract painting, sculpture, dance and installations were used to tell stories about women's oppression and struggle for identity, a new way of becoming in the world. A mass of cultural objects was created, to testify this research.

Similarly, the auto/biographical approach has drawn on 1980s feminist scholars to research relational subjects, creatively devising new methodologies and composing a panoply of paradigms to reflect the complexities of doing research (Merrill & West, 2009). Linden West's biographical research with GPs (family physicians) in southern England, for example, drew on psychoanalysis to interpret the gap between the myth of the doctor as an omnipotent and omniscient hero (clearly, a remnant of patriarchy), and the concrete struggles of these professionals in the everyday context of a multicultural, socially frag-mented landscape. They may assume an alienated position "partly as defence against fears of inadequacy and [their] own emotional difficulties" (West, 2004, p. 301). This can be true of many professionals, i.e. teachers, social workers, counsellors, doctors and nurses, and so on – who work with/within relation-ships, and need to meet otherness, first in themselves, but are asked to keep a distance and enact a role, not a whole person. Pierre Dominicé spoke of such workers as adult educators, applying the term beyond formal adult learning settings to cover "a diversity of professional activities including, beside teach-ing and group work, guidance and counselling as well as human resource" (Dominicé, 2007, p. 241). Recognising the educational work of a variety of pro-fessionals "helping other adults to acquire the tools which will help them to build their biographies" (Dominicé, 2007, p. 247) implies that more attention needs to be brought to how knowing and learning are understood and inform daily practice.

Professional socialisation into an overly intellectual model – not least by very rational and functionalist forms of training and continuous education – hinders the possibility to explore richer and more inter-subjective ways of knowing. Auto/biographical research can open possibilities and "illuminate more of what doctors, in reality, may need to know, including the place of self and emotional understanding" (Dominicé, 2007). However, speech-based professional reflection might remain tied up with abstract thinking and dis-embodied forms of reasoning (Fook et al., 2016). As feminists taught to us, propositional language is tacitly colonised by patriarchal themes. Besides, it takes time, good enough relationships, and courage to leave our comfort zone, to develop freedom and openness. This plays in favour of a workshop setting, as a reflexive training sustaining adult educators – professionals supporting other adults to learn from their own lives, as I am by training – to understand and take a position within "the social context in which learning takes place" (Dominicé, 2007, p. 248).

I shall now introduce my research workshop, but first I need to describe the auto/biographical imagination that helped me contextualise my own research epistemology in embodied relationality.

4   A Relational Aesthetic Auto/Biographical Imagination

Belenky and colleagues (1986) warned us that contextual, imaginative, sensuous, affective, and relational ways of knowing tend to be kept out (or mystified) in a patriarchal West. My research brought at the forefront that kind of knowing that "involves intimacy and equality between self and object" (Belenky et al., 1986, p. 100), and is marginalised by professional epistemologies. Professionals and researchers in education are trained to prefer alienated knowledge "based upon impersonal procedures for establishing truth" (Belenky et al., 1986, p. 102). Instead, an auto/biographical approach (Merrill & West, 2009), informed by feminism, relational theories and radical constructivism has the potential for self-reflexivity and self-subversion.

In order to better understand the complex interactions of knowledge construction, I use Donald Winnicott's (1971) approach to object relations to bring attention to how knowers continually negotiate who they are in relation to others and the world. Self-integration is the ongoing, never fully achieved result of the expression of different aspects of the self, intended as "a never complete product of relationships with actual people and diverse objects, including the symbolic" (Merrill & West, 2009, p. 70). The notion of transitional space illuminates learning settings where authenticity and playfulness can peak and sometimes flourish. As adults, thanks to biographical and educational work, we may have access to a space that is "good enough" – supportive and not exploitative:

> This intermediate area of experience, unchallenged in respect to its belonging to inner or external (shared) reality ... [is] retained in the intense experiencing that belongs to the arts and to religion and to imaginative living, and to creative scientific work. (Winnicott, 1971, p. 19)

The slash in auto/biography could be interpreted as such a relational space, a liminal space of difference, possibility, and transformation. Different ways of knowing may be conceived as different transitional objects, or spaces, that work as mediators of the dynamic interaction between self and world. They also represent different modes of self-existence – some of which are more highly regarded than others in our society. There are ways of knowing that nurture alienation and oppression, while others sustain freedom and connection, hence self-integration.

My thesis is that the multiplication of our ways of knowing can better support knowers to become creative and "use the whole personality" (Winnicott, 1971, p. 73). In this sense, Gregory Bateson's (1972) ecological understanding of art as the human "quest for grace" (Bateson, 1972, p. 129) points to the compositional and generative potential of our aesthetic engagement with the world, a way to overcome binaries between conscious and unconscious, body and mind, cognitive and emotional knowledge, self and the world.

By integrating artful languages in research (Formenti et al., 2019), and in relation to professional knowing, I want to challenge rationalistic universal claims to knowledge and common-sense ideas of educational good practices, hence I choose to look at the relational quality of learning and becoming. I feel the need to widen the stiff confines of knowledge, until it becomes meaningful to me, to our lives, countering the silencing of stories and ways of knowing that are marginalised by dominant discourses.

In sum, a relational aesthetic auto/biographical imagination includes:
- Spiralling – an ongoing recursive fluctuation between multiple modes of knowing (experiential, aesthetic, rational, practical, weaving imagination and intuition, consciousness and the unconscious);
- Self, voice and mind – celebrating the struggle for selfhood, recognition, and meaning imbued in our epistemological/ontological development (as professionals, researchers, etc.);
- Critical reflexivity – connecting knowing to the inter-subjective, material, and sociocultural contexts of its emergence (as feminists claimed: bring yourself with others);
- Art – engaging the senses (all of them!) in nurturing openness to experience, pleasure and pain; both in experiencing artful objects and in creating our own;
- Risk – by abandoning anaesthetised knowledge and drifting off into knowing as becoming, we encounter otherness and potential conflict within ourselves, with others and in the world.

Having somehow anticipated the end of the story, I shall now go back to present the research study that led me to widen my research imagination from more idealised to more processual and integrated knowing.

5   Practicing Multiplicity: Cultural Objects, Interpersonal
         Explorations, and Transcoding in My Research Design

How can an auto/biographical approach be used in a group setting to bring
about more holistic and complex ways of knowing for professionals in education? To answer my question, I implemented an auto/biographically oriented co-operative inquiry (Formenti, 2018; Heron, 1996) with two groups of
professionals, in Milan and Canterbury. A colleague and I facilitated them in
telling stories of knowing and becoming a professional, building explicit and
implicit theories of education, and discussing their relationship to knowing. I
was interested in exploring how a specifically designed setting of participatory
research might encourage participants to connect their thinking and acting,
narrated and enacted identities, and maybe sustain transformative learning to
contrast alienation.

Six monthly co-operative workshops were run simultaneously in Milan and
Canterbury from January to June 2015, with a follow-up four months later. The
participants in Milan were 4 professionals currently doing a PhD at the university, 3 social workers, 1 social-service coordinator, 1 teacher. The participants in
Canterbury were 2 professionals enrolled in a PhD programme, 2 lecturers, 1
art psychotherapist, 1 career counsellor. Each session took a repetitive format
based on Heron's (1996) 4 forms of knowledge, whereby the sensuous, imagi-
nation/intuition, and rational understanding are drawn together to develop
new lines of action. These kinds of knowledge are intertwined in a spiralling
process of inquiry that can be more or less chaotic, more or less ordered – Dio-
nysian vs. Apollinean – as Heron recognised (Heron, 1996, pp. 45–47).

I proposed a setting for shared exploration, using evocative objects (texts,
picture cards, and films) to stimulate the senses and memories, and asking
the participants to use writing as well as visual and performative languages
to shape them (what Heron calls "presentational knowledge", Heron, 1996, pp.
33, 54–55, 88–90). They discussed their learning lives, and interrogated experiences through their cultural representations, and vice versa. By "translating"
lived lives (Del Negro, 2019), or aspects of them, into different media (transcoding, intersemiotic translation), I hoped to foster different, complementary,
maybe disrupting modes of knowing and sustain novel thinking in the direction of transformation as an antidote to alienation.

The sessions involved writing, reading and discussing about life events, in
constant movement between individual and group, triggering reflection and
reflexivity (Formenti, 2018). The process proved messier than intended: letting
go of a controlling stance was a struggle with many dilemmas and a learning
path for me, as researcher. Critical incidents caused moments of displacement,

exhilaration and conflict in the groups, requiring all of us to find new creative compositions.

I propose here my reading of Federico's path in the group, to show how it raised conversations on difficult issues concerning the professional and the personal as connected sources of knowledge.

6   Federico's Narrative (or Mine?)

I chose to tell the story of a male participant to the Italian group, Federico, since it speaks to me auto/biographically (Merrill & West, 2009) about unlearning the idealisation of knowing and developing a more embodied understanding. This process started for me with the research. As it unfolds, it brings academic knowledge closer to my own life.

At the time of the research Federico was 31 (I was 30) and doing a PhD on literature and didactics. Specifically, he was researching the link between fictional immersive experience and learning with schoolteachers. A teacher himself, he coordinated teacher training courses on teaching literature, so perhaps he found the aesthetic and autobiographical approaches in my project strangely different from his own experience. All along the co-operative inquiry sessions, Federico came in and out of the process. Sometimes he was absent or arrived late and he wrote in a convoluted language. He was often a critical voice in the group, which I found challenging.

During the second session, as a starting point (Heron, 1996) I asked the participants to represent their learning biographies in the shape of a river. Federico produced this *Tangled Clump* (*Grumo Aggrovigliato, his original title*) (see Figure 12.1).

Following the drawing, I asked the participants to write, in the course of the day, three individual texts, which they read and discussed in the group after each writing session – the interpersonal theorising phase of the spiralling method, (Heron, 1996). Federico's first text (immediately after the drawing) was a piece of creative writing on his river learning biography metaphor.

> I am the Tangled Clump, clumped we don't know when, we don't know why, we don't know where, down there, there in the middle, burning persistent lit up, infected magnetic intermittent.
>
> The numerically finite alternative branching, tributaries-emissaries, nurture it above the swallowing swamp that hides it from sight, from senses, sometime from reason. They disperse me in 14066 regular rivulets: meanders, forks, lost times, straight lines, non-aims, non-direction,

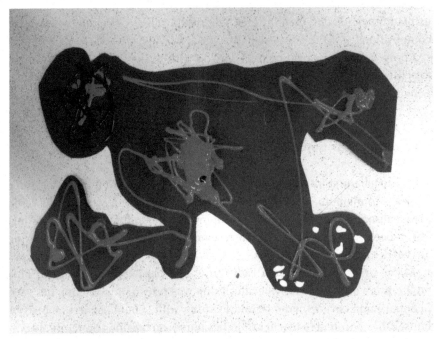

FIGURE 12.1 Federico's river of learning, Bicocca, 13/02/2015 (from Del Negro, 2018, p. 132)

clump indeed. Infernal skein that makes us suffocate, that eats my oesophagus.

I am not trapped from outside, no opportunity of otherness, rotten swamp that swallows and fakes, abstracting me.

The white, illusory, the white. (Federico, text "Let me introduce myself", Milan-Bicocca University, 13th February 2015, author's translation)

Federico's second text was an epistemological (Fabbri & Munari, 1990) yet poetic writing, a reflective text that pinned down a first personal theory of learning:

If a learning biography were a river
It would not exist
As it would not project itself into the ocean,
Nor into an artificial lake-reservoir,
Nor into a black sea,
Nor into a red sea.
It would flow ad-infinitum
So it would be
Non-definable

Non-croppable
Non-learnable.
So maybe the question is
To water, then
Placate the swallowing anxiety
Without sea salt
And then disperse it
Through the hypostatic channels. (Federico, text "If a learning biography were a river", Milan-Bicocca University, 13th February 2015, author's translation)

The third text was a biographical account on a learning experience – "That time when ..." – a personal recollection in relation to what had emerged on the learning biography. Federico wrote a story about fishing(?), from which he only read aloud the final part:

It was a question of meticulous movement of the wrist and sight. An issue of a few micro-millimetres and hundred-mill-thousands. The "mojarda" had to fall in the deadly trap, he saw it, just above water. Quick and with frantic movements and those hungry eyes with a fire in the pupil. And then wham, a sudden movement to take it unguarded, the tail risen, and the line loosen, bringing up the plumb ... knowledge? (Federico, text "That time that", Milan-Bicocca University, 13th February 2015, author's translation)

What is my relationship with Federico's texts? In my PhD thesis, I practiced different forms of analysis, in order to multiply the possible interpretations of a complex, mysterious and messy process – a more ecological approach (Bateson, 1972). Among these forms of interpretative analysis, I used a poetic re-writing of the participants' texts. This creative writing from research material is a critical-relational form of writing as inquiry, in which the researcher owns her interpretation and engages creatively with the words of others in order to open possibilities (Richardson & St Pierre, 2005). Poetic re-writing helped me to explore and open up the "/" between Federico's story and mine, how Federico's narrative could connect with my understanding of my own, and how my understanding of my own life could inform my interpretation of his.

The poem at the start of this chapter is my composition from Federico's texts. After circling out words from the texts, based on personal resonance, I placed the words on a white page and brought some order based on rhythm, spatiality, and meaning. The resulting poem prompted me to reflect on my understanding of his initial texts. This is a self-reflexive as well as critical process.

Federico's texts spoke about being confronted by countless alternatives that provided no direction. My poem presents themes of abstraction and embodiment, framing them within a dichotomy of knowing/not knowing, in which an ideal knowledge, regular and infinite, becomes nonsensical and threatening to the person.

Writing the poem, reading it, pushed me to consider the risk of abstracting the self from the professional. Do we take into account, as professional researchers, the anxieties related to making sense of things? In my academic work, I was socialised into thinking that intellectual knowing is the highest form of knowledge (Belenky et al., 1996; Charlot, 1997; Heron, 1996). This sums up with my biography as a first-generation student in HE, drenched in anxieties linked with questions of class, gender, and not feeling like you belong (Merrill & West, 2009). And yet the "clump" in the title of the poem (a word used by Federico himself) evokes nature and blood that nurtures our biological life. Was Federico, or better was I through Federico, telling a story about my desire of embodiment as an academic researcher?

During the last research workshop, Federico represented his learning from the inquiry process by drawing three concentric shapes of white, yellow and red on a black board. He then said in the group that

> ... The dynamics between power and transformation and care have been theorised throughout the 20th century. But I see the generative aspect represented as a very female figure ... a female genital organ ... which explores in me a female part that is present, and maybe this pedagogical and formative dimension emerges more clearly. (Del Negro, 2019, pp. 148–149)

The feminine element now stands out to me as particularly significant.

After initially describing learning in dichotomic terms and associating it with feelings of anxiety ("Infernal skein that makes us suffocate, that eats my oesophagus"), Federico uses here a generative representation of knowledge, explicitly referring it to a "female part" and connecting power with transformation and care. At the same time, he maintains a strong connection with his disciplinary knowledge. His present and past selves seem connected within his theorising, maybe bringing him nearer to a constructivist position – able to connect pockets of knowledge, personal experience and sociocultural reference, acquiring a new voice (Belenky et al., 1986). This seemed to make him quite happy.

When Federico and I met for a one-to-one follow-up to discuss my findings a year after the events, and afterward produced a collaborative piece of writing,

FIGURE 12.2 Federico's object representing the changed self, Bicocca, 16/10/2015 (from Del Negro, 2018, p. 143)

Federico did not disagree with my interpretation. He expressed appreciation for my courage in writing myself openly into my text (which I had not done much during the co-operative sessions!). In his part of the collaborative text, still, he played his academic self, inviting me to go further in my investigation; I hear in his words some traces of positivism:

He recommended that I read a book about neuroaesthetics and embodied cognition he believed could help me to further develop these ideas. He suggested that if I had focused on a smaller number of aesthetic objects, I could have provided a more in-depth analysis of how they had functioned as creative/formative dispositives. (Del Negro, 2019, p. 245)

Could I not provide a better – "more scientific" – theory to prove my argument? What I hear irritates me. When I listen for a while longer, I also hear my own subjectivist knower (Belenky et al., 1986), saying "praxis praxis praxis!" and closing her ears off to theory, out of exhaustion with the demands of academic standard, out of painful memories about learning and care in my family. There is richness here.

Keeping close to my ambivalent feelings, I have tentatively moved towards the uncertainties of auto/biographical imagination (Miller, 2007), and work neither to "demonstrate" nor to reject, but to explore and eventually nurture both theory and experience, knowing and living (Maturana, 1990), and their dynamic connection.

7   Conclusions

In this chapter, I began a discussion about the relationship between professional knowing and becoming, and professionals' alienation of the self from knowing in the education sector and educationally sensitive professions (Barnett, 2008, 2011; Gewirtz, 2009; West, 2004). Starting from a more traditional study, I narrated of how I ended up facilitating a cooperative, auto/biographically oriented workshop with adult education professionals like me. Whilst I had anticipated that rich stories could originate from such a design, the full potential of a multimodal group setting emerged during the research. As Federico's story shows, engaging in a relational aesthetic space of mutual learning can counter professionals' alienation: the disconnect of emotions, perceptions, intuitions, from professional knowledge. My own interaction with Federico illuminates for me the anxieties, as well as joys, that can be associated with professional knowing and becoming, a stratified and non-linear process to which different needs, desires, and sensations contribute in a messy way.

The journey illuminates the irreducible uncertainty of professional knowledge, but also all the different dimensions and resources we can draw on. For me, auto/biography started to mean that we can celebrate complexity – stratification, interaction, co-implication – and wholeness, by bringing every dimension of our lives into our way of knowing: the personal and the professional, conscious and unconscious, mind and body, knower and known. The unfolding process of becoming escapes dichotomic views of professional knowing and development (Fook et al., 2016). This can be messy, but messiness is, in the end, a feature of life itself.

Translating between media challenges our relationship to knowing, connects disciplines and parts of oneself playfully, and is aesthetically and ethically engaging because it creates a transitional space: it stands on the slash between self and other, where creative living happens. This is an ecologically sound approach to professional knowing, and it could support professionals to learn from their lives, bringing all of their artfulness into their professional journeys.

As I say this, I feel the risk to *"predicare bene e razzolare male"*, as the saying goes – not live as I teach. How many more spirals will I have to go through to come closer to that ecology? How often do I stick with what I know? I take Federico's invitation and the irritation is causes me, and let it work.

References

Bainbridge, A. (2015). *Becoming an education professional: A psychosocial exploration of developing an education professional practice.* Palgrave. doi:10.1057/9781137566287

Barnett, R. (2008). Critical professionalism in an age of supercomplexity. In B. Cunningham (Ed.), *Exploring professionalism* (pp. 190–208). Institute of Education, University of London.

Barnett, R. (2011). *Being a university.* Routledge.

Bateson, G. (2000). *Steps to an ecology of mind.* The University of Chicago Press. (Original work published 1972)

Belenky, M. F., Clinchy, B. M., Goldberger, N. R., & Tarule, J. M. (1997). *Women's ways of knowing: The development of self, voice and mind.* Basic Books. (Original work published 1986)

Belenky, M. F., & Stanton, A. V. (2000). Inequality, development and connected knowing. In J. D. Mezirow & Associates (Eds.), *Learning as transformation: Critical perspectives on a theory in progress* (pp. 71–102). Jossey-Bass.

Campbell, M., & Vidal, R. (Eds.). (2019). *Translating across sensory and linguistic borders.* Palgrave Macmillan. doi:10.1007/978-3-319-97244-2

Charlot, B. (1997). *Du rapport au savoir: Éléments pour une théorie.* Anthropos.

Del Negro, G. (2018). *An auto/biographical, cooperative study of our relationships to knowing* (Unpublished doctoral dissertation). Canterbury Christ Church University.

Del Negro, G. (2019). Transitional/translational spaces: Evocative objects as triggers for self-negotiation. In M. Campbell & R. Vidal (Eds.), *Translating across sensory and linguistic borders* (pp. 311–334). Palgrave Macmillan. doi:10.1007/978-3-319-97244-2

Dominicé, P. (2007). Educational biography as a reflective approach to the training of adult educators. In L. West, P. Alheit, A. S. Andersen, & B. Merrill (Eds.), *Using biographical and life history approaches in the study of adult and lifelong learning: European perspectives* (pp. 242–254). Peter Lang. doi:10.3726/978-3-653-03237-6

Fabbri, D., & Munari, A. (1990). Cultural psychology. A new relationship with knowledge. *Cultural Dynamics, 3*(4), 327–348. doi:10.1177/092137409000300401

Fook, J., Collington, V., Ross, F., Ruch, G., & West, L. (Eds.). (2016). *Researching critical reflection: Multidisciplinary perspectives*. Routledge.

Formenti, L. (2018). Complexity, adult biographies and co-operative transformation. In M. Milana, S. Webb, J. Holford, R. Waller, & P. Jarvis (Eds.), *The Palgrave international handbook on adult and lifelong education and learning* (pp. 191–209). Springer.

Formenti, L., Silvia, L., & Del Negro, G. (2019). Relational aesthetics: A duoethnographic research on feminism. *RELA, 10*(2), 123–141. doi:10.3384/rela.2000-7426.rela9144

Gewirtz, S., Mahony, P., Hextall, I., & Cribb, A. (Eds.). (2009). *Changing teacher professionalism: International trends, challenges and ways forward*. Routledge.

Heron, J. (1996). *Co-operative inquiry: Research into the human condition*. Sage.

Laing, R. D. (1977). *The politics of experience and the bird of paradise*. Penguin Books. (Original work published 1967)

Lonzi, C. (1996). Let's spit on Hegel (G. Bellesia & E. Maclachlan, Trans.). In P. Jagentowicz Mills (Ed.), *Feminist interpretations of G. W. F. Hegel* (pp. 275–298). Penn State Press. (Original work published 1970)

Maynard, M., & Purvis, J. (2013). *Researching women's lives from a feminist perspective*. Routledge.

Maturana, H. R. (1990). The biological foundations of self-consciousness and the physical domain of existence. In N. Luhman, H. Maturana, M. Namiki, V. Redder, & F. R. Varela (Eds.), *Beobachter. Konvergenzen der Erkenntnistheorien?* (pp. 47–117). Wilhelm Fink Verlag.

Merrill, B., & West, L. (2009). *Using biographical methods in social research*. Sage.

Miller, N. (2007). Developing an auto/biographical imagination. In L. West, P. Alheit, A. S. Andersen, & B. Merrill (Eds.), *Using biographical and life history approaches in the study of adult and lifelong learning: European perspectives* (pp. 167–186). Peter Lang. doi:10.3726/978-3-653-03237-6

Richardson, L., & St. Pierre, E. A. (2005). Writing: A method of inquiry. In N. Denzin & Y. S. Lincoln (Eds.), *A handbook of qualitative research* (3rd ed., pp. 959–978). Sage.

Scotini, M., & Perna, R. (Eds.). (2019). *The unexpected subject. 1978 art and feminism in Italy*. Flash Art.

Verhaeghe, P. (2014). *What about me? The struggle for identity in a market-based society* (J. Hedley-Prole, Trans.). Scribe. (Original work published 2012)

West, L. (2004). Doctors on an edge: A cultural psychology of learning and health. In P. Chamberlayne, J. Bornat, & U. Apitzsch (Eds.), *Biographical methods and professional practice: An international perspective* (pp. 299–311). Policy Press.

Winnicott, D. W. (1971). *Playing and reality*. Psychology Press.

CHAPTER 13

The PhD and Me: A Liminal Space

Paula Stone

Abstract

In this chapter, I share the experience of how undertaking feminist auto/biographical research, for a doctoral thesis, has had an impact, not only on my professional identity as an emerging researcher, but most importantly on my personal identity as an academic from working-class origins. It is wrongly assumed that doctoral writing is by and large a lonely enterprise; in reality it is a complex undertaking for both the student and the supervisor(s). Using Axel Honneth's work on recognition as a framework to analyze my experiences within the academy I show how studying for a PhD, using auto-diegetic narrative, enabled me to enter a third space (Bhabha, 1994, p. 28) to bring about transformation, not only at an intellectual and cognitive level, but at a spiritual and emotional level as well.

Keywords

une miraculée – auto/biography – Honneth – social class – third space

• • •

I am *une miraculée*, an academic from working class origins.
BOURDIEU and PASSERON (1990, p. 175)

••
•

1   Introduction

Having completed my PhD whilst working in higher education as a senior lecturer, I have travelled so far from the life in which my habitus was formed it could even 'be described as miraculous' (Bourdieu, in Bourdieu & Eagleton, 1992, p. 117).

© PAULA STONE, 2021 | DOI: 10.1163/9789004465916_014

In this chapter, I share the experience of how undertaking auto/biographical research, for a doctoral thesis, has had an impact, not only on my professional identity as an emerging researcher, but most importantly on my personal identity as an academic from working-class origins. I illustrate how studying for a PhD, using auto-diegetic narrative, can bring about transformation, not only at an intellectual and cognitive level, but at a spiritual and emotional level as well. This chapter will illustrate how complex inter-relationships, both real, and 'imagined' (Quinn, 2010, p. 68) are fundamental to the formation of the 'self' (Mead, 1934) as the pathway from one class to another is travelled. My story is set in a post-1992 university which contains a statistically higher proportion of 'non-traditional' students, (first-generation university attendees from working-class or minority backgrounds and mature students, those aged over 23 years), yet still predominantly employs middle-class academics.

I employed my doctoral thesis, entitled 'Confronting Myself: An auto/biographical exploration of the impact of class and education on the formation of self and identity' (Stone, 2018), to explore the relationship between class transition and education based on my own experience. Being both the researcher and the researched; the subject and the object; the narrator and the protagonist enabled me to create a 'third space' in which 'the transformational value of change lies in the rearticulation, or translation, of the elements that are neither the One ... nor the Other but something else besides which contests the terms and territories of both' (Bhabha, 1994, p. 28).

I argue that my analysis of my own class transition reaches beyond my personal experience to present a 'collective story' 'a story which tells the experience of a sociologically constructed category of people in the context of larger socio-cultural and historical forces' (Richardson, 1997, p. 14) in this instance female academics from non-traditional backgrounds.

2   Theorizing the 'Self' Using Auto/Biography

Feminist scholars argue that if society hopes to address issues around misrepresentation and exclusion, women must build knowledge from their own actual life experience (Brooks, 2007). So, when starting my research, I sought an approach that could help me to confront my 'self' within broader ecological interactions, including my past, my family, and my work to celebrate the connectedness of family and social networks in influencing and shaping my life (Stanley, 1995).

It was Stanley (1995, p. 3) who first appropriated the term 'auto/biography'; an approach that enters the contested space between the socio-cultural and the psychosocial, and biography and autobiography, instead recognizing their symbiosis (Stanley, 1995). Stanley's (1995) conception of auto/biography encapsulates the key elements of feminist approaches to research, in which the enquiry is guided by a feminist epistemology grounded in women's everyday experience (Stanley & Wise, 1993), which for me were not just gendered but are also 'classed'. My aim was to create an authentic and accurate understanding of what the life of an academic from working-class origins life was like, so that readers could understand from the insider's point of view the lived experience of class transition and class oppression. As such, my research approach challenged the dominant research practices that typically denigrate 'feminine' cognitive styles and modes of knowledge, instead celebrating 'women's ways of knowing' (Belenky et al., 1986, p. 3).

Auto/biography disputes the conventional distinctions between self/other, public/private, immediacy/memory, personal and political (Stanley, 1993) recognizing that knowledge is contextual, situational and specific. Thus, writing about the 'self' entails acknowledging the variety of social networks of others that a life moves between (Stanley, 1995, p. 50). In this way auto/biography challenges the idea of a single, stable or essential self and emphasizes the construction of a reflexive account of self through the writing process.

> There is 'the self who *writes* constructs a self who *was* (an other self for biography, a past self for autobiography); but there is also a self who is, outside of the text as it is written, who continues to grow older and to change after it is completed but is prototypically unmentioned'. (Stanley, 1995, pp. 131–132, original emphasis)

Through my auto/biography, paying attention to the subjective dimensions of classed experience, I was able to provide insights into mechanisms of class, and class' 'hidden injuries' (Sennett & Cobb, 1977, p. 1), which may have been missed by more conventional, objectivist approaches.

Drawing Stanley's (1995) distinct concept I wrote auto/biographically, building a first-person account of the significant moments in my history, and the people in it, to chronicle my life experiences sharing the intimate and often hidden details of my life. This is what makes auto/biography distinctive; the power of the auto/biography lies not in nostalgia but in the courage to confront painful memories – and this is what I did. But to avoid the risks of hedonistic and narcissistic self-indulgence, always levelled at autobiographical writing, and to achieve an insightful analysis, I interpreted my account theoretically using Axel Honneth's psychosocial theory of recognition.

Honneth's theory of recognition (1995) provides a conduit between structure and agency which connects a theory of psychic development with a theory of social change (Fleming & González-Monteagudo, 2014). The theory determines that identity is constructed intersubjectively, through a process of mutual recognition in which citizens morally require recognition in order that their identities be fulfilled. As such, recognition is simultaneously an individual and social need. Honneth takes from Hegel the idea that human flourishing is dependent on the existence of well-established ethical relations – love, law and ethical life. He suggests that through three different types of social interaction: loving concern, mutual respect and societal solidarity, individuals develop three differentiated forms of relation-to-self: self-confidence, self-respect, and self-esteem, respectively (Anderson in Honneth, 1995). The first, and most basic form of relation-to-self, self-confidence, gained in primary affective relations of love and friendship is based on the right to exist. Honneth (1995) argues that if an individual experiences love, an ability to love one's self and others is developed. In this, a positive image of one's abilities, self-confidence is developed and the individual is then capable of forging an identity by receiving recognition from others. The next form of positive self-relation, self-respect, derives from an awareness of being a morally accountable subject through the moral respect and recognition of the other as a moral agent, in the context of civil society. The final level of relation to self relates to self-esteem or self-worth. This, claimed Honneth (1995, p. 129), is dependent on an awareness of having capabilities that are good or valuable to a concrete community. In this context one can achieve self-esteem by being recognized as a distinct individual with traits and abilities that contribute positively to the shared projects of that community (ibid.).

Whilst engaged in the research process, three unplanned phases emerged naturally and organically from the writing activity. I identify phase one as the process of writing auto/biographically about my experiences up until I became a teacher educator; during phase two, I examined my current context as an educated working-class woman working within the academy; and only during phase three, towards the end of the research process, I started to critically analyze my data through a collaborative narrative approach (Arvay, 2003), engaging myself in a reflexive process with my 'imagined social network (Quinn, 2010, p. 68) and my supervisors to examine the process of 'becoming' an academic. I aimed for a self-conscious approach to writing, weaving together the research process, the writing process and the ongoing construction of my 'self' in a layered account (Ronai, 1995), which emphasized the emotional and personal dimensions of research alongside the cognitive (Coffey, 1999).

3   My Narrative and Struggling about Class

My story starts in 1963, my mum was just 17 years old when she gave birth to me out of wedlock. I am 'illegitimate'. Fifty years ago, mothers who had children but were not married were considered immoral and often consigned to reserved homes or mental institutions and deprived of their children. This meant that I grew up knowing that my family was abnormal. I was born in my grandad's house in London. Despite his absence, my mum still had strong affection for my dad, who by then had formed yet another new relationship. Notwithstanding this, a son, my brother, followed fewer than two years later. In this context, I developed my habitus, as stated by Bourdieu (2002):

> [...] a system of dispositions, that is of permanent manners of being, seeing, acting and thinking, or a system of long-lasting (rather than permanent) schemes or schemata or structures of perception, conception and action. (p. 43)

My habitus, then, was formed in the context of low economic, social and cultural capital coupled with the stigma of being illegitimate. Primary school was a happy place; we were all poor and lived locally. I was clever and I flourished and managed to secure a place at a selective senior school. It was here that I realized that the assumptions held by middle-class children and adults about those from lower socio-economic groups carried consequences.

My first memory of 'classed' humiliation was at senior school. The Senior Mistress, a middle-aged, middle-class woman, gave an observable sniff of distain when she met my mum for the first time: the single-mother with two illegitimate children who was too young to be a mother, and inappropriately dressed in her mini skirt. It was clear to me, from that moment on, that she felt I had no right to be in that setting. Founded on feelings of illegitimacy and inferiority, during my first year at senior school I suffered what I now recognize to be an episode of childhood depression. In a short space of time I had gone from a clever, cheerful child to emotionally demanding and problematic; my mum did not cope well with this situation.

It was during this time that my mum met the man she was later to marry. The relationship was unstable, and alcohol featured heavily, there were intra-family disputes; physical and verbal assaults and police visits. At the age of 13 and 15 years respectively, although our basic needs were met, my brother and I were left to depend on ourselves. We reacted differently; he started to hang out with friends on the streets 'doing nothing and getting into trouble' (Corrigan, 1979, pp. 119–121), and I turned to academic study. My room with my school books became a sanctuary.

It is widely recognized that the kind of person we are is strongly influenced by our relationship with our parents and in particular with our mothers (Lawler, 2000). As Dowd (1999) points out, the negative social construction of the single mother is not a burden borne solely by the mother, children also lose out because of the stigmatization and isolation of single-parent families. Because of our circumstance, my mum unconsciously transmitted to me that we were seen as valueless in society.

My mum's longing to be seen as respectable and valuable in society initially propelled my class transition; educational achievement was imperative to gain and maintain her love and affection. Through writing my life history, I now realize that my class transition was initiated to overcome the stigmatization of illegitimacy my mum faced as a single mother. My duty as her daughter was to show the community that her illegitimate children were educated and she was making a valid contribution to society (Honneth, 1995, p. 164). This proved to be a significant element of my story.

However, like many mothers in Lawler's (2000) study, as I became educated, mine found it difficult to accept who I was becoming, when, over the years, my beliefs and values started to diverge from hers. I now carry the burden of being expensive, ungrateful, and not good-enough (Steedman, 1986) and we have endured long periods of estrangement over the years, right up until the present time. Indeed, much of my adult life has been spent in a 'spiral of emotional conflict' (Eichenbaum & Orbach, 1982 in West, 2010).

Despite leaving school at 16 years, at the age of 27 I returned to college to gain a professional qualification, which gave me access to Higher Education, and training to be a primary school teacher. The critical analysis of that period of my life, using Axel Honneth's (1995) theory of recognition, enabled me to realize, for the first time, that behind those choices there was a quest for respectability, legitimacy, and recognition – a way to show that I had the capacity to contribute to the community.

Despite higher education institutions in the 21st century hosting a diverse population, the institutional habitus of the university is still strongly racialized, gendered, and classed (Reay et al., 2010). When I entered the field of higher education, as a teacher educator, those well-established feelings of illegitimacy and inauthenticity, grounded in my primary cultural identity, became even more apparent. I felt, and still feel, that I must work harder and longer than many of my peers to prove myself as equal, despite completing my PhD. I continue to live in fear of being found out as a fraud, thus, denying myself legitimacy. Sadly, this is not an predicament I face in isolation; over the past four decades working-class academics have been writing about the 'cruel duality' (Law, 1984, p. 1) of being a working-class academic in higher education; collections of stories edited Ryan and Sackrey (1984), Dews and Law (1995), Mitchell,

Wilson, and Archer (2015), and Binns (2019) have illuminated the enduring middle class myopia and sense of displacement when entering academia.

Bourdieu (1986, p. 241) contended that the intellectual field generates its own type of legitimacy with their own particular 'logic of practice' or 'game'. Entry into that field is dependent upon at least an implicit acceptance of the 'rules of the game'. The analysis of my auto/biographical data showed that, while I have attempted to adapt to the field by adopting the cultural disposi- tions valued in my new cultural milieu, for example through ways of dressing and speaking, I have often felt undermined by tacit and subtle distinctions of class difference based on lack of social and cultural capital.

Linguistic practices, above all, are measured against what is legitimate. I know I practice a direct communication style, which is often more expressive of my feelings than most of my colleagues; I can't help but challenge silence and obedience to authority. In my institution, the right to speak seems to be appropriated by those agents who possess the 'right' type of capital and, as such have become spokespersons for the dominant ideology. There have been many occasions, in which I perceived speaking my mind and sharing my opin- ions as evidence of passion, honesty, and integrity, that were received as being confrontational and truculent. My contributions in the academic context have been dismissed or even undermined, mostly by white middle-class men who take offence at what I am saying and misrepresent me. These small but signifi- cant acts of symbolic violence (Bourdieu, 1994) in the form of a lack of recogni- tion or disrespect, even within the most intimate of intellectual spaces, have created a barrier to ward off dissent, and for me these 'classed' experiences con- tinue to resurrect early childhood experiences of exclusion and humiliation.

As I wrote about these experiences, writing became an ethical practice for me that went beyond the pure mechanics of completing a doctorate. The activ- ity of writing strengthened the connections between body, mind and spirit which enabled me to recover fragments of my life, to re-educate myself, and to create a new story. My thesis exemplifies how the process of writing was not a merely cognitive or intellectual activity, a disembodied action removed from questions of gender and class; it was, in fact, an embodied ecological endeavor with all the complex, emotionally difficult, and messy experiences that under- pin the process of becoming a Doctor of Philosophy. I spent many sleepless hours regretting my decision to undertake the PhD and specifically to write auto/biographically, which had left me doubly exposed: as an academic and as a human being. Indeed, my research was filled with tensions, challenges and moments of intense emotion because of the personal nature of the data. But, it soon it became a way of working myself out; providing a source of hope and promise. Writing auto/biographically about class transition and feelings of illegitimacy in the academy provided a unique opportunity to analyze the interplay of history and my current struggle for recognition and legitimacy (Honneth, 1995). Indeed, my early explorations, as I chronicled my life and theorized my assumptions, started to reveal aspects of my life and self that I had never dared to consider before. In this space, my life and work became entwined – I began to explore, during the academic activity itself, how my own participation with the doctoral process, and the impact it was having on me, was shaping who I was 'becoming' (Dall' Alba, 2009).

As I began to share my research with others at conferences, my narrative revealed how internalized feelings of oppression, inferiority and vulnerability (Pheterson, 1986) would resurface, as this extract from my research diary shows:

> I always feel vulnerable in these settings [a conference]. Not because of my gender but always because of my class [...] despite working within a university for 10 years I always feel illegitimate, like I am here under false pretences. I feel people can sense the lack of social, cultural and educational capital. Rather than feel proud that I am here by my own virtue, I must remind myself what is good for me. (Research Diary, March 2016)

Serving to illustrate how enduring these feelings are.

4   Finding Solidarity – My Theoretical Friends

My research sits within an important body of theoretical work that illustrates the experiences of women like me, academics from working-class backgrounds. I have found comfort in their work since I can identify myself with them, having shared experiences. Beverley Skeggs; Pat Mahony; Christine Zmroczek; Valerie Walkerdine; Helen Lucey; Carolyn Steedman; Anne Oakley; Diane Reay; Steph Lawler; Liz Stanley; Sue Wise; Louise Morley; Gillian Plummer; Lisa Mckenzie and Lynsey Hanley, writing mostly in the zeitgeist of the women's movement in the 1990s, and some recently, have shared through their own autobiographies the feeling of being oppressed because of both their gender and class. At a time when I was feeling illegitimate and marginalized in the university setting, these women became my imagined social network (Quinn, 2010), engendering both social and cultural capital. These educated working-class women, who have embodied being a feminist working-class intellectual, proved to be good collaborators in my doctoral journey; affirming, provoking and critiquing my own thoughts and feelings. With their help, I was able to 'engage in a simulated conversation' (Brookfield, 1995, p. 187) about my/our experiences that has enabled me to reclaim my past and articulate the subjective experience of class, illegitimacy and education, as both a learner and an educator. As I wrote, I was able to reconcile, for the first time, the contradictions between my values and beliefs and the demands of the academy on my personhood.

5   Love, Rights, and Solidarity – The PhD

It is wrongly assumed that doctoral writing is by and large a lonely enterprise; in reality it is a complex undertaking for both the student and the supervisor(s). Supervision of doctoral students is the development of the 'becoming' scholar, but it is equally a process of continuing development of the experienced academic (Bryant & Jaworski, 2015). This intersubjective relationship, which suggests a dialogically co-constructed self in relation to others, is more than important to the ecology of doctoral research (Bryant & Jaworski, 2015). It involves each subject recognizing the other, and allowing the possibility of identifying with the other (ibid.). Whilst it is important to acknowledge that my doctorate came to life within the confines of a neoliberal university setting, which generally necessitates the denial of emotions in the process of achievement, both my supervisors, recognizing how gender, and class affected my position in the research, adopted what I would call a feminist approach to supervision, based on a 'collaborative relationship that is characterized by mutual respect, genuine dialogue, attention to social contextual factors, and responsible action' (Szymanski, 2003, p. 221).

The relationships with my supervisors, both white middle-class, one female and one male, have been crucial to my survival in very different ways. The male supervisor recognized something deep within me, even before I could see it myself. Like me, he has working class origins and is interested in people's lives. The female supervisor, acting from her middle-class position, often inadvertently 'misrecognized' (Bourdieu, 2000) my working-class habitus, provoking me to challenge and question my assumptions. By her own admission, she struggled to see how academic success is not a simple case of upward social mobility, as a path of redemption or empowerment for those who have a working-class identity. I am confident that these relationships were borne out of intersubjective love, rights and solidarity (Honneth, 1995). From the outset my supervisors considered, and indeed celebrated, my humanness, my emotions and values, enabling me to go beyond 'the process' of engaging in research and writing a doctorate per se; instead, they helped me to focus on how the self is being (re)constituted and (re)negotiated in the process of doctoral research (Petersen, 2014, pp. 823–834).

The fact that we valued each other's qualities despite differences has made me feel accepted for who I am. This relationship was significant in my successful completion of doctoral study because the supervision meetings played a significant and integral role in the development of who I am as a researcher and academic and indeed as a woman from the working-class in academe. Resisting the 'care-less culture' (Bryant & Jaworski, 2015) of doctoral supervision in a neo-liberal university, the 'undertaking' of my supervision was deeply embodied; there was a strong sense of reciprocity and through sharing our lived experiences, there became a sense of deeper understanding of self for all of us. Over time, through the love and recognition of my supervisors, I began to have trust in myself; and to see myself as worthy of the doctorate and my position in the academy. Being valued as an academic has led to a more secure, stable, and self-esteem (Honneth, 1995). This contrasted with how I felt in other areas of the faculty, in which I believed I could only achieve relational value, belongingness, or acceptance by behaving inconsistently with my natural inclinations.

However, like any long-term liaison, the supervisory relationship was complex and inevitably, and properly, challenging at times. Over the years, our meetings have involved surprise, passion, disappointment and euphoria; all of which have provided emotional and intellectual sustenance during the long marathon of the PhD in which the emotional histories of both candidate and supervisors are lived and relived in fragmented moments (Bryant & Jaworski, 2015). Some of our exchanges inevitably aroused feelings on both sides, as we challenged each other's perspectives; 'these became interactional moments that left marks on all of our lives' (Denzin, 1989, p. 15) as this extract from my field notes illustrate.

> A: [Talking about our last meeting] You just became angry
>
> PS: I wasn't angry. I was … It wasn't anger … although I know it came across like that … it wasn't anger … I don't know what it was … it was complete and utter frustration, impotence. I felt out of control. I was not angry … not for a moment did I feel anger at anybody … even myself. I just didn't know what to do with myself. I honestly didn't know what to do with myself … I felt backed into a corner by you all. (Collaborative Narrative, February 2017)

With the support of my supervisors, as my self-confidence developed, I had enough courage to present a paper at the Life History and Biography Network. This group of scholars welcomed me as an emergent researcher.

> [European conference] I am now entering a cultural space that is very
> frightening. Who am I to share my thoughts about the research process –
> I am merely a novice. I read an extract from my doctoral research as it
> existed at that point. [The auto/biographical content (which is clearly
> illustrated in this thesis) would make anyone feel slightly exposed]. At
> this point the 'Reader' as I will call her detected a hole in my research –
> her challenge was relentless. Thankfully some experienced academics
> offered their support– I was truly grateful for their support. Later, I cried
> a lot! (Reflective Diary, March 2015)

Once again returning to Honneth (1995), he argues that moral growth
flourishes only when the development of three psychological self-relations
is guaranteed: self-confidence, self-respect and self-esteem. Over the years,
I have become part of this affiliation of scholars who recognize me as a distinct individual with traits and abilities that can contribute positively to the
shared projects of that community which has proved vital for my academic
and human flourishing.

6   Emerging from the Third Space

So, despite being born into structures of inequality which could have cir-
cumscribed my academic and professional success, I have begun to thrive in
academe. But as my story tells, class transition is not simply an escape from
disadvantage to a more privileged situation, it is also associated with pain,
estrangement and feelings of illegitimacy.

Traditional research methods easily neglect the moral character of life and
experience. But, in the spirit of feminist epistemology, through an auto/bio-
graphical narrative, I was able to enter a third space (Bhabha, 1994) to embark
on a journey into myself to tell the story of who I was to who I am now. As I
wrote and re-wrote I began to recognize and understand myself in a different
light; I saw a human experience – a woman, filled with fear, anxiety, denial
and ambivalences, struggling with notions of self. And whilst I wrote tentatively at first; as I found my voice and garnered the courage to write about the
emotional and personal dimensions of my life, and how this was intrinsically
connected to the research process, the relationship between the research process, the writing process, and the 'self' became stronger. The auto/biographical
examination of my childhood enabled me to look beyond my own experience
to begin to understand that my own desire for educational attainment was not
about escape, a desire for a better life and 'bettering the self' (Lawler, 2000,

pp. 105–112), but instead was based on gaining legitimacy or what Honneth (1995) would call recognition, in the form of love, rights and solidarity. My narrative also revealed that 'policy micro politics' (Hoyle, 1982, p. 88) is still enacted within the institution, by which the culturally marginal are sometimes identified as the 'other', and treated as irrelevant and/or inferior as a status group.

Emerging from the third space (Bhabha, 1994), I can now recognize that my thesis went far beyond a piece of academic work and became an important part of my 'self' as writing became a way of working myself out; identifying and challenging feelings of inferiority and illegitimacy. The thesis itself, proving to be a dynamic, creative process; a method of discovery (Richardson, 1994), and a source of agency. Being both the researcher and the researched; the subject and the object; the narrator and the protagonist has afforded me a double consciousness; a unique 'mode of seeing' (Brooks, 2007, p. 11) which made visible the ecological mechanisms that have constructed 'self' and identity. Becoming a Doctor of Philosophy has served as a powerful space of resistance and a 'site of radical possibility' (hooks, 1989, p. 149).

But the story does not end there; my struggle to gain a place in the academy is still ongoing, but I am starting to make a difference for and on behalf of working-class students and colleagues who are all striving to find their place in higher education. Since completing my doctorate, through my work, I have been breathing new life into conversations about equality and diversity within the institution so that they include consideration of those us who come from lower socio-economic status (SES) groups and non-traditional backgrounds. These are important incursions into once unimagined territory of the academy, in which classed inequalities are deeply imprinted despite continued efforts to narrow the gap between the privileged and disadvantaged. Thus, auto/biographical writing has become a social action which linked knowledge production with healing and reconstruction (Walsh, 1997).

References

Arvay, M. (2003). Doing reflexivity: A collaborative narrative approach. In L. Finlay & B. Gough (Eds.), *Reflexivity: A practical guide for researchers in health and social sciences* (pp. 163–175). Oxford Blackwell Publishing.

Belenky, M. F., Clinchy, B. M., Goldberger, N. R., & Tarule, J. M. (1986). *Women's ways of knowing: The development of self, voice, and mind.* Basic Books.

Bhabha, H. (1994). *The location of culture.* Routledge.

Bourdieu, P. (1984). *Distinction: A social critique of the judgement of taste.* Routledge and Kegan Paul.

Bourdieu, P. (1986). The forms of capital. In J. G. Richardson (Ed.), *Handbook of theory and research for the sociology of education* (pp. 241–258). https://www.marxists.org/reference/subject/philosophy/works/fr/bourdieu-forms-capital.htm

Bourdieu, P. (2000). *Pascalian meditations*. Stanford University Press.

Bourdieu, P. (2002). Habitus. In J. Hillier & E. Rooksby (Eds.), *Habitus: A sense of place* (pp. 27–34). Ashgate.

Bourdieu, P., & Passeron, J. C. (1990). *Reproduction in education, society and culture* (2nd ed.) (R. Nice, Trans.). Sage Publications.

Brookfield, S. D. (1995). *Becoming a critically reflective practitioner*. John Wiley and Sons.

Brooks, A. (2007). Feminist standpoint epistemology: Building knowledge and empowerment through women's lived experience. In S. Nagy Hesse-Biber & P. (Eds.), *Feminist research practice* (pp. 53–82). Sage Publications Inc.

Bryant, L., & Jaworski, K. (2015). *Women supervising and writing doctoral thesis: Walking on the grass*. Lexington Books.

Coffey, A. (1999). *The ethnographic self: Fieldwork and the representation of identity*. Sage Publications.

Corrigan, P. (1979). *Schooling the smash street kids*. Macmillan Press Ltd.

Dall'Alba, G. (2009). Learning professional ways of being: Ambiguities of becoming. *Educational Philosophy and Theory, 41*(1), 34–45. https://doi.org/10.1111/j.1469-5812.2008.00475.x

Denzin, N. (1989). *Interpretive interactionism*. Sage Publications Inc.

Dews, B., & Law, C. L. (1995). Introduction. In B. Dews & C. L. Law (Eds.), *This fine place from home: Voices of academics from the working class* (pp. 1–12). Templeton University Press.

Dowd, N. E. (1999). *In defense of single-parent families*. NYU Press.

Fleming, T., & González-Monteagudo, J. (2014). Theorising student experience: Structure, agency and inequality. In F. Finnegan, B. Merrill, & C. Thunborg (Eds.), *Student voices on inequalities in European Higher Education: Challenges for policy and practice in a time of change* (pp. 13–24). Routledge.

Honneth, A. (1995). *The struggle for recognition: The moral grammar of social conflict*. Polity Press.

hooks, b. (1989). Choosing the margin as space of radical openness. *Framework, 36*(15).

Hoyle, E. (1982). Micropolitics of educational organizations. *Educational Management, 19*(2), 213–222. https://doi:10.1177/174114328201000202

Lawler, S. (2000). *Mothering the self: Mothers, daughters, subjects*. Routledge.

Mead, G. H. (1934). *Mind, self and society*. University of Chicago Press.

Petersen, E. B. (2014). Re-signifying subjectivity? A narrative exploration of 'non-traditional' doctoral students' lived experience of subject formation through two Australian cases. *Studies in Higher Education, 39*(5), 823–834.

Pheterson, G. (1986). Alliances between women: Overcoming internalized oppression and internalized domination. *Signs, 12*(1), 146–160.

Quinn, J. (2010). *Learning communities and imagined social capital.* Continuum Publishing Group.

Reay, D., Crozier, G., & Clayton, J. (2010). Fitting in' or 'standing out': Working-class students in UK higher education. *British Educational Research Journal, 36*(1), 107–124. https://doi.org/10.1080/01411920902878925

Richardson, L. (1994). Writing: A method of enquiry. In N. Denzin & Y. Lincoln (Eds.), *Handbook of qualitative research* (pp. 516–529). Sage.

Richardson, L. (1997). *Fields of play: Constructing an academic life.* Rutgers University Press.

Ronai, C. R. (1995). Multiple reflections of child abuse: An Argument for a layered account. *Journal of Contemporary Ethnography, 23*(4), 395–426. https://doi.org/10.1177/089124195023004001

Sennett, R., & Cobb, J. (1977). *The hidden injuries of class.* Cambridge University Press.

Stanley, L. (1993). On auto/biography in sociology. *Sociology, 27*(1), 41–52. https://www.jstor.org/stable/42855039

Stanley, L. (1995). *The autobiographical I: The theory and practice of feminist auto/biography.* Manchester University Press.

Stanley, L., & Wise, S. (1993). *Breaking out again: Feminist ontology and epistemology* (new ed.). Routledge.

Steedman, C. (1986). *Landscape for a good woman: A story of two lives.* Virago Press.

Stone, P. N. (2018). *Confronting myself: An auto/biographical exploration of the impact of class and education on the formation of self and identity* (Unpublished thesis). Retrieved August 16, 2019, from http://create.canterbury.ac.uk/17736/

Szymanski, D. M. (2003). The feminist supervision scale: A rational/theoretical approach. *Psychology of Women Quarterly, 27*, 221–232. https://doi.org/10.1111/1471-6402.00102

Walsh, V. (1997). Auto/biographical imaginations and social change. In P. Mahony & C. Zmroczek (Eds.), *Class matters: Working-class women's perspectives on social class* (pp. 152–174). Taylor and Francis.

West, L. (2010). Challenging boundaries: An auto/biographical imagination and the subject of learning. *International Journal of Continuing Education and Lifelong Learning, 2*(2), 73–87.

An Evolution of Ideas: The Transformative Ecological Imagination in Adult Learning, Education, and Research

Alan Bainbridge, Laura Formenti and Linden West

The main objective of this book has been to chronicle the recent evolution of narrative and auto/biographical methods in research on adult education and lifelong learning, as well as of narrative forms of intervention in professional fields with a variety of groups. Contexts and communities constantly evolve and asking new questions is existentially essential. Furthermore, we have engaged in this book with an evolving community of scholars – the ESREA network – consisting of a mixture of experienced and early career scholars, to explore, with them, their evolution, in relationship, as narrative researchers. We have posed a question as to the extent to which the Network itself is a good enough ecology of learning, and thus life enhancing in its own right. This in a world in ecological, cultural and political crisis, where entities are often viewed in isolation, and where learning and education are often reduced to narrow, instrumental purposes. There has been neglect of understanding our interactions with the natural world, in our patterns of consumption, or our engagement with others, and otherness, including otherness within. We offer no claim to neutrality, certainty of approach or outcome in these pages: all of us are engaged researchers, in varying ways, struggling towards using research and narrative methods to create a better, more ecologically aware, sustainable, and socially just, egalitarian world.

While writing this conclusion, or rather what is merely a marker on a larger journey of methodological and epistemological pilgrimage, the idea of evolution came firmly to mind. Evolution as a kind of viaticum, defined as a supply of provisions for an onward, never ending journey. Evolution, we suggest, is intrinsic to ecology: life is dynamic, ever-changing, striving to create new forms – of which some persist and blossom, and others die. Life, however – at least any life worth living – is deeply relational, and life-based research methods engage us within unprecedented, complex relationships, one with another and whole worlds. The relationships can eventually bring us to the new and life enhancing, as our perspectives and relationships broaden and deepen, in heartfelt, embodied as well as intellectual ways. If life is complex: narrative research is (or should be?) respectful of the complexity. The contributions presented in this book tell a lively, dynamic story, intrinsically generative and transformative, in which complexity is respected. They demonstrate the evolution of our methodological family towards greater complexity and the power of illumination, bringing creativity, relationships, connections, epistemological and ethical subtlety to life. We suggest, on the evidence of these pages, that the work is both necessary, and often beautiful and life enhancing. This is a big, but justified claim, especially if, as we believe, this book will speak to many others struggling to be, to know and connect with others in difficult and disturbing times.

Ecology as a topic revealed itself powerfully when bringing together various threads: the biological and the social, natural and human-built environments, the capacity (or resistance) of organizations and communities to change, and the openness (or closedness) of individuals to learning. Lights and shadows. Hate and love. Hope and desperation. And yet there is determination in the writing to keep on keeping on in the work, to live with uncertainty rather than close this down in false, forced and premature ways. And also, to speak truth, however provisional this might be, to power; many if not all our authors are committed to forms of learning and education that are deeply dialogical and emancipatory. There is an implicit, at times explicit challenge to instrumentalism: to the idea of targets, as well as a calculus that sets instructions as to how this is achieved and objectifies the other. Rather the research and learning at the heart of the book are grounded in the importance of relationship and trust, which are not amenable to simplistic technical solutions. It is about living and acting in ways that evoke trust and mutual respect in the perpetual experiment called life and learning.

An ecology of life is strong and flourishing when it evolves, and when the obstacles to flow are removed or minimized: we have challenged, in these pages, a mainstream conceptualization of learning and education disconnected from the ecology of natural and social life, or as simple cause/effect instructional processes, ignorant of the many hindrances that intervene in lives and learning. What is rigid, fixed and unchanging, dies. A narrative is not 'a photograph', but is a constant, evolving series of questions, a quest, in short, in which meaning making lies at the heart. This is the essential basis for good enough adult education and research.

Our authors embody and bear witness to an extraordinarily strong ecological and evolutionary sensibility, deployed though diverse narrative studies, auto/biographical and psychosocial theories and methodologies. There has been a diversity of perspectives finding expression across these pages. There is a sensitivity to suffering in the work, mindful as we are of writing this 'conclusion' in the time of Coronavirus. Not only are people suffering, but so too is the natural world and diverse species, while our cities, towns and villages are often in pain. Our governments too seem on the rocks, while the arts can be relegated to museums. So, we infuse our final reflections from the perspective of biodiversity, and care-full-ness, as a common thread across the book, and as an imperative in our lives and times. We will list the values we have found in reading the chapters, and which seem essential to a healthy research and learning community; in short, to an ecology of life and learning.

1   Biodiversity as a Value Celebrated in Narrative Research

Biodiversity, which is necessary to maintain life on the planet, is also the engine of historical and cultural evolution: without it, civilization would never have happened, and today both are at risk. We are not only confronting ecological disaster and life-threatening events (there were many, during the crafting of the book), but the shrinking of cultural, linguistic, expressive diversity too. Even individually, a closed, monothematic, saturated story is anti-ecological, minimizing desire and hope. Cultural evolution, as well as personal growth, is deeply rooted in meeting, merging, and the clashing of different ideas, practices, identities, selves, and communities. But the clash can be destructive and a retreat from any learning from the other and otherness. This is the very opposite of what adult education, historically and constructively, has sought to achieve.

Narrative research is a powerful means to chronicle the role of difference – a "difference that makes a difference", as Gregory Bateson would say (1979, p. 250) – in triggering awareness, reflection, reflexivity, and transformation, over time. Not only at the individual level, but in relationships, in proximal systems and communities (Formenti, 2018). Across these chapters, most adult learning seems to happen while engaging with the Other, which can mean another social actor, another idea or paradigm, another species, or the environment itself as otherness. One that challenges our existence, or balance; and – last but not least – the other that lies within our psyches, perhaps at an unconscious, repressed level. Personal struggles, for example with colonial pasts, familial relationships, or professional demands, are well documented in many chapters, each entailing the author's struggles to re-compose divergent aspects of his/her life and learning as well as to understand more of the other.

Plurality, then, is what makes us come alive; it nurtures our needs as individuals and as a species and offers potential solutions when we get stuck. When we tell a story, we can compose and respect the differences without blurring, recognize, name and celebrate them, we can name them, openly, and then see the patterns connecting them. We can be deeply respectful to different lives, different cultures, and ways of being and seeing. But ultimately, noting a common humanity, vulnerability, and power to act for good or ill. Private and public selves, personal and professional identities, rational and emotional reasons for our choices merge: narrative methods have a deeply inclusive aesthetic quality that transcends binary ideas. We can tell multiple stories, from many points of view, and engage with many actors with different interests and stories to tell. Stories, as the writer Elif Shafak (2020) makes clear, can be the means to sanity in an insane world. When we feel able to tell our stories and are listened to, we can then learn to listen to others. This process of self/other recognition has always characterized the best of adult education.

2   Telling One's Life Story Illuminates the 'Collective'

The collective stories of specific human groups (working class academics or students, adult educators, women, migrants, health workers, Palestinian and Israeli Jewish educators) are revealed by interviewing individuals, encouraging them to be personal, to talk in the first person. Macrophenomena like cultural difference, power and oppression, genocide and cultural domination/colonialism are illuminated in these individual biographies, in ways that no distant, more abstract historical account can do. The personal is historical, cultural, social, relational, psychological and political at one and the same time.

The tension between individual and collective life is extraordinarily strong in the contemporary world. "My rights", "my freedom", "my idea" are too often opposed to the interests of society, or of another group. 'Our' own group, team, family, gang or even militia, is what really matters. We have tried to illustrate how personal and environmental dis-ease, illness, disconnection emanate from troubles, tensions and differences that have not been addressed. Neoliberalism positions one against the other, in a competitive war, hindering dialogue and significant learning. The only collective we understand is 'us': my people, my generation, my family, my gang. Ultimately, we are the chosen or the historically exceptional, supposedly superior, in various ways. Ours too is most often a time of wall building rather than the opening of gates to welcome another.

Alan and Linden painfully reflect, in their chapter, on the difficulty, or even impossibility, of providing a good/safe space for dialogue when deeply held assumptions and unresolved histories meet, and where there is resistance to change and questioning. Conflict is more often the norm. His, and her story, particularly of Palestinian peoples, often go unheard, while the deep, unre-solved trauma of the Holocaust still plays out at the individual and collective level in the seductions of colonialist exceptionalism. Similarly, Rob Evans speaks of the post/communist experience, where stories often go unheard outside the countries affected. What do we do with our past, individually and collectively, when the story is saturated (White & Epston, 1990) by problems, blame, hate, or hopelessness, rather than curiosity and respect? Narrative methods offer no simplistic solutions for meaningful dialogue: a dialogical narrative space is difficult and hard fought for. Dissonance and difference will find space: what matters is our response to it, and the genuineness and self-knowledge with which we encounter the other. The best of narrative inquiry and adult education asks not less than everything.

Sometimes, it allows us to cross boundaries, of time (see Evans on memories and the reconnection with past micro, meso and macro structures), of space (see Sawyer on using dialogue with and through places to deconstruct the past and imagine other possible futures), of structures and organizations (church and family, in Moen's chapter; the health system in Mazzoli Smith's); and of specific events like a conference (Wright & Høyen); or even cultural bounda-ries (see Chan, and her caution about cultural appropriation and colonialist incursion). Crossing boundaries may be good and exhilarating but it may raise fears of being hurt, rejected, despised, and of losing one's bearings and doing damage to self and the other.

3   Narratives Are about Meaning Making

A common preoccupation for narrative researchers is taking proper care of transcription, translation, and interpretation (as Rob Evans shows in his detailed and thoughtful micro-analysis). We are aware that meaning is already partly lost when the spoken word is written down, and even more so when we must use a different language. Our network's community has been bilin-gual French/English for a long time, but now the English language often pre-vails. However, most authors in this book do not speak English as their first language, nor do their participants. There is a need to be critically reflexive about the non-linear, asymmetric power relationships in speaking, listening, and writing. Different cultural assumptions and personal meanings will be in play for the listener, the speaker, and the reader of a narrative text. Power cir-culates within all the processes, for good or ill.

All of which happens, even before we start analyzing, coding, categoriz-ing, and interpreting. From an ecological, complex, circular perspective, the researcher is not a God in the machine, all-controlling, and all-knowing. In a way, we are but part of the circular game of narration; however, this too can be a source of meaning and new life.

Hervé Breton warns us, that the researcher must be mindful of different levels of (self) narrative: a level of phenomenological description, where experience is captured by senses, and perception is at the forefront; and a narrative or historicized level, devoted to represent an ecology of experience, or a complexity of life, via meaning-making. Hervé shows us what can be gained by interweaving these two levels in our effort to make meaning out of experience. He plays with 'double' or 'multiple' description, which creates a sense of depth, or 'perspective' (Formenti & West, 2018).

For Mazzoli-Smith, the construction of meaning entails moving from the powerful but reductive medical categorization of illness or ageing, to sensitivity towards the particular other's experience – especially of patients but also practitioners – hence creating new learning opportunities for everyone, practitioners and patients alike. Multiple knowledge is better knowledge for everyone. Del Negro follows this principle, by using multimodal methods to invite professionals to explore their ways of knowing, which can challenge ultimately reductive certainties of professional expertise; and bring to problems and possibilities a more diverse, imaginative, richer and satisfying, personal as well as professional aesthetic.

4   A Story Is a Composition and Re-Composition

Ecological diversity and plurality are celebrated and re-composed by narrative researchers in many ways. For example, by taking life-as-a-whole into account. We read in Kjetil Moen's contribution that life and death are umbilically linked; far from being opposed, the one does not exist without the other; and yet, stories of death can be silenced in our cultures, as are many other topics linked to spirituality, meaning, wisdom and even religion in secular contexts. Mainstream accounts of life tend to be sanitized and the messiness, ugliness, unpleasant and uncertain feelings, and the search for meaning, integral to living, are washed away.

Adrienne Chan's chapter is maybe the most "ecological" of the book: her analysis of indigenous metaphors and stories, and even more so the practices of action research, are aimed at reconnecting people to the land, to their cultural roots, as well as to nurturing dialogue between older and younger generations. Experiences of genocide and cultural annihilation must be named and recognized if we want to heal disconnections. We may ask questions of youth:

are they, or can they be fully immersed in the indigenous narratives? Or have they been incorporated into the colonializing mentality in which they live, work, and study? The composition of different roots, weaving them together into more of a whole, is a learning dimension of trans-migratory societies, but it can also be a story of the colonized psyche. There is an important task here for many of us, at a time of mass migration and new manifestations of colonialism. Capitalism itself can be a form of colonialism, the worship of Mammon, which seduces us to accept a one-dimensional and ultimately anti-ecological way of being.

Rick Sawyer is the inventor of a method – duoethnography – that is based on the composition of different experiences and perspectives, embodied and enacted by the involved researchers/participants (Norris, Sawyer, & Lund, 2012). They learn and accept to stay with the tension provoked by place and difference and to re-compose resistant and often unhelpful narratives. In this chapter, he explains how stories of place can reveal a diversity of elements of culture, power, ethnicity, racism and abuse; only by looking at the bigger picture, past and present, can we gain a deeper, more satisfying and maybe healing way of knowing.

Paula Stone celebrates the unity and complexity of life by including her whole self in her autoethnographic effort. She does not hide from the uncomfortable or uncanny aspects that we often learn to remove from our official, edited self-narration. But the feeling of not fitting in, despite our attempts to do so, via editing and conformity, is ultimately a rebuke to anti-ecologic and oppressive practices of exclusion, subjugation, and mystification, so common in the academy and across society. Here finding your own place, voice, and identity, can be a life wrenching struggle against the power of class, privilege or particular ways of knowing.

5   We Do Not Silence Challenges and Struggles

Stories can also teach us about the challenges of encountering diversity, or the lack of a sufficiently diverse culture. As in our own conferences, where Hazel Wright and Marianne Høyen see the Network as a community of mostly aged/ experienced researchers, predominantly female, and many UK-based scholars, which can be a problem for a network celebrating diversity. How do we facilitate the necessary encounter with diversity and create a more eclectic family in which to learn? The Network has sought to meet the challenge and to create a space quite different from historically dominant university cultures. In the latter, there has been emphasis on mastery, individual displays of achievement, of competition and a survival of the fittest. Doubt, the personal and emotions are often silenced. In the Network, emphasis has been given to cooperation, to equality, to mutual exchange across differences of discipline, methodology and personal inclination; to listening and mindfulness about language, place, and subjective life. This includes the geographical and symbolic places of our conferences, and their complex histories of inclusion, exclusion, and silencing. It is a never-ending struggle to be sensitive to what is unsaid, erased or unheard. And the fact of the continuing vitality of our work suggests, despite failures, that we have been ecologically good enough in creating a space in which many can thrive.

Alan Bainbridge and Linden West reflect on struggles – for researcher and researched – to stay in the presence of radical, almost violent, expression of difference and refusal. We question, legitimately, if a research method can be extended into pedagogic practice, and used as a healing tool, or to create a facilitating environment, when conflict is so harsh, and some histories denied? What are the ethics entailed by 'exposing' the other, through narratives, to possible confrontation, challenge and blame by the relatively powerful? Ethical questioning of this kind is a necessity in narrative research, and in creating ecological sensibilities, because we must learn to treat difficult material delicately, in our responsibilities to those with whom we work, and toward a wider world full of danger as well as possibility.

The vulnerability, uncertainty and precarity of the human condition are engaged with, not expunged, in narrative inquiry. It may be the uncertain nature of professional knowledge in a neoliberal world, as in Gaia Del Negro's chapter, or as a result of the Palestinian/Jewish conflict, and the desperate search for safety and security, as in Alan Bainbridge and Linden West's writing; and or in the complex and uncertain nature of human experience, given the power of oppressive and destructive forces chronicled in many of the chapters. The point here is to keep on keeping on, and not to give up, in the face of those who would diminish our humanity.

6   Seeking to Overcome Reductionism and Simplification

Ours is a complex research methodology that needs and takes time, not only to collect authentic narratives and to be with the participant(s), but also to engage sensitively with emerging issues. It demands re-learning, again and again, and to be with the other in the here-and-now of such a process.

The principle of accountability, a pillar of positivistic research, may be useful, but only if balanced with the recognition of the partiality of any account.

Mere rationality or conscious purpose – Bateson warns us (1972) – needs to engage with the reasons of the heart, play, art, dream, and the workings of the unconscious, or what he calls 'thinking in terms of stories' (1979, p. 14). Accountability alone cannot represent how life works, in good enough ways. Even Bronfenbrenner's model – used by Wright and Høyen to evaluate a conference – is only one tentative solution to representing experience in a complex, systemic way. Its form is concentric and rigid. Who, what and why is 'in the centre' of collective encounters? Who and what are excluded from the frame?

Laura Mazzoli Smith criticizes simplistic cause/effect 'evidence-based' biomedical models, since they cannot give a good enough or sufficient explanation of the experience of illness: hence, the need to foster narrative knowledge of patients' (and one's own) illness and wellness stories, to enable practitioners to better understand the other, and themselves.

Feminist informed methodologies (used by Barbara Merrill with working-class university students) acknowledge complexity including spheres of influence, power relations and the need for good enough spaces, and listening, for, and to, frequently silenced voices. Class and gender in this work refuse to be silenced.

7   In the End, Our Research Asks, "What Is a Good Life?"

Different cultural perspectives have different expectations of 'the good life'. Narrative workshops can be places where different perspectives on notions of the good are shared. Thanks to narratives, it is possible to imagine the good life across time: past, present, and future. As Paula Stone states, 'Working reflexively is not nostalgia but courage to confront pain and difficulty'. Fergal Finnegan observes, we will never fully know or capture what exists, and is real, but narrative methods still generate deep and rich insight into individual and collective experience. And into what is good, beautiful and life-enhancing as well as what is destructive, life-constraining, and ugly. To work in good enough ways requires courage, not least to think outside boxes, and our own lives. When Lake Eerie is polluted, we are polluted too, if we turn our backs and refuse to see and know, as Laura and Linden wrote. Refusing to recognize our responsibilities in what we do and perceive at micro, meso and macro levels, is proving catastrophic. Recognizing, for instance, our complicity in the pain of species extinction, in the harm we do to others, in turning our backs to the vulnerable migrant, or to the violent abuse of women and people of colour, really does matter. As does what can be our willful ignorance in refusing to see how the problems of our planet relate to what we greedy humans consume and pollute. Doing narrative and auto/biographical or autoethnographic research in ecologically sensitive ways, and making connections between environmental degradation, psychological health, and meaningful learning, really does matter.

References

Bateson, G. (1979). *Mind and nature. A necessary unity*. Bantam Books.

Formenti, L. (2018). Complexity, adult biographies and co-operative transformation. In M. Milana, S. Webb, J. Holford, R. Waller, & P. Jarvis (Eds.), *The Palgrave international handbook on adult and lifelong education and learning* (pp. 191–209). Palgrave Macmillan.

Formenti, L., & West, L. (2018). *Transforming perspectives in lifelong learning and adult education: A dialogue*. Palgrave Macmillan.

Norris, J., Sawyer, R. D., & Lund, D. (Eds.). (2012). *Duoethnography. Dialogic methods for social, health, and educational research*. Left Coast Press.

Shafak, E. (2020). *How to stay sane in an age of division*. Wellcome Collection.

White, M., & Epston, D. (1990). *Narrative means to therapeutic ends*. Norton Press.

Index

adult education/learning   1, 3, 7–10, 14, 18, 24, 27, 28, 33–36, 54, 62, 63, 66, 122, 123, 129, 137, 144–148, 155, 158, 159, 200, 217–221

adult educators   7, 17, 27, 28, 31, 32, 34, 36, 79, 88, 148, 157, 186, 188, 191, 192, 220

aesthetic experience   17, 192, 193

alienation   17, 102, 113, 166, 172, 186–189, 193, 194, 200

auto/biography   1, 3, 7, 14, 16, 29, 32, 36, 122, 124, 127, 130, 131, 133, 136, 137, 187, 188, 191, 192–195, 200, 204–206, 209, 213, 214, 218, 226

autoethnography   96, 223, 226

biographical interview   16, 39, 41, 42, 145, 148, 154, 166

biographicity   6, 11, 39, 40, 44, 45, 49, 50, 128

class   27, 43, 108–113, 114, 145, 160–164, 169, 176, 190, 237, 302, 323, 328, 381, 425, 427, 429, 436

colonialism   16, 134, 135, 172, 174, 175, 220, 223

context   1, 3, 8, 10–12, 14–17, 24, 26, 28, 32, 33, 39, 40, 42–45, 49, 61, 62, 65–71, 74, 75, 77–80, 83, 84, 95, 96, 103–105, 109–111, 113, 114, 116–118, 123, 126, 127, 133–135, 144–146, 149, 158, 162–165, 171–173, 177–179, 183, 188–193, 204–207, 209, 217, 222

COVID-19   29, 35, 77, 83

critical theory   128, 158–161, 163

critical realism   15, 158, 161

cure   14, 127, 132

dialogue   1, 7, 10, 12–14, 18, 26, 28, 34, 36, 42, 44, 54, 55, 98, 100, 104, 111–115, 117, 121–124, 126, 127, 129–131, 133–137, 159, 161, 166, 182, 183, 211, 220–222

ecologies of learning   10, 42, 50, 108, 137

ecoformation   53

ESREA   1, 2, 5, 8, 36, 41, 63, 78, 82, 127, 144, 158, 217

equality   29, 88–90, 124, 158, 160, 192, 214, 224

environment   13, 16, 18, 26, 27, 30, 31, 34, 42, 43, 53–55, 57, 58, 60, 62, 63, 78, 80, 98, 100, 102, 104, 105, 114, 117, 127, 149, 154, 183, 218, 219, 224

gender   9, 15, 18, 43, 87, 144, 147–149, 151–153, 198, 205, 208–211, 225

healing   16, 24, 30, 35, 36, 122, 126, 137, 171, 172, 177, 182, 214, 223, 224

health (care)   13, 14, 66, 68, 70, 71, 73, 74, 107–111, 113, 114, 116–118, 189

higher education   15–17, 48, 87, 114, 130, 143, 144, 148, 149, 157, 162, 163, 165, 189, 203, 208, 214

identity   5, 15, 16, 29, 42, 46, 49, 54, 61, 63, 99, 103, 145, 150, 153, 154, 171, 172, 176, 177, 183, 190, 191, 204, 206, 208, 211, 214, 223

Israel   14, 122, 123, 125–127, 130, 136

knowing   13, 14, 17, 25, 31, 84, 102, 112, 116–118, 134, 167, 173, 176, 178, 186–195, 198, 200, 201, 205, 207, 222, 223

languages   1, 6, 16, 17, 27, 31, 34, 36, 40, 42, 43, 45, 48–50, 54, 58, 66, 67, 86, 96, 97, 110, 112, 116, 123, 132, 133, 135, 147, 170–172, 176, 177, 179, 188, 190, 191, 193–195, 221

macro, meso and micro worlds   9, 11, 12, 15, 26, 27, 31–33, 65, 66, 71, 73, 112, 117, 118, 129, 144–146, 149, 150, 154, 225

Mezirow   113, 117

microphenomenology   11, 54, 59

migration   18, 26, 86, 134, 137, 223

multimodality   186–188, 200, 222

narrative   1–3, 6–9, 11–15, 17, 18, 25–27, 29, 30, 34, 36, 40–44, 46–50, 53–63, 66–69, 72, 74, 79, 85, 88, 96, 99–102, 104, 105, 107–118, 122, 124, 126–133, 135–137, 144, 148, 149, 160, 164, 171, 174, 178, 180–182, 190, 195, 197, 204, 206, 207, 210, 213, 214, 217–226

neoliberal   12, 18, 33, 82, 87–89, 189, 211, 212, 224

Palestine 123
peace   10, 121–125, 127, 130–134, 137
pedagogy   13, 15, 28, 102, 105, 107, 112–116, 118,
    134, 158, 159, 171, 178
perspectives of meaning   183
power of stories   63
pragmatism   5, 13, 107, 108, 110–112, 114–118
precariat   88
psychoanalysis   11, 28, 31, 32, 36, 128, 191
psychosocial   25, 32, 42, 122, 128, 205, 218

reflexivity   35, 40, 44, 115, 116, 122, 128, 163,
    192–194, 219
resistance to learning   105, 220

Solastalgia   29, 30

synthesis   11, 42, 43, 48, 50
systemic theory   28

transformative learning   28, 107, 110, 112–117,
    194
trauma   14, 16, 122, 123, 125, 131, 133–135, 137,
    221

unconscious   6, 28, 32, 34, 36, 97, 129, 193,
    200, 208, 219, 225

verbalization   11, 48, 49
violence   14, 35, 122, 135, 137, 209

women (adult students)   9, 41, 143, 144, 148,
    149

.